Rumor and Communication in Asia in the Internet Age

New communication technology has transformed the way in which news about key events is communicated. For example, in the immediate aftermath of catastrophic events such as the Mumbai attacks or the Japanese tsunami, partial accounts, accurate and inaccurate facts, rumor, and speculation are now very rapidly disseminated across the globe, often ahead of official announcements and formal news reporting. Often in such situations, rumors take hold, and continue to characterize events even after a more complete, more accurate picture eventually emerges. This book explores how such rumors are created, disseminated, and absorbed in the age of the internet and mobile communications. It includes a wide range of examples and, besides considering the overall processes involved, engages with scholarly debates in the field of media and communication studies.

Greg Dalziel is a Research Associate at the Global Security Research Institute in Tokyo, while also completing his doctoral studies at the Graduate School of Media and Governance at Keio University, Japan.

Media, Culture, and Social Change in Asia

Series editor
Stephanie Hemelryk Donald, University of New South Wales
Editorial board
Devleena Ghosh, University of Technology, Sydney
Peter Horsfield, RMIT University, Melbourne
Chris Hudson, RMIT University, Melbourne
K.P. Jayasankar, Unit for Media and Communications, Tata Institute of
  Social Sciences, Bombay
Michael Keane, Queensland University of Technology
Tania Lewis, RMIT University, Melbourne
Vera Mackie, University of Melbourne
Kama Maclean, University of New South Wales
Anjali Monteiro, Unit for Media and Communications, Tata Institute of
  Social Sciences, Bombay
Laikwan Pang, Chinese University of Hong Kong
Ursula Rao, University of New South Wales
Gary Rawnsley, University of Leeds
Ming-yeh Rawnsley, University of Leeds
Jo Tacchi, RMIT University, Melbourne
Adrian Vickers, University of Sydney
Jing Wang, MIT
Ying Zhu, City University of New York

The aim of this series is to publish original, high-quality work by both new
and established scholars in the West and the East, on all aspects of media,
culture, and social change in Asia.

1 Television across Asia
Television industries, programme
formats and globalisation
*Edited by Albert Moran and
Michael Keane*

2 Journalism and Democracy in Asia
*Edited by Angela Romano and
Michael Bromley*

**3 Cultural Control and Globalization
in Asia**
Copyright, piracy and cinema
Laikwan Pang

**4 Conflict, Terrorism and the Media
in Asia**
Edited by Benjamin Cole

5 Media and the Chinese Diaspora
Community, communications
and commerce
Edited by Wanning Sun

**6 Hong Kong Film, Hollywood and
the new Global Cinema**
No film is an island
*Edited by Gina Marchetti and
Tan See Kam*

7 Media in Hong Kong
Press freedom and political change
1967–2005
Carol P. Lai

8 Chinese Documentaries
From dogma to polyphony
Yingchi Chu

9 Japanese Popular Music
Culture, authenticity and power
Carolyn S. Stevens

10 The Origins of the Modern Chinese Press
The influence of the Protestant missionary press in late
Qing China
Xiantao Zhang

11 Created in China
The great new leap forward
Michael Keane

12 Political Regimes and the Media in Asia
Edited by Krishna Sen and Terence Lee

13 Television in Post-reform China
Serial dramas, Confucian leadership and the global television market
Ying Zhu

14 Tamil Cinema
The cultural politics of India's other film industry
Edited by Selvaraj Velayutham

15 Popular Culture in Indonesia
Fluid identities in post-authoritarian politics
Edited by Ariel Heryanto

16 Television in India
Satellites, politics and cultural change
Edited by Nalin Mehta

17 Media and Cultural Transformation in China
Haiqing Yu

18 Global Chinese Cinema
The culture and politics of hero
Edited by Gary D. Rawnsley and Ming-Yeh T. Rawnsley

19 Youth, Society and Mobile Media in Asia
Edited by Stephanie Hemelryk Donald, Theresa Dirndorfer Anderson and Damien Spry

20 The Media, Cultural Control and Government in Singapore
Terence Lee

21 Politics and the Media in Twenty-first Century Indonesia
Edited by Krishna Sen and David T. Hill

22 Media, Social Mobilization and Mass Protests in Post-colonial Hong Kong
The power of a critical event
Francis L.F. Lee and Joseph M. Chan

23 HIV/AIDS, Health and the Media in China
Imagined immunity through racialized disease
Johanna Hood

24 Islam and Popular Culture in Indonesia and Malaysia
Edited by Andrew N. Weintraub

25 Online Society in China
Creating, celebrating and
instrumentalising the
online carnival
*Edited by David Kurt Herold and
Peter Marolt*

**26 Rethinking Transnational
Chinese Cinemas**
The Amoy-dialect film industry in
Cold War Asia
Jeremy E. Taylor

**27 Film in Contemporary
Southeast Asia**
Cultural interpretation and social
intervention
*Edited by David C.L. Lim and
Hiroyuki Yamamoto*

28 China's New Creative Clusters
Governance, human capital and
investment
Michael Keane

**29 Media and Democratic Transition
in South Korea**
Ki-Sung Kwak

30 The Asian Cinema Experience
Styles, spaces, theory
Stephen Teo

31 Asian Popular Culture
Edited by Anthony Y.H. Fung

**32 Rumor and Communication in
Asia in the Internet Age**
Edited by Greg Dalziel

Rumor and Communication in Asia in the Internet Age

Edited by
Greg Dalziel

LONDON AND NEW YORK

First published 2013
by Routledge
Published 2014 by Routledge
2 Park Square, Milton Park, Abingdon, Oxfordshire OX14 4RN

Simultaneously published in the USA and Canada
by Routledge
711 Third Avenue, New York, NY 10017

Routledge is an imprint of the Taylor and Francis Group, an informa business

First issued in paperback 2015

© 2013 selection and editorial material, Greg Dalziel; individual chapters,
the contributors

The right of the editor to be identified as author of the editorial material,
and of the authors for their individual chapters, has been asserted in
accordance with sections 77 and 78 of the Copyright, Designs and Patents
Act 1988.

All rights reserved. No part of this book may be reprinted or reproduced or
utilised in any form or by any electronic, mechanical, or other means, now
known or hereafter invented, including photocopying and recording, or in
any information storage or retrieval system, without permission in writing
from the publishers.

Trademark notice: Product or corporate names may be trademarks or
registered trademarks, and are used only for identification and explanation
without intent to infringe.

British Library Cataloguing in Publication Data
A catalogue record for this book is available from the British Library

Library of Congress Cataloging in Publication Data
Rumor and communication in Asia in the Internet age / edited by Greg
Dalziel.
    pages cm. – (Media, culture and social change in Asia ; 32)
    Includes bibliographical references and index.
    Summary: "Explores how rumours are created, disseminated and
absorbed in the age of the internet and mobile communications. It includes
a wide range of examples and, besides considering the overall processes
involved, engages with scholarly debates in the field of media and
communication studies"– Provided by publisher.
    1. Rumor–Asia. 2. Communication–Social aspects–Asia. 3. Internet–
Social aspects–Asia. 4. Public opinion–Asia. I. Dalziel, Greg, editor of
compilation. II. Series: Media, culture, and social change in Asia series ; 32.
    HM1241.R845 2013
    302.2–dc23
                    2012047977

ISBN 978-0-415-64127-2 (hbk)
ISBN 978-1-138-95660-5 (pbk)
ISBN 978-0-203-40332-7 (ebk)

Typeset in Times New Roman
by Taylor & Francis Books

Contents

List of illustrations	ix
Contributors	x
Acknowledgments	xiv
Introduction	1
GREG DALZIEL	
1 Rumor, gossip, and conspiracy theories: pathologies of testimony and the principle of publicity	20
AXEL GELFERT	
2 Have you heard? The rumor as reliable	46
MATTHEW DENTITH	
3 Triangle of death: strategic communication, counterinsurgency, and the rumor mill	61
DANIEL BERNARDI AND SCOTT W. RUSTON	
4 The politics of informal communication: conspiracy theories and rumors in the 2009 (post-)electoral Iranian public sphere	78
BABAK RAHIMI	
5 Rumors, religion, and political mobilization: Indonesian cases, 1965–98	94
MARK WOODWARD	
6 Rumors of terrorism: social cognitive structures, collective sense-making, and the emergence of rumor	106
GREG DALZIEL	
7 Rumor, culture, and strategic communication across old and new media in Southeast Asia: the case of terrorist Noordin Top	124
CHRIS LUNDRY AND PAULINE HOPE CHEONG	

viii *Contents*

8 Anxiety and rumor: exploratory analysis of Twitter posts during the Mumbai terrorist attack 143

ONOOK OH, MANISH AGRAWAL, AND H. RAGHAV RAO

9 Rumor—the evil twin of strategic communication: what "white" propaganda can learn from "gray" 156

ANTHONY OLCOTT

Conclusion 167

GREG DALZIEL

Bibliography 181
Index 206

List of Illustrations

Figures

7.1	A *produser*'s manipulated images of Noordin Top's "wanted" photo	132
7.2	A variety of remixed versions of the Noordin Top "wanted" photo	133
8.1	Representation of rumor and emotional tension/anxiety	151

Table

8.1	Rumor word and anxiety word list defined	150

Contributors

Manish Agrawal is an Associate Professor in the Department of Information Systems and Decision Sciences of the College of Business Administration at the University of South Florida in Tampa, Florida. Dr. Agrawal teaches classes on Web applications development, information security, and computer networks at both graduate and undergraduate levels. His current research interests include information security, software quality, and the use of IT during extreme events. His articles have appeared or are forthcoming in journals including *Management Science, INFORMS Journal on Computing, IEEE Transactions on Software Engineering, ACM Transactions on Information Technology, Communications of the ACM,* and the *Journal of Management Information Systems.* He completed his PhD at SUNY Buffalo. Dr. Agrawal is a member of AIS and INFORMS.

Daniel Bernardi is Professor and Chair of the Cinema Department at San Francisco State University (SFSU). He is also the Director of the Documentary Film Institute at SFSU. Bernardi's research explores the representation and narration of cultural difference, including race, gender, and sexuality, in media and popular culture. He is currently extending this work to address the cultural dimensions of counterinsurgency operations, where he uses critical theory, narratology, and ethnography to study rumors as narrative IEDs. He is the author of *Star Trek and History: Race-ing Toward a White Future* (Rutgers University Press, 1998), co-author of *Narrative Landmines: Rumors, Islamist Extremism and the Struggle for Strategic Influence* (Rutgers University Press, 2012), editor of four books on whiteness in American cinema, and the author of numerous articles on early cinema, US television, and new media.

Pauline Hope Cheong (PhD, Annenberg School for Communication, University of Southern California) is Associate Professor at the Hugh Downs School of Human Communication, Arizona State University. Her research focuses on the social and cultural implications of communication technologies, including aspects concerning religious authority and community. She is lead editor of *Digital Religion, Social Media and Culture: Practices, Perspectives and Futures* and *New Media and Intercultural Communication:*

Identity, Community and Politics. She is also co-author of *Narrative Landmines: Rumors, Islamist Extremism and the Struggle for Strategic Influence.* Her award-winning research has been published in multiple journals, including *New Media and Society, Journal of Computer-Mediated-Communication, The Information Society, Information, Communication and Society, Journal of Media and Religion, Journal of International and Intercultural Communication,* and the *Journal of Communication.*

Matthew Dentith recently completed his PhD in Philosophy at the University of Auckland. His dissertation, "In defence of conspiracy theories" was an examination of when, if ever, it is rational to believe conspiracy theories. Matthew is a regular New Zealand media commentator on conspiracy theories and wacky beliefs in general and consequently receives a lot of hatemail calling into question his academic credentials and accusing him of being a member of the One World Government, which may or may not be true. Matthew is currently working up a new research project on the epistemological and ethical question of when we might be obligated to investigate conspiracy theories.

Axel Gelfert is an Assistant Professor in the Department of Philosophy at the National University of Singapore and Co-Chair of the Science, Technology, and Society (STS) Research Cluster at the Faculty of Arts and Social Sciences. Since 2011, he has also been an Associate Fellow at Tembusu College. He completed his PhD in History and Philosophy of Science at the University of Cambridge in 2005, after which he spent a year as a Junior Fellow at Collegium Budapest (Institute for Advanced Study). In 2009 and 2011, he was a Visiting Research Fellow at the Institute for Advanced Studies in the Humanities (IASH), University of Edinburgh. Most of his research revolves around issues in the philosophy of science and technology, social epistemology (especially its history and potential applications), and the history of philosophy.

Chris Lundry is an Assistant Research Professor at the Hugh Downs School of Human Communication at Arizona State University and the Chair of the Southeast Asia Council. He has published in journals such as *American Behavioral Scientist, Studies in Conflict and Terrorism, Inside Indonesia,* and *Waskita: Jurnal Agama dan Masyarakat,* and has written chapters in several edited volumes. His dissertation (Arizona State University, Political Science, 2009) focused on rebellion, separatism, and state cohesion in Indonesia, and was supported by Blakemore Freeman and Fulbright fellowships. His current work with the Center for Strategic Communication, where he is the group's Southeast Asia expert, focuses on the use of narrative in extremist and counterextremist communication. His other interests include religion and politics, and democracy and democratization in Southeast Asia, and he monitored the 1999 referendum in East Timor under United Nations accreditation and the 2004 Indonesian Presidential election with the Carter Center.

xii *Contributors*

Onook Oh is a doctoral candidate in the School of Management at the State University of New York at Buffalo. He is also a Visiting Research Associate in the Center for Collaboration Science at the University of Nebraska at Omaha. His research interests are in the areas of new modalities of information exchange and social media, crowdsourcing, and the use of social media in information assurance and extreme events. His papers have been published in *Communications of AIS, Information Systems Frontiers, AIS Transactions on Human-Computer Interaction* and *Information Systems Management*. He has also presented his papers at ICIS, HICCS, and other international and national information systems conferences.

Anthony Olcott has recently retired from the Center for the Study of Intelligence, where he was part of the Emerging Trends team. Prior to that he was an Officer in Residence in the Institute for the Study of Diplomacy at Georgetown University, where he taught open source intelligence and propaganda. Originally an academic (PhD, Stanford University), Olcott taught Russian more than 20 years at Colgate University before entering government as an open source analyst with the Foreign Broadcast Information Service (which later became the Open Source Center). He is the author of *Russian Pulp: The Way of Russian Crime*, which was judged Best Book of Literary or Cultural Studies by the American Association of Slavic Studies in 2003. More recently he published *Open Source Intelligence in a Networked World* (2012). He has also published five novels, many translations, and a large number of scholarly articles

Babak Rahimi is Associate Professor of Communication, Culture, and Religion at the Department of Literature, University of California, San Diego. He received a PhD from the European University Institute, Florence, Italy, in October 2004. Rahimi has also studied at the University of Nottingham, where he obtained an MA in Ancient and Medieval Philosophy, and the London School of Economics and Political Science, where he was a Visiting Fellow in the Department of Anthropology, 2000–2001. Rahimi has written numerous articles on culture, religion, and politics and regularly writes on contemporary Iraqi and Iranian politics. His book, *Theater-State and Formation of the Early Modern Public Sphere in Iran: Studies on Safavid Miuharram Rituals, 1590–1641 C.E.*, studies the relationship between ritual, social space, and state power in early modern Iranian history. He has been a Visiting Scholar at the Internet Institute, University of Oxford, and the Annenberg School for Communication at the University of Pennsylvania. He has also been the recipient of fellowships from the National Endowment for the Humanities and a Jean Monnet Fellowship at the European University Institute, and was a Senior Fellow at the United States Institute of Peace, Washington DC, 2005–6. Rahimi's current research project is on the relationship between digital culture, politics, and religion.

H.R. Rao is a SUNY Distinguished Service Professor at SUNY Buffalo and WCU Visiting Professor at Sogang University, S. Korea. He has published more than 150 archival papers and has received several best paper or best paper runner-up awards at conferences such as AMCIS, ICIS, and journals such as ISR. He has edited several books, the most recent of which is *Information Assurance, Security and Privacy Services.* He has been a Fulbright scholar, and his research is funded by NSF, DOD, and others. He is co-editor-in-chief of *Information Systems Frontiers* and is (has been) associate editor or guest senior editor at MISQ, ISR, DSS, IEEE Trans on SMC, ACM Trans on MIS, CACM, etc. He has a PhD from Purdue University, an MBA from Delhi University, and a B. Tech from IIT Kanpur.

Scott W. Ruston is currently an Assistant Research Professor with Arizona State University's Center for Strategic Communication, where he specializes in narrative theory and media studies. He received his PhD in Critical Studies from the University of Southern California's School of Cinematic Arts, and has published on narrative, story-telling, and new media in international journals including *Refractory: A Journal of Entertainment Media*, *The International Journal of Technology and Human Interaction*, and most recently, in *Storyworlds: A Journal of Narrative Studies.* He combines this media studies expertise with past military experience to address real-world problems of strategic communication. He is the co-author of *Narrative Landmines: Rumors, Islamist Extremism and the Struggle for Strategic Influence* (Rutgers University Press, 2012), and has presented widely on topics intersecting media, narrative/counter-narrative, and terrorism.

Mark Woodward received his PhD in cultural anthropology from the University of Illinois in 1985. He is Associate Professor of Religious Studies at Arizona State University, USA, and Visiting Professor of Comparative Religion at the Center for Religious and Cross-cultural Studies at Gadjah Mada University, Indonesia. His research focuses on Javanese Islam and on Islam and politics in Indonesia, and in Southeast Asian more generally. He is the author of *Islam in Java: Mysticism and Normative Piety in the Sultanate of Yogyakarta* (1989) and *Java, Indonesia and Islam* (2010).

Acknowledgments

This volume arose out of a workshop, *The Political & Social Impact of Rumors*, held in Singapore. All but one of the chapters in this book was originally presented there. The workshop was organized by the Center of Excellence for National Security (CENS), a research unit of the S. Rajaratnam School of International Studies (RSIS) at Nanyang Technological University, Singapore. In addition, the workshop would not have been possible without the support of the National Security Coordination Secretariat (NSCS), Prime Minister's Office, Singapore.

The editor would like to gratefully acknowledge support from Kumar Ramakrishna, Norman Vasu, Yvonne Lee, and the rest of the staff at CENS.

Information on the above organizations can be found at:

CENS: www.rsis.edu.sg/cens

RSIS: www.rsis.edu.sg

NSCS: www.nscs.gov.sg

The contributors, editor, and publishers have made every effort to trace the owners of copyright material in this book, and would be happy to hear from any rights holders whose work may have been used without proper acknowledgment.

Introduction

Greg Dalziel

> Rumor, I believe, is a practical necessity of human existence. It is founded upon the human longing for knowledge, it appeals to and satisfies that social instinct which has welded individuals into communities.
>
> (Chadwick 1932: 8–9)

The devastating March 3, 2011 earthquakes and tsunamis in Japan created swathes of destruction along its northeastern coast. Directly causing the deaths of tens of thousands and dislocating hundreds of thousands, the disaster indirectly disrupted and brought uncertainty to the daily lives of those living outside the immediate disaster zones. These multiple events, coupled with ongoing aftershocks and a nuclear emergency at reactors in Fukushima, created an environment of extreme uncertainty.

Under such conditions, normal patterns of daily life become disrupted. The expectations of the day ahead, one's sense of relative certainty about the future, are quickly ruptured. What the situation means for one's self, community and for the future are uncertain. Decisions need to be made. For some, these decisions are vitally important. For others, the compression of time brought about by the terror of crisis creates a sensation of immediacy in the need to make a decision, any decision. However, lacking adequate information, one supplements. People talk to each other. They engage in trying to find out what is going on, attempting to piece together the significance of events and what may come next. These two sets of behavior, of information-seeking and meaning-making, are often taken together and called sense-making. Whether with one's family and neighbors or via internet channels, information is shared. Sometimes, it is presented as rumor; at other times, it is not until later that this information acquires such a label. In the case of Japan, information—however labeled—circulated that Japanese political elites were sending their families out of Japan (Ito 2011); the royal family had been evacuated to Kyoto; or that "toxic rain" was going to occur and one should not go outside (Sasaki 2011). However, this kind of information was not only confined to Japan. Information quickly circulated globally about a variety of health-related effects of radiation or "toxic rain." Reports of different varieties of these messages circulated in China, South Korea, the Philippines, Singapore and the United States.

2   *G. Dalziel*

Crisis, often typified as a temporal period of heightened uncertainty, requires us to figure out why a particular event occurred, what it means and what might happen next. They are examples of sense-making, of people attempting to make sense of and bring meaning to the world around them (Weick 1995). In looking at variations in rumors, we engage in exploring and discovering the boundaries of meaning and truth that can often vary between communities. At the same time, these boundaries of meaning can be problematic for state efforts to either communicate or persuade policy and action to differing communities.

The broad goals of this volume are to explore the phenomenon of rumor, its social and political impacts, and how such study can inform our understanding of state communication practices. The authors presented in this work come from a variety of different academic and professional backgrounds, often with distinct ontological and epistemological stances, using differing methods to explore the subject.

As a topic of study, it is within the fields of sociology and social psychology that rumor research is most prevalent. They make appearances in anthropology along with other fields such as folklore studies. This book features chapters using these perspectives as well as those of philosophy, communication studies, and religious studies. Alongside theoretical and historical pieces sit case studies drawn from Asia writ-large. This spread of countries is the result of both a conscious effort on the part of the editor as well as, in no large measure, serendipity.

Cases are drawn from field work in Iraq (exploring rumors circulating during counterinsurgency efforts), Iran (rumors and conspiracy theories during the 2009 election period), India (the diffusion of rumors via Twitter during the 2008 Mumbai terrorist incidents), Singapore (online discourse after the escape of a suspected terrorist from detention) and two cases from Indonesia (rumor and myth during a twenty-plus year period of the Suharto era and a more recent case of rumor surrounding the death of a suspected terrorist).

The book is divided roughly into three sections: the first explores the philosophical terrain of rumor and testimony; the second part examines rumor using a narrative approach and the strategic use—or exploitation, if one prefers—of the sense-making process in the form of rumors; the final section looks at the implication of rumor for strategic state communication efforts.[1]

Why rumors

Why do rumors matter? Often what drives interest and research is the frequently negative meaning of rumor and the associations of having a negative impact on decision-making in society. Their role has been negatively associated in, for example: (1) episodes of collective violence (Adams 1999; Bubandt 2000; Engineer 1995; Knopf 2006[1975]; Mackey 1996[1841]); (2) fomenting resistance to public health campaigns (Butt 2005; DeClerque *et al.* 1986; Dodoo *et al.* 2007; Feldman-Savelsberg *et al.* 2000; Kaler 2009;

Kroeger 2003); (3) having a negative impact on decision-making in financial markets (Koenig 1985; Kosfeld 2005; Rose 1951; Schindler 2007); or (4) decreasing levels of trust between social groups (Bubandt 2008; Kirsch 2002; Musambachime 1988; Odum 1997[1943]).

Such studies not only focus on the presumed social ills that either accompany or are directly caused by rumor, but often reveal an implicit belief that, if everyone had access to "true" information, it would improve decision-making, or alleviate conflict. Such logic often permeates state communication practices as we shall see. Studies of rumor also highlight everyday concerns that people have over what constitutes information that they may take to be true and, perhaps, a simple desire not to be deceived. Indeed, this focus on "truth" in information is highlighted precisely by the status that some information holds by being classed as "rumor."

Labeling information as rumor may be one way in which we mark distinctions in knowledge between either the perceived facticity of information or the credibility of the information source. Making this distinction can enable comparisons between items of information; but the manner in which this distinction is made can be modulated by power, authority and boundaries between institutions, social groups or publics. Whether and when a state organization, for example, categorizes information as rumor or not inherently makes a distinction between officially sanctioned truth and falsity, acceptable and unacceptable discourse, and between what is remembered and forgotten. This is seen most markedly in the manner in which rumor was conceived of and studied during World War II in the United States (Faye 2007). Similarly, certain institutions such as financial markets legislate against rumor because of a concern that falsehood can lead to poor decision-making with a negative effect on financial gains.[2] As such, one can see how states might perceive rumors to have a negative impact on strategic communication efforts. If rumor can influence people's beliefs or behavior, then it can influence people in ways contrary to those in power.

The basics of rumor

Rumors are a dynamic and propulsive part of the discourse of both the unusual and the quotidian. As a concept, it is also one that is cunningly tricky to define, often varying based on the lens through which they are viewed. The term "rumor" is commonly used as a synonym for falsehood, or to describe some information we are undecided is true or not. That is, rumor is used as a form of classification to differentiate a piece of information that is considered "not true" (or "not yet true") from one that has attained the status of truth. Similarly, if we do not trust the source or the information itself, or if it turns out in hindsight to be false, we may call it "rumor" (see Shibutani 1966: 3).

Often the concept overlaps, both definitionally and in practice, with that of gossip, urban or contemporary legend, and conspiracy theory. We can identify five common ways that boundaries are made to differentiate rumor from

4 G. Dalziel

other forms, or genres, of communication. These are merely ideal types, and any of the following may be used in combination: (1) *communication channel* (e.g., rumor spread via word-of-mouth, generally confined to the early twentieth-century definitions); (2) *syntax* (e.g., statements beginning with "Did you hear ...," etc.); (3) *temporality* (rumors differ from other genres in that topics are based on current events and diminish in time as the event is no longer of importance to the community in which the rumor spreads); (4) *contextual* (rumors are prevalent during particular periods, e.g., uncertainty, ambiguity, crisis, disaster; or rumors vary based on cultural and/or social context); (5) *functional* (rumors serve an individual- or social-level function that differs from other genres; most prevalent in psychological research into rumor).

The "classic" and most influential definition of rumor is that put forward by the psychologists Gordon W. Allport and Leo Postman (1947: ix) as a "proposition or belief, passed along from person to person, usually by word of mouth, without secure standards of evidence being presented."[3] The context of Allport and Postman's research was World War II. The concern at the time was the US government's desire to monopolize the information space in order to bolster the American public's morale (with rumors seen as having a negative impact), and to ensure that the populace listened to, trusted and (most importantly) followed directives issued by the authorities. The study of rumor, then, was effectively the study of social control. Publications from the time are indicative of popular rumor meanings:

> Of all the virus [sic] that attack the vulnerable nerve tissues of a nation at war, rumor is the most malignant. Breeding sometimes in the stinkholes of enemy propaganda, sometimes in the muddled minds of gossips and show-offs, it spreads through a community with the rapidity of measles. It damages public morale as effectively as infectious disease damages public physique. Its most dangerous carriers are innocent folk who love to tell a tale.
>
> (*Life Magazine* 1942)

Rumor here is seen as either a product of enemy propaganda (always false, of course) or to be the product of pathological human processes. In both cases, rumor is seen to negatively affect the community in which it circulates, the body politic, and ultimately the modern nation-state and its righteous cause. The above example exemplifies how rumor—at least how state authorities categorize information as such—has long been a concern of those tasked with state communication (however such practices are themselves categorized). However, beyond its historical and social context—and notwithstanding issues of power and values—there are numerous problems with Allport and Postman's definition (and those inspired by this foundational concept of rumor). For instance, people often do not put forward secure standards of evidence for the propositions they communicate (Coady 1992). As the sociologist Tamtosu Shibutani (1966: 94) noted, most of the information upon which we either make decisions or form beliefs could be pejoratively classified as rumor (here, false information) using Allport and Postman's concept.

Indeed, the prevalence of rumor is often associated with the plausibility of the information at hand. However, the mere existence of rumor (as defined by Allport and Postman) reveals variations within a public of what counts as "secure standards of evidence." In addition, "secure standards of evidence" may, in fact, be present in the rumor communicated (e.g., the rumor may reference state officials or the media as the source [Fragale and Heath 2004]).

Shibutani takes the definition of rumor in a different direction. A student of Herbert Blumer at the University of Chicago, Shibutani saw rumor simply as part of people's "routine social processes" (Miller 2006: 508). Instead of basing such a definition on the potential truth value of a proposition, Shibutani looked at the social dynamics of communication interactions (Shibutani 1961). He defined rumor as "communication through which men caught together in an ambiguous situation attempt to construct a meaningful interpretation of it by pooling their intellectual resources" (Shibutani 1966: 17). Shibutani termed this phenomenon *improvised news* as he surmised that this informal communication typified undefined or ambiguous situations, especially where official news sources were either partially or completely absent, or perceived as untrustworthy. In such situations, then, people acted in interaction as "pragmatic problem-solvers" (Miller 2006: 508).

Although Allport and Postman (1946: 503) noted that rumor was the product of people's "effort after meaning," their research tended to emphasize a mechanistic view of rumor, taking them as discrete, isolated bits of information removed from the broader cultural system in which they circulate. As distinct pieces of information, rumors, then, are akin to physical objects with inherent properties rather than resulting from human interaction. Shibutani (1966: 8) argued that rumors in this sense are often "treated as something that can be passed around from person to person—somewhat like a brick." The best example of this is the serial transmission studies conducted by Allport and Postman examining how the content of word-of-mouth communication changed as it was passed from individual to individual (we discuss serial transmission studies in greater detail in the next section).

We can see from this discussion that the study of rumors is extremely "fuzzy" with no clear consensus on what rumor means or does (albeit falsehood seems to be a common property contained in either the concept itself or the data collected). While this lack of agreed-upon definition is problematic for those hoping for some epistemic certainty, it is, in part, a natural function of the variety of disciplines—psychology, social psychology, sociology, anthropology—that have attempted to study rumors. It is also a reminder that meanings can and do vary (Swaffield 1998); this is something that people encounter every day without a problem but one that can often trouble particular professions and professionals, such as a bureaucrat or an academic (or, even more frighteningly, one who is both of those things). Conversely, this inability to come to agreed-upon definitions of rumor itself provides new

6   *G. Dalziel*

opportunities for research and a largely unexplored terrain in looking at both variations in rumor meanings and their consequences, but also into the sociology of rumor research itself. What is more useful to keep in mind when studying rumor is Shibutani's (1966: 17) suggestion that "the reality to be studied ... is not distortion in serial transmission but the social interaction of people caught in inadequately defined situations."

Studying rumor

We purposely did not set out for participants at the beginning of this project any strict methodological guidelines for the study of rumor, nor rigid definitions of rumor itself. This was to make transparent the variety of ways in which different disciplines approach the study of rumor, something that itself is a useful exercise for understanding rumors. Secondly, the inherently contextual nature of rumors means that the best approach is one that is methodologically flexible and fits the question at hand (Flyvbjerg 2001). Historically, studies of rumor (predominantly within social psychology) have gone for methodological rigor in attempts to find epistemologically pure and predictive theories of rumor. There is nothing inherently wrong with such an approach; it is simply an example of the assumptions at work within a particular academic field, and such works are liberally cited within this volume along with a case study that explicitly utilizes such methods (Oh *et al.*, Chapter 8). The overall aim, however, is to present a rich picture of the different ways in which rumors are seen to operate in different societies, within different social groups, and by different academic fields.

Methods of studying rumor vary almost as much as its meaning. Not surprisingly, the manner in which rumors are defined, collected and analyzed depends greatly in which academic field a researcher is situated. Those based in psychology and social psychology tend towards laboratory experiments, testing specific hypotheses about a variety of assumed variables in the dynamics of rumor diffusion. Within sociology (often within the tradition of symbolic interactionism) and anthropology, we see a reliance on ethnographic and narrative approaches often couched in the framework of case studies. These tend towards researching environmental contexts in which rumor spreads (generally environments that can be characterized temporally and spatially as being post-disaster or -crisis periods) and the variety of rumors that spread within such a space, or examining the diffusion of a particular rumor across a community.

At this point, however, we will attempt to sketch out the range of approaches that have historically characterized rumor research. Early rumor studies cleaved off from psychological research into the vagaries and limits of human memory in relation to testimony (see Bartlett 1932; Hart 1916; Stern 1902). This work heavily influenced the path that Allport and Postman (1946, 1947) took in their research. These methods largely involved testing students' ability to recall pictures, staged events or written materials at a later date and then tracking distortions in recall. Here, one can see a connection between these serial transmission studies of rumor with contemporaneous research into information theory (Shannon 1948) and the *sender—message—receiver* model of communication that still underpins strategic state communication practices today (Corman *et al.* 2007).

Focusing on the fallibility of memory, however, implies that rumors are simply the product of distortion or error brought about by cognitive limitations. Hart (1916: 14), in fact, was an early critic of the type of investigation for which Allport and Postman became so influential and argued that, "most of the experimental work on rumor hitherto attempted has failed to produce much illumination. The experiments have been limited to the serial transmission of reports, and naturally no new facts have emerged other than those already ascertained." Peterson and Gist (1951: 161) also criticized the route taken by Allport and Postman with regard to the experimental serial transmission studies:

> Allport and Postman proceed on the assumption that rumor basically results from distortion in perception and in *unilateral* verbal communication. Thus in the course of their experiments they completely rule out changes in meaning and in motivation which occur in the give and take of informal discussion. They also overlook the possibility that the same individual, transmitting rumor to a succession of persons, may communicate a different version in each instance, not just because of faulty memory, but because of differences in his relationship with them
>
> [emphasis in the original].

Indeed, this criticism that experimental work creates not only a linear and mechanistic treatment of the communication process but also the idea that the information itself remains static and unchanging is an important and often overlooked point. As Peterson and Gist point out, in the process of communication, different versions of accounts may proliferate not because of distortions due to fallible cognitive processes but also because people alter what they say depending on to whom they are speaking and in what context such interaction is occurring. Although the topic of a rumor may remain static, the manner in which it is communicated can alter, something not captured by serial transmission studies. Such studies fail to pay attention to the social context within which communication interactions take place (Shibutani 1961).

Further research into rumor located within the psychology and social psychology field often attempts to ascertain *why* rumors spread in the first place. What is the motivation to spread rumor? Often particular underlying emotional states—anxiety being the most popular—are posited as being behind such motivation. It is unclear from early psychological investigations into rumor, such as those by Prasad (1935, 1950) and Jung (1964), whether the psychological bases for why people spread rumor were deduced from asking those participating in rumor diffusion or if they were assumed by the analyst

8   *G. Dalziel*

from analyzing the content of the rumors. Knapp (1944: 31) writes, for example, that "regardless of their manifest content, [all rumors] may be regarded as expressions of underlying anxiety." Another work of that period states that, "Rumor ...is a more common medium of anxious hysterias" (Jacobsen 1948). These sorts of sweeping assumptions on the part of the analyst, however, point to one of the failings of rumor studies taking this path. It is remarkably similar to the same weaknesses prevalent in psychoanalytical analyses in general, typified by the analyst being dismissive of reports given them by the subjects under study (see Martin 2011 for more on problems in psychoanalytical explanations).

Knapp's (1944: 23) heavily cited work utilized a classification system for rumors based on "the already observed fact that rumors almost invariably gratify some emotional need." How he arrived at such a conclusion is not clear, nor is it entirely clear how rumors differ from other forms of communication with regard to the types of emotional needs they satisfy. Whether via intuition, assumption or otherwise, Knapp (1944: 23) derived three ideal-type categories that all rumors fit into based on the emotions of "fear, wish, and hostility" (Allport and Postman [1946, 1947] utilize a similar scheme). Collecting rumors sent in by readers of a popular weekly magazine, along with those passed on by a pre-selected group of rumor "wardens" (bartenders, mostly, it appears), Knapp then sorted these incoming rumors into the three main (emotional) categories before creating new sub-categories to sort the rumors into based on their themes (Higham 1951 used a similar method). More recent work in this regard is that of Kelley (2004, 2005) and others at the *Baghdad Mosquito*. This publication by the US Armed Forces working in Iraq collated "rumors" found in local and regional newspapers along with those passed on by friendly Iraqis.[4]

Many early studies, in addition to the laboratory work previously discussed, attempted to conduct experiments in more naturalistic studies. This often involved intentionally introducing (false) rumors into an environment such as a classroom, school (Schachter and Burdick 1955) or an entire town (via leaflets dropped from a plane [Buckner 1965]). Although an interesting approach, it is not entirely clear whether such methods would pass university institutional review boards today.

Smith (1947) took a different tack with experimental work, presenting fictitious news reports to undergraduates and labeling a variety of the reports as "rumor," "fact," or with no label at all. But, as Smith notes, the test itself created a situation that students tried to make sense of. This sense-making process generated a number of hypotheses (and rumors!) among the student body as to why this survey was being passed around and, more importantly, they were trying to work out what was expected of them in answering the questionnaire.

These experiments suggest that labeling something as "rumor" does not imply to others that it is something not to be believed, or that it is a falsehood (Smith 1947). On the one hand, there is the act of labeling information that is false as "rumor" and, on the other hand, there is the fact that people do not necessarily take the label "rumor" to mean falsehood. In fact, there are two different meanings at work here for the concept of rumor. There may not be a large gap between the two; statements labeled as "rumor" need not be taken as being *not true*, but rather they may be assumed to be *not false*. Whether statements labeled as rumor are believed may be dependent on the frame used to analyze them, the frame being arranged by the plausibility of the statement. Smith highlights this variance in meaning when he writes that, while a newspaper columnist might dismiss some seemingly incredulous information circulating as "rumor" does not mean that people will disbelieve it (Smith 1947: 86); in fact, they make take such information to be true based merely on reading it (Gilbert 1991; Gilbert *et al.* 1990, 1993).

Beyond advertizing in magazines, as Allport, Postman and Knapp did, how does one go about collecting rumors? Some studies simply try and see whether a sample of respondents have either heard a particular rumor or a set number of pre-defined rumors found by researchers to be circulating in a particular geographical location. Allport and Lepkin (1945), for example, conducted a study asking respondents whether they had heard one of twelve statements classified by researchers in advance as "rumor." Respondents were queried on whether they had heard the rumor and to what degree they believed it. In addition, the questionnaire posed such questions as, "Are you satisfied that we have the best men in office now for leading positions of the national government and army? Do you think that all classes and occupations of Americans are working as hard in the war effort as could be expected?" (Allport and Lepkin 1945: 4).

Not surprisingly, one finds work situated in sociology and anthropology uses methods and techniques that are common to those fields. These often take the form of case studies that track the diffusion of particular rumors or narratives. In rare bits of "luck," a researcher may hear of a rumor persistently circulating in a particular location and be able to get there soon enough to conduct a study. Danzig *et al.* (1958) examined a rumor (defined by the researchers as a "false report") circulating in a town recently affected by a disastrous flood. They used interviews to garner responses to a specific rumor. Notably, however, these researchers were solely interested in studying the dynamics and effects of one particular rumor (that the dam had broken and the town was going to flood again). The context of their research was in rumor control in a post-disaster situation, and hence the researchers were concerned about what actions people took (or did not take) after they heard the particular rumor, rather than examining variations in the content of the rumor itself.[5]

Morin's (1971) study, *Rumor in Orleans*, is another example, albeit one not concerned with rumor control. Focusing largely on a single rumor circulating in the town of Orleans, Morin and his team used interviews and analyses of primary documents to investigate possible reasons for how the rumor began in the first place, where it spread geographically, and possible reasons why it was plausible to certain members of that community.

10   G. Dalziel

A more common experience, it appears, is of a researcher finding them-selves in felicitous circumstances, in the right place and at the right time. This is especially true of the case studies by sociologists and anthropologists (e.g., Brison 1992; Caplow 1947; Firth 1956; Kirsch 2002; Mains 2004; Pels 1992; Shibutani 1944, 1948; Tanner 1978). Shibutani, for example, was a *nisei* brought up in northern California who unexpectedly found himself caught up in the turbulence of the beginnings of America's entry into World War II.[6] Using questionnaires and interviews, Shibutani (along with some friends he enlisted) attempted to collect as many rumors as possible that were circulating in the Japanese community in the San Francisco area before he and the bulk of the Japanese community were interned (Shibutani 1944, 1948). Shibutani's later work (1966) would focus less on the underlying psychological motiva-tions behind the spread of rumors and more on the particular roles that people in a public played when diffusing rumors.

Bordia and Rosnow (1998) note the many problems with studying rumors in their natural environment including barriers to collecting time-sensitive data and analyzing such data. Internet-based communications have promised one way around this, albeit with some caveats. Bordia and Rosnow (1998) conducted one of what we believe to be the first academic researches into online rumors. However, it should be noted that they did not track either (i) the diffusion of a single rumor and/or (ii) the diffusion of many rumors. Instead, they analyzed Usenet group discussions where people discussed and tried to make sense of a single rumor. The sense-making at work here, then, was not utilizing rumors, but was about the (truthfulness or not) of a parti-cular set of informational items categorized as rumor. We discuss the role of the internet in rumor research in greater depth in the Conclusion.

Many of the methods and positions that researchers make use of are dependent on one particular aspect of how the rumor concept is constructed, and that is the manner of what kind of *problem* rumors are supposed to be. For wartime researchers such as Allport and Postman, Knapp and Caplow, rumors were examples of potentially dangerous communications that could damage morale and, overall, the war effort. For researchers in 1960s America, rumors were a source of racial unrest and riots. In the latter half of the 1960s, we begin to see more of a focus on rumors related to popular culture, for example with cases related to rumors of the death of Paul McCartney (Bird *et al.* 1976; Rosnow and Fine 1976; Suczek 1972), drugs in the popular media (Renard 1991), or consumer products (Burgess 2007; Burke 1998; Fine 1992; Lai and Wong 2002; McConnell 1989; Miller 1992; Turner 1987).

In this volume, for example, the type of problem that rumors present varies. Bernardi and Ruston's (Chapter 3) case study of rumors of bovine poisoning in Iraq sees them as not only false but also perceived as a hindrance to those tasked with communicating US policy and action to the local community. To Oh *et al.* (Chapter 8), rumors circulating on Twitter during the 2008 Mumbai terrorist incidents are seen to be impeding state authorities, possible sources of social disruption and bad for morale. Woodward (Chapter 5) and Rahimi

Introduction   11

(Chapter 4) show how rumors can be incredibly useful for people engaged in what some may call anti-state activities. The common linkage between the cases described by the authors is that often what discourse is categorized as "rumor" is dependent on those who have the power to make such distinctions in meaning *meaningful*.

Once we begin to notice these distinctions in meaning, and who is engaged in such meaning-creation (or-stabilization), we can begin to look at the effects of such actions. That is, what are the social and/or political implications of these activities when it comes to defining what is or is not categorized as rumor. One must also pay attention to the *absence* of a category for an item of information; a focus on marked categories means that unmarked ones are more likely to be accepted unthinkingly as the status quo (Brekhus 1998). The effects of such variations in meaning can be everything from social control (monitoring communication in order to impinge the spread of further "rumor") to how events are remembered (as information categorized as "rumor" may be viewed as untrustworthy or not part of official state-approved discourse).

Rumor and plausibility

The perceived truth or validity of information we come across can be an important subtext to rumor concerns (and often the choice by which data are chosen); even so, the truth value of statements classified as rumor is not of necessary importance for our purposes. Instead, a recurrent question in rumor research is why do particular rumors (or a set of rumors around a particular theme) propagate and not others? Here, we turn to the contours of belief to understand the propagation of rumors and two factors that are often seen to determine their spread: plausibility and credibility. For a rumor to spread, we often assume that it must cohere in some fashion with our beliefs and understandings of the world around us; it must be plausible to us. The credibility of the information source is also assumed to play a role in how plausible we might find a piece of information. The amount of credibility and plausibility is intersubjectively variable, and hence their relationship to rumor can be seen to reveal what Fine and Ellis (2010) call the "politics of plausibility." Distinctions in plausibility between different groups of people can make apparent different patterns in the way people make sense of the world around them; what Zerubavel (1999: 12) writes are "instance[s] of the considerable cognitive diversity that exists among different social groups even within the same culture." These groups of differing sense-making outcomes can be thought of as "cognitive subcultures" (Zerubavel 1999).

Although not directly addressing the *politics* of plausibility (something others address in this volume), Gelfert (Chapter 1) and Dentith (Chapter 2) explore in depth the concept of plausibility within a community from the perspective of philosophy, and whether rumors can be considered a reliable form of communication or testimony. Dentith moves our understanding of

12   G. Dalziel

rumors forward through his discussion of the role that perceptions of authority play in how we perceive the reliability of information and the distinction between conspiracy theories and rumors. It is this plausibility, coupled with their propagation, which leads Dentith (Chapter 2) to argue that, the more a rumor circulates, the more likely that people are to be justified in believing it:

> What makes the transmission process of rumoring a reliable one is that when a speaker transmits a rumor to a hearer we do not require the speaker or the hearer to believe the rumor is true, we only require that the hearer finds it plausible, which is to say it coheres with her other beliefs.

On the other hand, Gelfert (Chapter 1) disagrees with Dentith's position, writing that,

> the recipient of a rumor is typically in no position to tell just how much "filtering" has actually taken place. In reality, any *prima facie* entitlement he might have for believing that a particular claim has been deemed plausible by a large enough number of people, is insufficient to establish the reliability, *in general*, of rumor as a source of knowledge.

This is a theme that other authors take up throughout the book, highlighting some of the commonalities between disciplines in the study of rumor. Bernardi and Ruston (Chapter 3), for example, would seem to agree with Gelfert's position when they discuss the circulation of rumors in a particular community in Iraq:

> Insurgents, familiar with the culture and narrative ecosystem in which rumors evolve, actively spread rumors that they have concocted or that have arisen organically and serve their interests in order to advance their strategic messages. This does not mean that the content of the rumor is untrue, but it certainly also does not mean that, if it survives as the case of the bovine poisoning rumor, it is likely to be true.

Rumor and narrative

It may appear strange and rather perverse that, in an edited volume consisting largely of case studies, we start with two quite theoretical pieces from the somewhat staid and fussy field of philosophy. However, the chapters by Gelfert (Chapter 1) and Dentith (Chapter 2) extend our understanding of rumor and rumor research while also showing the real-world ramifications, the policy implications if you will, of their positions. In addition, both chapters reveal the ways in which philosophy and its study of testimony—the transmission of belief—often overlap with previous work on rumor. These philosophical

Introduction   13

investigations by Gelfert and Dentith give us a better understanding of why plausibility is important, the role that rumor should (or should not) play in social knowledge, and useful conceptual distinctions between rumor and other forms of social communication.

However, we get a much richer picture of rumor dynamics by combining the conceptual insights that philosophy brings to the table with a narrative approach to rumor. This narrative approach revolves around previous work in the social sciences that emphasizes the central role that narratives play in people making sense of the world around them (Berger and Luckman 1967; Bridger and Maines 1998; Fisher 1984, 1987; MacIntyre 1984; Somers and Gibson 1994; Tilly 2002; Weick 1995). This approach sees narratives as giving "meaningful form to our experiences" (Flyvbjerg 2004: 299).

A narrative focus on rumor is distinct in many ways from traditional behaviorist approaches to rumor that often think of rumor and narrative as being of a separate kind. A common thread through rumor research is that, by their very nature, rumors are too short in length to be considered "narrative." DiFonzo and Bordia (2007: 26), for example, state that "a narrative cannot be presented [in rumor statements] because the sense making is contemporaneous rather than post hoc." We would argue that the cases presented in this volume, as well as prior work on rumor, shows that sense-making is by its very nature an essentially *post hoc* exercise in narrative construction.

One cannot separate rumors from the narrative system in which they circulate; such an extraction seems far too artificial if we see narrative and rumor as being the products of social interaction. Indeed, it may be better to think of rumors and narrative as being "mutually constitutive" (Mohr 1998). Bernardi and Ruston introduce the concept of a "rumor mosaic" to describe how sets of rumor fit into broader narratives circulating within a community or public, helping to explain both their plausibility and their sense-making function (see Farge *et al.* [1991] for a historical examination of a similar process). They define a rumor mosaic as "the interlocking system of related rumors that function to support broader cultural narratives."

The benefits of this approach, besides being a better explanation of the social action that rumors represent, is that it helps us to understand the dynamics of rumor content while adding to previous research on plausibility. What the narrative approach in this volume adds to rumor research is in the incorporation of Fisher's (1987) concepts of "narrative probability" and "narrative fidelity" to work on rumor and plausibility. The former relates to the perceived coherence of a set of related stories (including rumor), whereas the latter is whether the set of stories coheres with socially shared schema or frames (Benford and Snow 2000; Bridger and Maines 1998, D'Andrade 1995; DiMaggio 1997; Lizardo and Strand 2010; Maines 1999; Ross 2004). We see this socially shared schema as akin to what some call a social cognitive structure (Hopf 2002; Zerubavel 1999).

Halverson *et al.* (2011: 25) describe the work that narratives do in our understanding of the world around us, "Narratives not only hang together

14   *G. Dalziel*

and make sense of the world …they also create expectations for what is likely to happen and what the audience is expected to do about it." Narratives are "the syntax of commonsense explanation" (Abbott 2004: 33). In this sense, we see the work that rumors do in a collective sense-making process during periods of crisis. That is, crisis represents a breakdown in the everyday "narrative trajectory" (Halverson *et al.* 2011: 19) of the world around us that requires resolving. Expectations about what will happen, and what one has to do, are shattered. Rumor as a collective activity is part of the work done in resolving such crises of meaning through information-seeking and meaning-making behavior that rumor diffusion represents.

In terms of what this approach adds for policy understandings of rumor in the context of strategic state communication, Bernardi and Ruston analyze the diffusion of a rumor about intentional bovine poisoning in Iraq by American forces, along with a separate rumor mosaic at work in the Iraqi town of Hillah. In doing so, they highlight the usefulness of a narrative-based approach:

> Crucial to understanding the ideological function and effects of rumors is a recognition of their operation within narrative systems. Approaching rumors with a cultural and narrative-based approach not only aids in understanding what rumors do, but helps identify how and why they circulate, repeat, and most importantly impede strategic communications.

In this sense, the circulation of rumors and rumor mosaics within a community are part of the broader narrative sense-making that people use to understand and make meaning of the world around them. Their use to those studying them is by the way in which they can reveal and shine a light on the often covert and invisible narratives of a group (Maines 1999).

Values, trust, and power

Woodward's essay (Chapter 5) is based on over twenty years of fieldwork in Indonesia and is a rich exploration of rumors circulating in Suharto-era Indonesia (confined here to the island of Java) between 1965 and 1998. He uses a narrative approach combined with the fine-toothed detail that typifies ethnographic accounts prevalent in anthropology. Through this combination of methods, Woodward looks at how religious and cultural myths can influence the types of rumors that resonate within particular cultural contexts and within particular communities. Comparing the rumors propagated by the state and those from its opponents, Woodward uses a Gramscian perspective on hegemonic and counter-hegemonic discourse to reveal how some rumors may attain the status of "history" or "truth" with very real and, in some cases, very negative consequences. Woodward's piece calls to mind Bourdieu's (1977: 650) essay "The Economics of Linguistic Exchanges," in which he writes that an understanding of the "hidden conditions are decisive for understanding what can and cannot be said in a group." Indeed, through Woodward's command

Introduction 15

of historical data, field work and Javanese myths, he shows the often "hidden conditions" of Java that shape the discursive boundaries of groups.

In Woodward's analysis, rumors over time can become part of sustained narratives through which not only the past is remembered but future events are understood. Woodward approaches this from two different directions: via (false) rumors apparently propagated intentionally by the Suharto political apparatus and those rumors that arose in opposition to the Suharto regime. In engaging in such a comparative study, he is able to show some of the impact this has on social memory.

Also based on extensive field work, albeit covering a shorter time period, Rahimi's research in Chapter 4 on the 2009 Iranian elections examines similar accounts of hegemonic and counter-hegemonic discursive practices. In this case, Rahimi explores the rumors and conspiracy theories that propagated in both pro- and anti-government circles. In his chapter, Rahimi notes this contestation of truth—and the strategic use of communication such as rumor and conspiracy—between two opposing publics:

> The main claim here is that rumors and conspiracy theories, as discourses of disbelief in an apparent reality, are disruptive performances and strategic communication through which political actors produce value-laden images of self and other in a complex set of network relations. It is primarily through the interpretative medium of rumors and conspiratorial languages produced in complex social networks that counterpublics shape the "collective text" of meaning.

However, as Rahimi and Woodward demonstrate in their work, state communication practices can be used for negative ends, harnessed in attempts to try and exploit people's sense-making routines. In a certain sense, Woodward's chapter shows a real-world case of Dentith's argument that the longer a rumor spreads, the more chance it has of attaining the status of "truth." What Woodward adds to this is the role that hegemonic, symbolic power (Bourdieu 2003[1991]) has in maintaining the boundaries of knowledge production, of what is considered "true" and what is remembered or forgotten in society. Bourdieu (2003[1991]: 170) writes of symbolic power:

> Symbolic power does not reside in "symbolic systems" in the form of an "illocutionary force" but that it is defined in and through a given relation between those who exercise power and those who submit to it, i.e., in the very structure of the field in which belief is produced and reproduced. What creates the power of words and slogans, a power capable of maintaining or subverting the social order, is the belief in the legitimacy of words and of those who utter them.

As Woodward demonstrates, although Suharto was able to exercise symbolic power in the enactment of certain myths about the post-1965 coup, this

16   G. Dalziel

symbolic power was exercised through very real coercive and punitive power. However, such a system of power is only hegemonic to a certain degree. The belief in Javanese mythic narratives gave the counter-hegemonic rumors percolating throughout Javanese society a symbolic power in and of themselves. The persistence, especially, of the sets of rumors (all linked to deep archetypal mythic schemas) in differing, oppositional cognitive subcultures highlights an important form of counter-hegemonic power and the role rumors can play as a form of resistance to such power (see also Guha 1983; Renne 1993; Scott 1985, 1990).

Rumor and new media

Lundry and Cheong's research (Chapter 7) is also influenced by a narrative approach to rumor, and looks at one possible way that the state may use rumor to try and exploit distinctions of plausibility for particular ends; here, an apparently intentional rumor allegedly started by state officials for propaganda purposes. This rumor, about the sexuality of Noordin Top, a man accused of terrorism who had been shot and killed by Indonesian security forces, was framed by a false narrative about the physical manifestations of homosexuality. Adding to their analysis, however, is a strong examination of the role that new media plays in the mediation and transmediation of rumor. In certain cases, this may help resonant rumors to propagate faster and wider than in previous periods.

Also examining the interaction of rumor and new media, Oh *et al.* (Chapter 8) use the framework established by the classic Allport and Postman studies to examine the affective content of Twitter postings during the Mumbai terrorist attacks of November 2008. Their content analysis of Twitter activity highlights one method by which to make sense of the large volumes of information being circulated online. During events representing high ambiguity, Oh *et al.* argue that this can cause problems for state authorities, especially given constraints on the amount of information that can be expressed in Twitter postings (although some languages such as Chinese and Japanese that use logographic writing systems can express more than English), along with trouble in verifying the credibility of sources and the validity of information circulating.[7]

An underlying current of Lundry and Cheong's chapter is that, although the propagation of the Noordin Top rumor may seem like a successful use of rumor for propaganda purposes, how people communicate and make sense of events is often uncontrollable and relatively unpredictable. The case shows that, at times, "propaganda occasionally recoils upon its user" (Schmeidler and Allport 1944: 144). In this episode, rumors surrounding the death of Noordin Top were not simply uncritically repeated by social media users; instead, Lundry and Cheong argue, they were utilized "to contest identities" between Indonesians and Malaysians online. The manner in which this phenomenon combines and recombines through the effects of transmediation is a demonstration of how a planned state communication campaign—overt or

Introduction 17

covert—can move quickly out of control. Lundry and Cheong's work echoes something that many governments are having to deal with in the context of state strategic communication practices. A report written by the Open Source Center (OSC), part of the US Office of the Director of National Intelligence (ODNI), for example, wrote:

> The complex network of formal and informal communications makes it increasingly difficult to plant and spin stories in a predictable way. Indeed, the digital nature of the format makes it easy for players across the system to take, chop, remix, and twist almost any message and pass it along in different directions. In this atmosphere, governments are more often finding themselves on the defensive, responding to news stories, accusations, and rumors that are challenging the official agenda.
>
> (Open Source Center 2007: 6–7)

Rumor and the practice of strategic state communication

One of the central questions framing the workshop that spawned this volume is: what effects can rumors have on state communication practices? As noted earlier, the common view is that rumors impede state communication because of, *inter alia*, their negative impact on decision-making. Bernardi and Ruston argue they can "impede strategic communication" and also be a "threat ...to counterinsurgency efforts." Oh *et al.*'s chapter on the Mumbai attacks posits that rumors have a deleterious effect on morale; rumors should therefore be carefully monitored—and rebutted if need be—during times of crisis.

Closing the volume, Olcott (Chapter 9) takes a positive and useful view of the efficacy of studying rumor for strategic state communication practitioners. His chapter takes the opposite approach from many in this book in that he does not look at the content or circulation of rumors in a specific context. Instead, Olcott presents a case study of an unsuccessful strategic state communications campaign—the *Shared Values Initiative* policy program initiated by President George W. Bush—and then works backwards to show a few ways that an understanding of the rumors and narratives circulating within the targeted communities might have led to a better crafted, or at the very least a better informed, communications strategy. Instead of "putting out an answer to a question no one had asked," Olcott argues that rumors can help give insight into the sense-making routines of people within particular communities: "Rumors, in other words, are one venue through which outsiders might learn what those with whom they would like to engage in conversation are already talking about."

Olcott's chapter and, indeed, most of the other work in this book implicitly or explicitly highlights that the understanding of communication as *information transmission* that forms the institutional logic of much state communication practices today needs to be replaced by a logic of communication as *meaning-making* (Corman *et al.* 2007). Viewing rumor as merely false or

18   G. Dalziel

distorted communication may be an easy—and natural—way to classify information. However, the essays in this volume speak to the idea that reifying such a concept of rumor may be far too simplistic an exercise. Such reification makes it easy to ignore the active roles people play in making sense of the world around them. It also works to minimize the manner in which power can shape the contours of knowledge in a society through both the ability to categorize information as rumor and the resources to make such boundary work meaningful.

The distinction between authoritative and non-authoritative information that underpinned many of the older rumor formulations may be breaking down, but this simply means that it may be more useful to utilize the rumor concept to understand distinctions in plausibility between differing communities. As such, many strategic state communication practices that assume one can simply transfer meaning between communities ignore the role that plausibility plays. These practices ignore the "effort after meaning" that people engage in, focusing on the product rather than the process of how people go about organizing and communicating their experience of the world around them.

Conclusion

In connecting some of the common threads between differing academic approaches to rumor, this volume extends previous work on rumor. However, a number of common themes motivate the essays connecting these different works through their examinations of the knowledge boundaries at work between different communities, the role that power and trust play in communication, and the tension between strategic state communication practices and genres of social communication such as rumor. This tension is between the temptation by state officials to try and harness the "power" (and cheapness) that appears to characterize rumor diffusion and the manner in which the rationalization of state communication practices often minimizes or backgrounds people's active agency in making sense of the world around them. As Lundry and Cheong demonstrate, such attempts by state organizations to try and harness rumors can often spin out of control. Woodward and Rahimi's writing also explores some of these tensions, showing the way that rumors can be used to actively resist state communication efforts.

The use of a narrative framework to understanding rumor, a theme used in a number of the essays herein, is especially important for improving our understanding of the work rumor does in the collective sense-making process and how plausibility is constructed and maintained within a community or cognitive subculture. The sum total of the work presented here highlights the boundaries at work in the construction of knowledge. How we notice and attend to certain pieces of information and not others, creating distinctions between credibility and plausibility, has consequences for how we engage in understanding the world around us.

Introduction 19

Notes

1 "Strategic communication" is a popular *term du jour* commonly used in government policy circles in the US and the UK; it is often equivalent (and less fraught with negative meaning) to "propaganda." However, here we use the term "strategic state communication" to differentiate from the type of organizational strategic communication commonly practiced in the commercial field. Even so, its meaning is highly variable. In the US government, it has often implied inter- and intra-organizational coordination of communication activities, for example. In this volume, we follow the notion of strategic communication as state communication in the service of particular policy goals. For more, see *Defense Science Board* (2007); Long (2008, 2011); Ramakrishna (2002); Taylor (2005); Taylor and Snow (2006).
2 It should be noted as well that the meaning of rumor can and does vary between institutional settings. So rumors circulating in specific communities are often deemed threatening, are false and deceptive, whereas in other contexts, they may be true just not widely known. Rumor in financial institutions, for example, does not necessarily mean false information but can also mean "unofficial" information.
3 This is very close to Robert Knapp's (1944) definition, also widely cited; he was a student assistant of Allport's at Harvard during World War II.
4 An issue of *The Baghdad Mosquito* from March 5, 2009 is available online (PDF) at www.antiwar.com/horton/05MAR2009_BM.pdf (accessed February 20, 2011)
5 The report has a useful and detailed explanation of their methodology and examples of surveys utilized, coding protocols and so forth in the appendixes.
6 *Nisei* is a rather outdated term for second-generation Japanese-American.
7 We discuss some other works that use online communications in the Conclusion.

1 Rumor, gossip, and conspiracy theories

Pathologies of testimony and the principle of publicity

Axel Gelfert

Introduction: testimony and its pathologies

Much recent work in social epistemology has focused on when, and how, we can acquire knowledge from the word of others, i.e., on the basis of other people's testimony. At the heart of this concern lies the realization that, upon reflection, there is little that we can claim to know entirely off our own bat: most of what we know, we know at least in part because we were told—by friends and family, in school, and at universities, through the media or through the grapevine. The testimony of others is, thus, an important source of knowledge.[1]

This then raises the question of whether testimony is a fundamental source of knowledge, or whether it is derivative in the sense that any epistemic justification that testimony-based beliefs might enjoy must ultimately derive from those epistemic sources—perception, memory, and inference—that, unlike testimony, do not depend on the sincerity and competence of others. The present chapter is not the place for a sketch of the general debates in the epistemology of testimony. What is important to note, however, is that the traditional philosophical concern has been with truth-oriented discourse ostensibly—if not always sincerely—aimed at conveying knowledge. On this conception, the paradigmatic case of testimonial success would be one of a hearer accepting on trust the sincere and reliable testimony of a competent speaker who, in turn, intends to share his knowledge with the hearer. Various modifications to this general model have been explored by epistemologists but, by and large, the main concern has been with truth-oriented discourse aimed at conveying knowledge.

Unfortunately, this general outlook runs into problems as soon as one shifts attention from idealized reconstructions of testimonial interactions to the messy realities of everyday communication. If "testimony proper" consists only of exchanges that are genuinely intended to convey knowledge from the speaker to a hearer, then many communicative practices—such as small talk, moralizing, gossiping, rumor—can hardly be regarded as instances of testimony; at best, they share some formal characteristics with true cases of testimony— such as the fact that they involve a source (the speaker) and an audience (the hearer). However, they do not—at least not generally—share the same epistemic goal of imparting knowledge; of course, they may serve other goals, such as

Rumor, gossip, and conspiracy theories 21

creating social cohesion or satisfying a speaker's desire to be the focus of attention.

Lying is perhaps the most extreme example of "mimicking" testimony, while also directly violating the goal of imparting knowledge; after all, the liar *knows* his pronouncements to be false and intends the hearer to adopt a false belief. As the clearest contrast to truthful testimony, lying has received its fair share of philosophical attention. However, little consideration has been given to those communicative practices that, while not outrightly deceptive, nonetheless show a significant departure from the goal of conveying knowledge. I am thinking here of cases of informal, sometimes speculative, communication such as gossiping, rumor-mongering, or simple small talk. Although some of these—such as small talk—are generally considered harmless (or perhaps even polite), others typically attract "moral or epistemic suspicion" and—adopting the terminology suggested by C.A.J. Coady—may be deemed "pathologies of testimony" (C.A.J. Coady 2006: 253).

Coady considers three examples of *prima facie* pathologies—gossip, rumor, and urban myth—and analyzes whether, in each case, the epistemic and moral suspicion generally directed at it is justified. One could, of course, settle the question by brute stipulation—for example, by *defining* gossip as always malicious (hence, morally blameworthy), rumor as unreliable (and hence, epistemically deficient), and urban myths as fictions. This, however, would not only beg important moral and epistemic questions, it would also be quite revisionist of ordinary linguistic usage of the terms in question, which tends to admit of a great deal more continuity between them than the stipulative approach would suggest. Gossip need not be unreliable, yet, as C.A.J. Coady (2006: 263) notes, "something that begins as gossip may well continue as rumor"; similarly, neither "benevolent gossip" nor "reliable rumor" appear to be incoherent notions.[2] Only with respect to urban myths—i.e., recurring stories that are preserved in considerable narrative detail (e.g., "the dotty grandma who tried to dry her damp poodle in the microwave"), but are variously attributed to different times, places, and sources ("the cousin of a friend")—does it appear to be a definitional truth that they should be considered fictions rather than reports of actual events. In general, however, as Coady rightly points out, "whether some communication is a degenerate form of testimony cannot simply be read off from the content or form of its telling, though either may give clues to this fact" (C.A.J. Coady 2006: 269).

I concur with Coady that the three phenomena he identifies—gossip, rumor, and urban myth—are clear *prima facie* cases of pathologies of testimony; however, as Coady argues with respect to gossip, it is not always clear whether the suspicion they attract is indeed justified. Rather than use the term "pathology of testimony" as an umbrella term for atypical forms of communication that can be characterized independently, I want to suggest a more principled account of what makes some forms of ostensibly (although perhaps only formally) testimonial interactions pathological.

I have argued elsewhere, on broadly Kantian grounds, that the term "pathology of testimony" should be used to designate *any type of overtly*

22   *A. Gelfert*

informative speech act that disrespects another person in their capacity as a rational being.[3] This suggestion finds some support in Kant's own discussion of rumors and (malicious) gossip. The wrongness of such speech acts, Kant argues, is quite independent of whether or not what is said actually happens to be true. What invites moral suspicion is the fact that such speech acts indicate a lack of respect for other people. This is obvious in the case of malicious gossip. As Kant puts it: "The intentional *spreading* (*propalatio*) of something that detracts from another's honour—[...] even if what is said is true—diminishes respect for humanity" (Kant 1996: 212). Less obviously, the same argument applies to rumors that are not about other people. The disrespect, in this case, is directed at the hearer himself. Any attempt to convince another person of a claim that one does not take oneself to know, can at best induce a state of *persuasion* in that person, never of knowledge. Hence, if a speaker, against his better knowledge, passes off a rumor as true to his audience, he is indirectly disrespecting them in their capacity as rational beings, by exploiting their gullibility.

Whether one prefers to use the expression "pathology of testimony" as an umbrella term for a class of independently characterizable communicative practices, or in the more principled way I have sketched, in both cases, there is by and large agreement about the extension of the term. Gossip, rumor, and urban myths are clear candidates for inclusion in any list of testimonial pathologies; an interesting borderline case, discussed later in this chapter, is the communication of conspiracy theories.

With respect to both the content and the mode of transmission, conspiracy theories lie at the opposite end of the spectrum from gossip. Whereas the content of gossip tends towards the local and the personal (even when it is about the private lives of celebrities that have become "household names"), conspiracy theories offer global explanations in terms of agents whose machinations typically transcend the messy details of ordinary human lives. Likewise, whereas gossip is typically directed at acquaintances only, conspiracy theorists actively seek out new audiences in order to convert them to their cause.[4] Importantly, however, conspiracy theories—more so than urban myths—pose considerable social and political challenges. In this respect, they are not unlike rumors in that they require attention to the conditions that give rise to them. In the next three sections, I shall characterize rumor (including urban legends), gossip, and conspiracy theories as distinct classes of testimonial pathologies, before addressing the epistemological issue of reliability. In the final two sections, I shall discuss the relation between rumor, secrecy, and the (Kantian) principle of publicity; the last, I argue, is key to the social and political challenge of how best to prevent rumors from spiraling out of control.

Rumor

Asserting that rumor constitutes, at least *prima facie*, a distortion of our usual epistemic practices of conveying knowledge, tells us what it has in common with other pathologies of testimony, but it does not tell us yet *what a rumor is*. As with any good definition, we are as much interested in finding out about commonalities as in getting clearer about specific differences. One might, therefore, be tempted to settle the matter by a stipulative definition but, as suggested earlier, this would likely preclude the outcome of our inquiry. In the present section, instead of offering my own proprietary definition of what should count as a rumor, I shall review some extant definitions and characterizations that can be found in the literature. In doing so, I shall also shed light on some of those aspects of rumors that will turn out to be especially relevant to the subsequent discussion. In the subsequent two sections, I shall first contrast rumor with gossip, then with conspiracy theorizing, thus contributing to a fuller understanding of the phenomenon of rumor.

Much contemporary rumor research traces its ancestry back to Gordon W. Allport's and Leo Postman's classic study *The Psychology of Rumor* (1947), which had grown out of wartime studies of the potentially disruptive effects rumors can have, especially in crisis situations. Allport and Postman defined rumor as "a specific (or topical) proposition for belief, passed along from person to person, usually by word of mouth, without secure standards of evidence being present" (Allport and Postman 1947: ix). On the one hand, this places rumor firmly in the realm of *prima facie* testimonial interactions between individuals; on the other hand, it suggests—although, to be fair, does not entail—that the dominant mode of transmission of rumors is strictly linear in character. The latter point is borne out by several of the laboratory studies conducted by Allport and Postman, in which an "eyewitness" to an event recounted the situation to another, who in turn described it to another, and so forth—until the report reached a research associate who carefully noted the content and analyzed any deviations from the original account. Transmission of rumor—or, indeed, regular testimony (if the original eyewitness report is taken to be authoritative)—was thus "idealized" as a linear series of simple, unidirectional acts of communication; more complex interactions, which might involve the recipient questioning the speaker's reasons for the telling, or corroboration by reports from multiple speakers, were abstracted away in the set-up of the study.

Based on their study of wartime rumors, Allport and Postman formulated what they called "the basic law of rumors," according to which "first, the theme of the story must have some *importance* to speaker and listener; second, the true facts must be shrouded in some kind of *ambiguity*" (Allport and Postman 1947: 33). Importance and ambiguity were regarded as "essential conditions" of the occurrence of rumors, and were thought to contribute directly to the overall transmission and circulation of rumors. In quantitative terms, $R = I \times a$, where R represents the amount of rumor in circulation, I stands for the importance of the subject matter, and a refers to the ambiguity of the evidence. Apart from the difficulty of quantifying any of these factors, let alone establishing a law-like mathematical relationship between them, Allport and Postman's approach has been criticized for being too narrow in

24   *A. Gelfert*

its focus on how rumors can be passed along a chain of interlocutors, each of whom adds to the distortion of the truth. Thus, Dan Miller (2006: 507) argues that "Allport and Postman ignored the social context within which rumors develop, spread, and gain meaning", whereas Ralph Rosnow (1991: 485) emphasizes "that there are variables besides importance and ambiguity that influence the origins and perpetuation of rumors."

Challenges to the idea that "importance" and "ambiguity" are the determining factors in determining rumor circulation arise from both conceptual and empirical considerations. At the conceptual level, it is important to distinguish between the objective ambiguity of available evidence (in the sense of its being inconclusive) and a generalized sense of ambiguity that also encompasses subjectively experienced "personal anxiety" (Rosnow 1991: 487).[5] At the empirical level, several researchers have reported that, under certain conditions, subjects are "more inclined to rate the rumors they spread as *unimportant* rather than important" (Rosnow 1991: 486). Two possible explanations for this last effect come to mind. First, when the stakes are sufficiently high—for example, when a community's physical survival depends on ascertaining the truth or falsity of a matter—a rumor may tend to elicit *more*, rather than *less*, critical examination before it is passed on. Second, to the extent that people also pass on rumors in order to simply pass time, rather than convey knowledge—that is, to the extent that rumor is continuous with gossip or ordinary small talk—people may prefer to pass on rumors they regard as by and large inconsequential.

The collective character and social function of rumor was emphasized by Tamotsu Shibutani in his 1966 book *Improvised News*, which drew on the author's experience as a Japanese-American—interred in "relocation centers" in 1941—who witnessed the role of rumors in resolving ambiguity and psychological tension. In his book, Shibutani (1966: 17) characterizes rumors as "a recurrent form of *communication through which men caught together in an ambiguous situation attempt to construct a meaningful interpretation of it by pooling their intellectual resources*" [italics in original]. In particular, he analyzed the process by which "improvised news" evolves to fill a gap in a community's collective understanding of problematic situations. Whenever the collective need for understanding is not satisfied by the information available, shared norms of accuracy, objectivity, and fact-finding will be relaxed, thereby allowing rumors to emerge as attempts at collective sense-making. This has direct consequences, among others, for the individuation of rumors. Rather than treating rumors "as stand-alone statements" (Miller 2006: 516)—as "an object that stimulates one person, undergoes certain modifications while passing through him, and then departs to stimulate someone else" (Shibutani 1966: 8)—a rumor is "something that is shaped, reshaped, and reinforced in a succession of communicative acts"; it is "not so much the dissemination of a designated message as the process of forming a definition of a situation" (Shibutani 1966: 9). Whereas Allport and Postman questioned the faithfulness of serial transmission to the original statement, Shibutani argues that rumors "cannot be identified in terms of any particular set of words," but only "by abstracting from dozens of communicative acts ... Rumor is not so much distortion of some word combination but what is held in common" (Shibutani 1966: 16).

The definitions and characterizations of rumor discussed thus far point to different aspects of the concept of rumor. In particular, it makes sense to distinguish the question of how rumors *originate* from their mode of *transmission* and *functional role*. This is not to say that these dimensions of rumor are unrelated to one another. For example, Shibutani's thesis that rumors are collective attempts at sense-making asserts both that rumors originate in situations of ambiguity *and* that they fulfill a social function by alleviating (social and cognitive) pressures arising from such situations. Likewise, if one regards as primary the quasi-testimonial role of rumor as conveying (unofficial or suppressed) knowledge, then one will naturally be drawn to a picture of serial transmission that conforms to standard sender—receiver models of communication. In any case, despite their differences, most theoretical approaches to rumor have operated "on the commonsense premise that rumors are essentially public communications that are infused with private hypotheses about how the world works" (Rosnow 1991: 488):

> Steeped in theory-driven attitudes and idiosyncratic expectations, rumors give vent or expression to anxieties and uncertainties as people attempt to make sense of the world in which they live.
>
> *(ibid.)*

Interestingly, what little attention rumor has received in contemporary philosophy has been directed at the problem of ascertaining its reliability (a topic to which I shall return shortly) rather than at definitional issues. Thus, David Coady contents himself with stating two necessary (and, he claims, jointly sufficient) conditions on when a communication constitutes a rumor, namely "that it has passed through many hands (or lips), and that it has unofficial status at the time and place in question" (D. Coady 2006a: 49). Such a minimalist account of rumor is not without problems of its own. For one, it says nothing about the conditions under which rumors originate or about their function. It also raises the question of why there could be no such thing as "officially sanctioned rumors" (e.g., as part of a rogue government's disinformation campaign). Too much also appears to hinge on which sources are to be regarded as authoritative, i.e., as conferring "official" status to certain informational narratives. Consider the case of urban myths, which are frequently reported as factual by (let us assume, otherwise reliable) local newspapers. Clearly, urban myths remain an epistemically problematic subclass of testimony (and may well be recognizable as such by a more discerning reader), even when a gullible editor reprints them in good faith.

The case of urban myths deserves special discussion, as many authors either regard urban myths as simply more of the same—that is, "cases of

26   *A. Gelfert*

rumors: unofficial information circulating in society" (Kapferer 1990: 9)—or cite examples of urban myths as "exemplary" cases of rumor (Merten 2009: 26). Others regard urban myths, or legends, simply as persistent rumors that have become divorced from their specific origins. Thus, Allport and Postman (1947: 162) write: "A legend may be regarded as a solidified rumor," and Shibutani (1966: 130), although reluctant to equate the two entirely, none-theless suggests they are of a piece when he writes that "some rumors persist and become incorporated into popular lore." And yet, we typically face no difficulty when it comes to distinguishing, at least retrospectively, urban myths (e.g., reports of snakes biting customers in the produce section of super-markets) from rumor (e.g., concerning the impending bankruptcy of a savings bank). For one, urban myths often make use of highly stylized narrative ele-ments. Indeed, as folklorists have pointed out, urban myths are the modern equivalent of legends, aimed at conveying the moral of the story rather than factual knowledge. Typically, as with urban myths concerning dangers to children (such as the legend of LSD-coated "lick and stick" tattoos [Renard 1991]), they depict "conflicts between the apparent conditions of modern society and the traditional values of individuals and families" (Miller 2006: 510).

As stories, urban myths conform to their own (albeit variable) narrative conventions; whatever basis in fact they may have had has been transformed beyond recognition, via "a form of collaborative storytelling that is meta-phorical in character not bound by time and space limitations"; rumors, in contrast, are "temporally and locally situated" (Miller 2006: 508). To the extent that urban myths "travel"—and, for example, are reported in local newspapers as "recent" occurrences in a "neighboring" town—they may, of course, take on a local flavor, as it were. However, the details of their spatio-temporal location, as well as concerning the source ("a friend of a friend"), are virtually always incidental and matter only to the extent that they keep up the illusion of newsworthiness. This is, of course, cold comfort for anyone who has been gullible enough to believe a news report that turned out be a case of urban legend. The various ingredients of an urban myth—such as locales, protagonists, or brands—are constantly being updated to make them virtually indistinguishable from, say, fact-based rumor. For the most part, then—and especially from the epistemic vantage point of a moderately gulli-ble recipient of rumors and urban myths—their similarities in terms of mode of transmission outweigh their dissimilarities in terms of narrative structure:

> Both rumors and urban legends are forms of communication found in networks of informal social relationships. Both are communicative acts in which the content of the stories is imbued with cultural meaning that resides in the communities and social relationships in question.
>
> (Miller 2006: 510)

Although it is true that, as Alan Dundes (1965: 247) puts it, "Rumor is similar to folklore but usually consists of nontraditional material," it is also true that "some legends become rumors and some rumors become legends" (Mullen 1972: 98).

Gossip

Several authors have proposed definitions of gossip, sometimes in direct contrast to rumor. Thus, Klaus Merten (2009: 16) claims that gossip can be distinguished from rumor by "four precise conditions." Unlike rumor, gossip (1) occurs only among acquaintances, (2) is always about a particular individual, who (3) is known to—and, in turn, knows—everyone in the group, but (4) is not present at the time. Similarly, Nicholas Emler (1994: 136f) characterizes gossip as informal speech "between acquaintances," typically "one-to-one" (and almost always "face-to-face"), which may or may not be "unscheduled." In Jörg Bergmann's (1993) fortuitous turn of phrase, gossip consists of "discreet indiscretions." Whereas gossip, on the one hand, "possesses relevance only for a specific group" and—*pace* the existence of celebrity gossip—"is disseminated in a highly selective manner within a fixed social network," rumors spread "unauthorized messages that are always of universal interest and accordingly are disseminated diffusely" (Bergmann 1993: 70).

Traditionally, philosophy has paid scant attention to gossip, and to the extent that it has, it is fair to say that it has viewed gossip—and those who engage in it—with moral suspicion. Interestingly, both the purveyor of gossip and the one who believes it (perhaps uncritically) are typically regarded as sharing the blame. On one construal of the traditional view, the gossiper "shows a lack of respect for persons" (Taylor 1994: 43), in that he treats the private life of the gossipee as fair game for the amusement and delectation of others. In this sense, the gossipee is being treated as a "mere means," even though gossip need not be intended as being of instrumental value in manipulating others. Unlike lying, gossip is often truthful and sincere and, in this sense, does not appear to be in direct violation of epistemic norms. And yet, some philosophers have argued that, even though gossip should be able, in principle, to function as a source of knowledge, it does not *in general* merit belief. According to Kant, malicious gossip [*Nachrede*], *even when true*, ought to be dismissed (see the earlier discussion). In his *Anthropology from a Pragmatic Point of View*, Kant (2006[1798]: 194) makes clear that not only is the gossiper at fault, but also the recipient who believes what is manifestly gossipy information. Thus, he demands: "Not to pay attention to gossip [*Nachrede*] derived from the shallow and malicious judgments of others; for paying attention to it already indicates weakness [of character]."

In the very recent philosophical literature on gossip, there has been a trend towards rehabilitating gossip, both as a legitimate activity and as a source of knowledge.[6] This development appears to be motivated by three distinct general concerns, each of which indicates a break with, or at least some departure from, the received view. I shall refer to them as (1) the grooming analogy, (2) the argument from empowerment, and (3) the challenge to hypocrisy.

28 *A. Gelfert*

Let us first turn to the grooming analogy. According to this view, the primary function of gossip is not to convey knowledge, or to present information about the gossipee, but to establish and reinforce friendships among the gossipers. Although some gossip may titillate by virtue of what it is about, it is the frisson of being part of an intimate group of gossipers that makes gossip enjoyable. As Max Gluckman puts it, "the right to gossip about certain people is a privilege which is only extended to a person when he or she is accepted as a member of a group or set" (Gluckman 1963: 313). Gossiping among humans is thus a linguistic equivalent of sorts to grooming among other social primates; it has even been argued that language itself evolved in response to pressures arising from our social environment, rather than as an adaptation to informational needs in relation to the natural environment (e.g., Dunbar 1996). As Gabriele Taylor (1994: 41) puts it, "good personal relationships are an important value in our lives, and the circumstances of gossiping clearly foster such relationships"; gossip, much like the practice of grooming in the case of non-human primates, provides *social glue*—in addition to "the pleasure of recognition" (Taylor 1994: 41) that comes with being able to empathize with the experiences of others. Given such beneficial effects of the practice of gossiping, it is perhaps no surprise that defenders of the grooming analogy have come to a very different assessment of the moral permissibility of gossip. Taylor, in particular, claims that "the Kantian objection need […] not be taken seriously" as "it is absurd to put so much weight on attitudes [on the part of the gossiper] that may have no practical effect, particularly when we consider the concrete social benefits of gossiping in the form of generating comfortable relationships" (Taylor 1994: 44).

A second, more ambitious defense of gossip is based on recent feminist epistemology and takes its cue from the historical connotations of the term "gossip." As Louise Collins (1994: 114) notes, "the association of gossip with the feminine and a negative evaluation have a long history; in the English language, the term 'gossips' historically referred to a woman's circle of female friends."[7] The casualness and informality of "female" gossiping was frequently contrasted with the serious business of men. As Nicholas Emler characterizes this view, with some (ironic) exaggeration for dramatic effect: whereas "women chatter, tattle, gab, rabbit, prattle, nag, whine, and bitch," men open their mouths only in order "to accomplish something of consequence—to discourse, debate, philosophize, exchange ideas, conduct business, or engage in politics" (Emler 1994: 118). That such a "femininization" of gossip does not do justice to social reality goes without saying. More importantly, however, any distinction along gender lines overstates the degree, and permanence, of the contrast between informal ways of knowing—such as knowledge gained from the casual testimony of everyday conversation (which may or may not include gossip)—and official pathways of learning, such as formal education and scientific inquiry, both of which have historically been male dominated.

Rather than reconceptualize gossip as itself a mechanism of inquiry, as some commentators have attempted (Ayim 1994: 85–99), a more thorough-going

Rumor, gossip, and conspiracy theories 29

defense would be based on the observation that informal communication may exhibit certain positive epistemic qualities—for example, by being more egalitarian, nuanced, and imaginative—that render it superior to traditional forms of knowledge, in particular when it comes to such areas as ethics, politics, and knowledge of the social world at large. The very "unruliness of gossip" (Code 1994: 104) may expose some official "knowledge" as mere prejudice, while bringing to the fore previously overlooked interests and injustices. Gossip may have an empowering effect at the epistemic level as well as, ultimately, in the political domain.

This last point finds its clearest expression in the defense of gossip as a challenge to hypocrisy. Thus, in a 1994 paper, Ronald de Sousa argues for a radical rethinking of the public/private distinction. In an argumentative move that may seem prescient, given that it foreshadows some of the challenges to privacy in connection with electronic social networks, de Sousa argues that the principle of "freedom of information" should perhaps be extended from the public realm to the private sphere. That part of our life that is considered private may "in terms of the actual quality of our lives [...] well be the most important one, [and so] accurate knowledge about it is crucial" (de Sousa 1994: 30). In some cases, gossip may be society's best shot at exposing hypocrisy or uncovering cases of abuse and discrimination. As de Sousa (1994: 31) puts it:

> La Rochefoucauld taught us that hypocrisy is the tribute that vice pays to virtue. But what is discretion but hypocrisy in the third person? [...] I suggest that the indiscretion of gossip is, in a small way, a saintly virtue.

Rehabilitating gossip as a source of knowledge and legitimate social activity is, of course, one thing, praising it as a "saintly virtue" is quite another. It is perhaps worth noting that gossip itself also has a potentially oppressive aspect—not so much for its intrusion into privacy as such, but because it provides an effective tool for disciplining those who challenge, or violate, the existing social order. In traditional oral societies especially, but also in what Ruth Benedict (1946: 223) has called "shame cultures," being the target of persistent gossip may permanently undermine a person's social reputation, or even group membership, sometimes driving the victim to suicide (Malinowski 1926: 77–79).

Conspiracy theories

Gossip, as the "social form of discreet indiscretion" (Bergmann 1993), is normally meant for a limited audience only, and may even depend for its success on the gossiper's remaining anonymous to the gossipee. Unlike rumor, gossip is not typically intended to be spread beyond the immediate group of gossipers.[8] The situation is quite different in the case of conspiracy theories. Conspiracy theorists often seek to attract large audiences and blame their failure to do so on the suppression of their views by the mainstream media.

30   *A. Gelfert*

Having drawn a line, in the previous section, between rumor and gossip, it is important also to demarcate rumor from another "close cousin": conspiracy theories.

Unlike rumor and gossip, conspiracy theories have received considerable philosophical attention. In *The Open Society and Its Enemies*, Karl Popper (1945: 104) sketches in very general terms what he calls "The Conspiracy Theory of Society":

> It is the view that an explanation of a social phenomenon consists in the discovery of the men or groups who are interested in the occurrence of this phenomenon (sometimes it is a hidden interest which has first to be revealed) and who have planned and conspired to bring it about.

Whereas Popper targets what he regards as an ideologically misguided way of analyzing social phenomena in general, subsequent discussion has focused on the social, epistemic, and structural features of conspiracy theories that are invoked as alternatives to specific "official stories." Among the historically most virulent are the various anti-Semitic conspiracy theories that blame events in world history on the alleged aim of "Jewish world domination"; more recent examples of conspiracy theories range from the euphemistically named "9/11 Truth movement" to the pop-cultural speculations surrounding the deaths (or not!) of figures such as Elvis Presley and Michael Jackson.

By focusing on "*unwarranted* conspiracy theories," such as the examples just mentioned, one might be tempted to think of them as a unitary class of explanations "that can be distinguished analytically from those theories that deserve our assent" (Keeley 1999: 111). As Brian Keeley (1999: 111) puts it, this reasoning gives rise to the "idea that we can do with conspiracy theories what David Hume did with miracles: show that there is a class of explanations to which we should not assent, *by definition*." Just as Hume argued that one should never believe a witness who claims to have experienced a miracle—as a violation of the laws of nature (which is how Hume defines a miracle, namely as an exception to our otherwise uniform experience of nature) is, by definition, always less likely than error or insincerity on the part of the witness—so one might argue that conspiracy theories, *by the very content of their claims*, defy belief.

However, in the case of conspiracy theories, things are not quite as simple as that. For one, no participant in the debate denies that conspiracies are possible and have occurred as a matter of historical fact. The Watergate affair really did happen, corporations have indeed been caught engaging in conspiratorial price-fixing or cover-ups of health risks associated with their products, and governments in Europe and the Middle East did conspire with the CIA in the abduction and torture ("extraordinary rendition") of a number of their citizens.[9] Which conspiracy theories are unwarranted and which merit belief is thus a matter of degree and cannot be decided on the basis of their content alone. Keeley's attempt to identify characteristics of (some) conspiracy theories—such as their reliance on "errant data" (i.e., data not accounted for by official explanations), their positing a secret cabal of decision-makers behind the publicly known line-up of politicians, and so forth—has been dismissed by some critics as "a strategy that systematically discounts conspiracy" to the point where the denial of conspiracy itself becomes "a superstitious or irrational belief" (Pigden 2006: 165).

A more fruitful way of approaching conspiracy theories is by abandoning the idea of a strict demarcation criterion in terms of the content of (unwarranted) conspiracy theories versus (legitimate) historical explanations, focusing instead on certain features of how conspiracy theories are developed and on the mechanisms of belief formation involved in the process. In other words, attention must be shifted from conspiracy theories, understood as abstracts sets of claims, to conspiracy theorizing (as an activity) and to conspiracy theorists and their psychology. Steve Clarke (2002: 143) has suggested that one should

> focus attention on the cognitive failures of a significant class of conspiracy theorists—those conspiracy theorists who continue to hold on to conspiracy theories even when these take on the appearance of degenerating research programmes.

In other words, it is the failure of conspiracy theorists to respond appropriately to evidence, or lack thereof, which renders their explanations epistemically deficient—not any epistemic flaw of conspiracy theories as such. Although Clarke (2006: 129–132) has since modified his position in response to criticism, he initially identified the social–psychological phenomenon known as the *fundamental attribution error* (FAE) as a potential explanation for the appeal of conspiracy theories (Clarke 2006: 144). According to the FAE, human reasoners systematically underestimate the importance of situational factors, while overestimating the significance of dispositional factors—such as intentions, character traits, and other long-term dispositions—in explaining the behavior of others. Although the FAE has been shown (not uncontroversially, one might add) to hold universally, it seems plausible to assume that some people will be more prone than others to the distorting effect it (along with other well-documented cognitive biases) may have on the process of belief formation. Perhaps, then, conspiracy theorists are simply more prone than the rest of us to attributing various historical and political events to the machinations of conspirators.

The thought that conspiracy theorists may be suffering, however subtly, from certain cognitive deficiencies has recently been developed further by Cass Sunstein and Adrian Vermeule. In particular, they emphasize the role of social feedback mechanisms—such as informational cascades and group polarization—which may exacerbate any pre-existing cognitive biases, leading to an overall *crippled epistemology* among conspiracy theorists (Sunstein 2002). As Sunstein and Vermeule put it, "members of informationally and socially isolated groups become increasingly distrustful or suspicious of the motives of others or of the larger society, falling into a 'sinister attribution error' [SAE]." In what is essentially a twist on the FAE and its possible role in the acceptance of conspiracy theories, in the case of the SAE "people feel that they are under pervasive scrutiny, and hence they attribute personalistic motives to outsiders and overestimate the amount of attention they receive" (Sunstein and Vermeule 2009: 218).

Although rumors and conspiracy theories are conceptually distinct, they are at the same time intimately connected, for "conspiracy theories can proliferate through rumors, although they need not do so" (Sunstein and Vermeule 2009: 203). Conspiracy theories typically spread along similar channels of informal communication as rumors, and individual rumors may often supply relevant factoids, which are then interpreted as supporting evidence for the conspiracy hypothesis. However, although it may be true that "conspiracy theories, in many cases, can originate as rumors," equating the two—that is, treating conspiracy theories as "a subgenre of rumor" (Singleton 2008: v)—seems too strong. For one, rumors are "temporally and locally situated" (Miller 2006: 508) in a way conspiracy theories need not be; after all, some of the most persistent conspiracy theories, such as those concerning the historical influence of Freemasons, have developed into elaborate explanatory frameworks that allege continuous, rather than episodic, conspiratorial activity at a global, not merely local, level.

Furthermore, there is a significant difference when it comes to the level of doxastic commitment on the part of those who spread rumors or conspiracy theories. Whereas a rumor need not itself be believed, or presented as such by the speaker, for it to achieve the intended effect of being spread, any conspiracy theorist worth his salt needs to assert, not merely report, at least the core ingredients of his pet theory.[10]

As far as content is concerned, rumors and conspiracy theories tend to differ insofar as rumors typically involve existence claims—concerning the presence or absence of causal (or, for that matter, personal) relationships, or the occurrence or non-occurrence of an unusual event—whereas conspiracy theories provide explanatory frameworks which, as Keeley puts it, "typically seek to tie together seemingly unrelated events" (Keeley 1999: 117).

Partly as a result of the last point, there appears to be a difference in the degree to which rumors and conspiracy theories (or rather, rumor-mongers and conspiracy theorists) are *responsive* to evidence. Whereas conspiracy theories are sufficiently complex to allow for *prima facie* counterevidence to be assimilated, as well as for lack of evidence of conspiratorial activity to be re-interpreted as evidence of a cover-up, rumors (all else being equal) take empirical evidence at face value: if no evidence materializes, a rumor will subside more often than not.

The termination of a rumor, however, is not a simple affair; as Shibutani noted, the phenomenon of rumor is best understood as a social process. Whereas "the process of rumor construction is terminated when the situation

Rumor, gossip, and conspiracy theories 33

in which it arose is no longer problematic" (Shibutani 1966: 139), this does not always mean that a rumor will immediately go out of circulation. Some rumors may, for example, "solidify" into urban legends, perhaps aided by the well-known "sleeper effect," by which people over time dissociate the content of claims from their initial evaluation of sources.[11] A final contrast between rumors and conspiracy theories concerns their status as *unofficial* accounts. Whereas rumors merely lack confirmation from official sources, conspiracy theories are put forward as *alternatives* to official stories. Indeed, if official confirmation were to be forthcoming, a rumor would simply cease to be a rumor and become an acknowledged fact, whereas a conspiracy theory—as in the Watergate case—would come to be accepted as a factual, yet nonetheless conspiracy-based, explanation (even if the conspiracy would, one hopes, by then have ceased to exist).

The problem of reliability

From the perspective of someone who receives a rumor, or encounters a conspiracy theory, what matters is the reliability of the claims he or she is confronted with. Whereas rumors tend to spread by diffusion, conspiracy theories are often disseminated actively by their proponents. It seems fair to suggest that, all else being equal, conspiracy theories must meet higher epistemic standards than rumors in order to warrant belief, precisely because they typically aim at overturning already well-confirmed alternative accounts. The point is not that blind trust in official stories is always rational—it clearly is not—but rather that conspiracy theories must be more explanatorily successful than their competitors, not just in terms of their completeness with respect to data, but also in terms of simplicity, coherence with undisputed background knowledge, and other explanatory desiderata.[12]

In the case of rumors, much depends on the chain of transmission by which a given claim has reached the recipient. As with testimony in general, at every intermediate step in the chain of transmission, deliberate or accidental distortion may occur as a result of possible insincerity, or lack of competence, on the part of the interlocutors involved. However, we do not dismiss all secondhand testimonial reports on the basis of the mere possibility of unreliable transmission; if we did, much of what we ordinarily take ourselves to know would lack a rational basis. How different kinds of rumors "travel"—that is, whether they are just another kind of second-hand report, or whether they "grow" via a "cumulative process" (Shibutani 1966: 84)—will therefore feature prominently in assessments of their reliability. However, it is not only the mode of transmission that is relevant in this context; just how reliable rumors are as sources of information also depends crucially on the conditions of their construction. Thus, in situations where "collective excitement is mild" and "unsatisfied demand for news is moderate," rumor construction "occurs through critical deliberation," which may involve close examination of available information, the collective appraisal of the plausibility of claims, and the placing of "a premium upon facts" (Shibutani 1966: 70f). In contrast, in situations where an identifiable dynamic of events is already unfolding, rumors may *extrapolate from*, rather than *contribute to*, the facts; as a result, "a total picture may be constructed that is quite inaccurate, but highly plausible" (Shibutani 1966: 77). When extrapolation from the facts is coupled with a general sense that nothing can be done to influence the unfolding dynamic—that is, when ego-involvement is low—the accuracy of information inevitably suffers: "Where action is impossible or not seriously contemplated, accuracy of definition is not decisive, and people may say things that please them" (Shibutani 1966: 91). Needless to say, any initial accuracy that rumors lack cannot later be compensated for by the reliability of the processes by which they are subsequently transmitted across social networks.

David Coady has recently argued that rumor does not deserve its bad reputation as an unreliable source of knowledge. The mere fact that a rumor has passed "through many hands (or lips)" (D. Coady 2006a: 49) need not count against its reliability—on the contrary:

> [I]f you hear a rumor, it is not only *prima facie* evidence that it has been thought plausible by a large number of people, it is also *prima facie* evidence that it has been thought plausible by a large number of reliable people. And that really is *prima facie* evidence that it is true.
>
> (D. Coady 2006a: 47)

The basic problem with *prima facie* accounts, of course, is that first impressions can be misleading. What, then, are Coady's reasons for holding that justification can *accrue* (rather than diminish) through transmission?[13] Coady rests his case on an example from anti-rumor campaigns carried out by the US military during World War II, which were aimed at "dispersing the normal channels along which rumors passed" (D. Coady 2006a: 48). However, by inhibiting the flow of information and, in effect, reducing the number of pathways by which rumors were transmitted, the campaigns had the paradoxical effect of making rumors less reliable. Coady, in support of his thesis, quotes Theodore Caplow's (1947: 301) account of why the break-up of stable networks of transmission led to a decrease in the reliability of rumors:

> Distortion in terms of wishes and avoidance seems to be an individual rather than a group characteristic. As channels solidified, this phenomenon became comparatively rare, because of the exclusion of persons associated with previous invalidity. When they were broken up [in the course of the anti-rumor campaigns], wish fulfillment again became conspicuous.

Coady interprets this as compelling evidence that "the survival and reproductive success" of rumors is "partly dependent on their being disseminated by people widely known to be reliable sources" (D. Coady 2006a: 47).

Rumor, gossip, and conspiracy theories 35

Reliable interlocutors thus act as "filters" of sorts, removing unsubstantiated rumors from circulation. Chances then are that, by the time we encounter a rumor, it will have gone through various stages of "filtering," thereby making it likely that it merits belief.

I believe that Coady's argument is flawed in several ways. Here, I shall only focus on the dynamics of rumor-mongering that, in my opinion, render Coady's "filtering" scenario unlikely. Note that the example Coady cites in support of his view—Caplow's case of wartime rumors—is a highly specialized one. In times of war, when one's own survival and that of one's community is at stake—that is, when ego-involvement is high and the action-guiding role of rumors dominates—any pressure towards truthfulness and accuracy of second-hand reports is likely to be greater than during less trying times. It therefore seems unjustified to extrapolate from the reliability of wartime rumors to the reliability of rumors *in general*. Furthermore, while rumors will often fail to spread beyond a speaker who is deemed unreliable by his peers— simply because nobody believes him—this effect can easily be masked by what has sometimes been called "informational cascades" (Sunstein 2008: 6). As Sunstein and Vermeule (2009: 215) emphasize, "affective factors, and not mere information, play a large role in the circulation of rumors of all kinds," with many rumors persisting and spreading "because they serve to justify or to rationalize an antecedent emotional state produced by some important event." Hence, rumors that stir up emotions, or relate to otherwise highly charged controversies, may enjoy a disproportionate amount of "airtime" as it were. Given further that rumors do not propagate uniformly in the linear fashion presupposed by Coady, but through multipliers—well-connected individuals who form important nodes in social networks of communication—the recipient of a rumor is typically in no position to tell just how much "filtering" has actually taken place. In reality, any *prima facie* entitlement he might have for believing that a particular claim has been deemed plausible by a large enough number of people is insufficient to establish the reliability, *in general*, of rumor as a source of knowledge.

Publicity, secrecy, and levels of public trust

The above analysis of pathologies of testimony—specifically gossip, rumor (including urban myth), and conspiracy theories—presents a mixed picture. On the one hand, there appears to be no strict demarcation criterion according to which such communications are *necessarily* unreliable; after all, they are typically received through testimony, which we consider an important source of knowledge. On the other hand, there seems to be a clear sense in which testimonial pathologies invite suspicion, if not on purely epistemic grounds then certainly for the reasons outlined in the discussion regarding rumor. The lack of a clear demarcation criterion—whether on the basis of content or by virtue of recognizable features of the source—poses an epistemic challenge to the recipient of associated testimony: should he, or should

36   *A. Gelfert*

he not, accept what he is told? At the social and political level, false rumors and conspiracy theories also pose a considerable challenge to policy-makers, who face a dilemma in responding to false or unsubstantiated claims. Take the example of a rumor or conspiracy theory that alleges the involvement of government authorities in a cover-up of some sort or another. Should the authorities respond to the allegations by denying them, thereby drawing additional attention to the rumor or conspiracy in question, or should they remain silent, thereby lending credence to the suggestion that the government has something to hide? In light of the absence of *a priori* arguments for or against the reliability of gossip, rumor, or conspiracy theories, I shall focus in this section on the general conditions of communication that may either contribute to, or inhibit, the occurrence of testimonial pathologies.

In developing my position, I take my cue from an argument by Brian Keeley concerning conspiracy theories which, although ultimately unconvincing, contains an important observation about the relation between public trust and the acceptance of conspiracy theories. Keeley (1999: 123) argues that, because conspiracy theories "throw into doubt the various institutions that have been set up to generate reliable data and evidence," acceptance of any particular conspiracy theory necessarily escalates into wholesale skepticism about all, or most, publicly available information. Conspiracy theories are thus self-defeating, because they would entail *public trust skepticism*; according to Keeley (*ibid.*), "we shall be forced to recognize the unwarranted nature of the conspiracy theory if we are to be left with *any* warranted explanations and belief at all".

Keeley's argument from public trust skepticism has attracted much philosophical criticism. Thus, Clarke (2002: 141) argues that, although it may be empirically true that conspiracy theories have a tendency to "escalate"—in the sense that they allege ever larger conspiracies, involving government agencies, corporations, the press, etc.—at best, this tells us something about "the fallacious reasoning patterns of some contemporary conspiracy theorists"; it is not a feature of conspiracy theories as such. Similarly, Coady points out that a conspiracy theory, unlike a skeptical hypothesis, is typically "offered as an actual explanation," not with the intent of "undermin[ing] belief as such" (D. Coady 2003: 205). It is indeed an overstatement on Keeley's part to claim that belief in *unwarranted* conspiracy theories would necessarily lead into a skeptical abyss; a person's web of belief is more robust than this. Nonetheless, there remains a legitimate worry about cognitive dissonance on the part of conspiracy theorists. What calls for an explanation is the ease with which many conspiracy theorists seem to be able to square their belief in conspiracy theories with leading otherwise perfectly ordinary lives.

Even if Keeley's argument is ultimately unsuccessful, it nevertheless points to an important connection between the general level of trust in public sources of information and belief in rumors and conspiracy theories. Even Keeley's critics do not disagree about the existence of such a connection. As Coady puts it, "whether the pervasive skepticism of people and institutions in

Rumor, gossip, and conspiracy theories 37

authority, that Keeley warns us against, is warranted depends on the kind of people and institutions in authority at the time and place in question" (D. Coady 2003: 204). In the remainder of this section, I shall steer a middle path between Keeley's dismissal and Coady's defense of the admissibility of rumors and conspiracy theories, while at the same time being more specific about the relation between levels of public trust and the reliability of such forms of communication. Instead of arguing, like Keeley, that belief in rumors and conspiracy theories necessarily escalates into wholesale public trust skepticism, I want to suggest the converse point: namely, that rumors and conspiracy theories deserve to be taken seriously if, and only if, one has good grounds for distrusting public sources of information. It is important, therefore, to identify and analyze factors that determine the level of public trust that is appropriate at a given place and time.

Sociological research has identified a variety of cultural, political, and socio-economic factors—ranging from degree of ethnic heterogeneity to historical differences in religious affiliations and income distribution—all of which contribute to the general level of trust in a society (Misztal 1996). Although there will often be a correlation between social trust in general and trust in public sources of information, it is the latter—which I shall henceforth refer to as "public trust"—that matters most in the present context.[14] I shall call levels of public trust "appropriate" if the degree of trust that people place in public sources of information, on average, reflects the actual reliability of those sources. As with trusting people, it is possible to be both *too trusting* and *too distrustful* with respect to public sources of information; correspondingly, gullibility and skepticism are the twin dangers that threaten to undermine successful processing of publicly communicated information. Indeed, as some authors have suggested, the presence of *some* rumor activity is to be expected in a healthy civil society, as "a moderate number of rumors suggests social participation, investment in collective order and social trust," whereas "rumor as dominant discourse or as nearly absent suggest either mistrust or apathy (or fear)" (Fine 2007: 17).

When it comes to public sources of information, reliability must be understood as comprising such desiderata as truthfulness, completeness, and relevance. For a public source to count as reliable, it must not only have a track record of disclosing truthful information, but it must also be the kind of source that an individual seeking information can reasonably expect to be able *to rely upon*.[15] It is easy to see that there are going to be tradeoffs between these desiderata. For example, a government agency might decide only to release information that meets its own, exceptionally high, standards of confirmation and accuracy; as a result, it might choose not to respond at all to a request for information, if giving a substantive reply would mean having to release information that does not meet its internal standards. On a narrow interpretation of epistemic reliability, such a policy would, in many ways, be exemplary; after all, one could be virtually certain that information received from the agency will turn out to be true. However, by ignoring many

38   *A. Gelfert*

legitimate requests for information, the agency could quickly earn a reputation as secretive and inefficient at communicating information. Although the information it actually releases would be impeccable, the agency itself could not be relied upon to provide the information in the first place.

Rumors, gossip, and conspiracy theories flourish wherever there is a lack of relevant and reliable information. Leaving aside momentarily the phenomenon of *"conspiracy entrepreneurs* who profit directly and indirectly from propagating their theories" (Sunstein and Vermeule 2009: 212), much speculative talk arises opportunistically in response to informational needs in the absence of relevant information. As Shibutani (1966: 62) puts it:

> Unsatisfied demand for news—the *discrepancy* between information needed to come to terms with a changing environment and what is provided by formal news channels—constitutes the crucial condition of rumor construction.

When informational deficits are no longer tied to particular situations, but are perceived to be pervasive or worsening (or come to be associated with long-standing collective tension), rumors may emerge spontaneously: "If unsatisfied demand for news is very great, collective excitement is intensified, and rumor construction occurs through spontaneous interchanges" (Shibutani 1966: 96). Under such conditions, once a rumor is out, even the subsequent release of relevant disconfirming evidence may not be sufficient to curb its spread. Rather than responding to rumors that are already in circulation, a policy aimed at minimizing the prevalence of rumors should seek to prevent their coming into existence—not primarily by suppressing the rumor-mongering activities of individuals (an effort that would quickly become self-defeating), but by maintaining conditions of communication that make reliance on rumors subjectively less attractive. At the most basic level, this would mean redressing informational deficits by ensuring that relevant information and data are made available—not *in response to* existing rumors, but *pre-emptively*. In other words, where avoidable, informational gaps should not be allowed to occur.[16]

Mere in-principle availability of authoritative information, however, is going to have little effect unless conditions are in place that ensure sufficient uptake by those most in need of the information. Furthermore, official information must be available in a format that can be easily absorbed, applied, and assessed by individuals with a range of epistemic and practical interests. In short, in addition to being available, official information must be reliable, relevant, and intelligible, and most importantly must be recognized as all of the above. It is important to note that what is required is relevance and intelligibility as they would be experienced by potentially any interested competent member of the public, and not merely as they are deemed appropriate for a particular "target group" by the supplier of the information (e.g., a government agency). As Onora O'Neill has emphasized, "many current examples of attempts by government and other institutions to communicate better with various publics fail" not for lack of trying, but for being cavalier about what it takes to achieve successful communication in the public sphere.[17] As a result, many official efforts at public communication display severe shortcomings:

> Often they oversimplify and so distort; sometimes their glossy presentations raise suspicions that realities and prospects are not as they are depicted; sometimes the consultations they undertake are seen more as public relations than as genuine inquiry.
>
> (O'Neill 2009a)

When official communication comes to be viewed as biased, "spin," or mere "PR," its perceived authority as a reliable source of knowledge is likely to suffer.

In order to get a better grasp of what is required for genuine communication in the public sphere, it is perhaps instructive to contrast *availability* (of information) with the philosophical concept of *publicity*. This is not the place to trace the history, or develop in detail the conceptual ramifications, of the philosophically rich notion of publicity and its cognate, public reason.[18] Instead, I shall content myself with a rough sketch of those aspects of the (Kantian) notion of publicity that are relevant to the present concern with communicative actions and their pathologies. The precise nature of the Kantian view of publicity as a criterion of validity is itself a matter of dispute, as it bridges the practical realm of action and the theoretical realm of knowledge. Thus, in the *Critique of Pure Reason*, Kant assigns publicity—in the form of *in-principle* communicability—a central role in grounding the claim to validity of judgments in general:

> The touchstone of whether taking something to be true is conviction or mere persuasion is therefore, externally, the possibility of communicating it and finding it to be valid for the reason of every human being to take it to be true.
>
> (Kant 1998a [1781]: 685)

In contrast, in the second appendix to *Perpetual Peace*, Kant (1991[1795]: 126) grants publicity the status of a criterion that any proposed course of practical action must satisfy: all actions affecting the rights of other human beings are wrong if their maxim is not compatible with their being made public.

The theoretical and practical dimensions of publicity for Kant are deeply intertwined, both conceptually and psychologically. Free and frank exchanges about differences in judgment fulfill a corrective function, insofar as they serve as checks and balances on—all too common—individual prejudice, ignorance, or misguided enthusiasm. Making it one's maxim to be indifferent "to the judgments of others in relation to [one's] own" would amount to blameworthy "logical egoism."[19]

40   *A. Gelfert*

At the same time, actively engaging in debate with others also fulfills a fundamental psychological need. As Kant (1998b) puts it elsewhere, "Man always wishes to test his judgment on others ... Everything is unimportant to us if we cannot communicate it to others." Importantly, Kant is not advocating here a rights-based approach to freedom of self-expression; instead, he is adamant about defending the possibility of participating in reasoned public discourse. All participants in such discussion and debate are subject to the same obligations—the twin constraints of truthfulness and respect for others being the two most important—from which no individual or agency can claim exemption. On the part of governments, this calls for an abstention from paternalistic interference—although not for wholesale abstention from public discourse in general. Policies that exclude certain groups from participating in public discourse are a particular target of Kant's (quoted in Gelfert 2006: 644) scorn:

> It is unfair to condemn people to keep all their judgments to themselves; for they must express themselves, lest they not lose the strong criterion of truth: to compare their judgments with the judgments of others.

The publicity test—which demands that any proposed course of action must be compatible with publicity before we may begin to assess its other merits—for Kant is a cornerstone of how to organize political and public life. If a maxim of action fails to pass the test, it indicates that acting upon it would be either self-defeating or unjust—or both, as in the case of declarations of preventive and pre-emptive war, which Kant famously rejects in *Perpetual Peace*. A threat, issued by one state in order to justify a pre-emptive attack on another, whose greater (or growing) power it fears, would only encourage the latter to launch an anticipatory attack of its own, thus precluding any outcome other than war: "This maxim of political expediency, if acknowledged publicly, necessarily defeats its own purpose and is consequently unjust" (Kant 1991[1795]: 128). What is true of relations among states governed by international right must also hold for the domestic affairs within a lawful state; hence, Kant's insistence on the following principle of public right: "All maxims which *require* publicity if they are not to fail in their purpose can be reconciled both with right and with politics" (Kant 1991[1795]: 130). If a policy could not be divulged publicly "without thereby inevitably arousing the resistance of everyone"—that is, if it requires secrecy *as a matter of principle* (rather than for individually justifiable contingent reasons)—then it violates the principle of publicity, and "the necessary and general (hence *a priori* foreseeable) opposition" arises because the policy "is itself unjust and thus constitutes a threat to everyone" (Kant 1991[1795]: 126).

One might think, in the light of this—admittedly brief—discussion of the significance of publicity that the best policy would be to make as much information as possible publicly available. Unfortunately, however, things are not as simple as this. Even within a Kantian framework, non-disclosure of some information may be permissible, prudentially advisable, or even morally desirable. In his *Lectures on Ethics*, Kant argues that "concealment, reservation, is a precaution that is approved of in ethics"; hence, not telling the whole truth is permissible "if we try by our action or utterance to promote the truth, or avert an evil" (Kant 1997: 426). It is worth keeping in mind that the publicity test only applies to *maxims of action*: under no circumstances must one lie about one's intentions, or pursue maxims of action that, if made public, would immediately be opposed as unjust. It does not follow from this injunction that information *as such* must always be volunteered and shared with others. When it comes to aspects of our own person, for example, it is permissible to "conceal our faults, and try to give a different impression, and [for example] make a show of politeness, despite our mistrust" (Kant 1997: 201). The suggestion seems to be that, if everyone knew everything about everybody else, perhaps respect for others in general would suffer.[20] As Kant puts it, "if men were all good, they could afford to be open-hearted; but not at present" (Kant 1997: 201). Some measure of personal privacy may be necessary to sustain individual autonomy, and thus may even be considered as contributing to the conditions that make reasoned public discourse possible.

Finally, it seems entirely possible that certain ways of making information available in principle may in fact contradict the spirit of publicity. One problem with recent freedom of information regimes around the world has been that information, even once it has been released in the name of transparency, remains unintelligible to those who lack the requisite legal, technical, or bureaucratic training to interpret complex pieces of legislation, technical guidelines, or administrative directives. O'Neill puts this point nicely when she writes:

> There is quite a lot to be said for transparency, but by itself it may not improve or even secure communication—let alone accountability. [...] Sometimes it is even used to maintain secrecy: one effective way to ensure that information is not communicated is not to keep it secret, but to "release" it with no fanfare.
>
> (O'Neill 2009b: 170)

The idea of publicity thus occupies a fragile place at the intersection of theoretical and practical philosophy—one that has to some extent been overshadowed by recent controversies about information technology's alleged assault on privacy.[21]

Promoting publicity, rebutting rumors: a conclusion and some implications for policy-makers

There are several lessons to be learnt from this discussion of publicity for the problem of rumor, conspiracy theories, and their rebuttal. If it is indeed the case that rumors typically arise in response to gaps in collective understanding

42 *A. Gelfert*

caused by lack of information, then the best long-term strategy for minimizing their occurrence may well consist of ensuring a constant flow and uptake of relevant information, allowing a diverse and critical public sphere to absorb and evaluate the information it deems reliable and trustworthy. Success at this level is difficult to measure, and will rarely consist of all individuals and institutional actors coming to share the same view; indeed, such unanimous agreement would likely be spurious and would merely indicate that reasoned discourse has not truly taken place. Ensuring that diverse viewpoints are not merely solicited and canvassed, but are allowed to develop of their own accord, is crucial to this process. At the same time, tendencies that are detrimental to genuine public discourse—such as group polarization (Sunstein 2002), concentration of commercial media ownership, or excessive litigation—must be monitored and kept in check.

The temptation on the part of governments to perpetuate monopolies of information—although superficially making top-down communication easier—masks a greater underlying vulnerability as rebuttals of rumors and conspiracy theories are then inevitably tied to government activities that undermine their authority in the eyes of those who already believe in the allegations. For official information to carry any significant weight in rebutting rumors, it is of crucial importance that the institutions in charge of rebuttal efforts be known and trusted. As Shibutani notes, "where institutional channels are not completely trusted, [...] rumors may persist even after formal denials, at least in part of the public" (Shibutani 1966: 132). If official responses are seen as erratic, selective, biased, or otherwise shrouded in mystery, the public will remain skeptical—and will continue to speculate over what has been left out. This is one of the dangers of censorship: "Institutional channels are then not fully trusted even when the censor is identified as a party with allied interests" (Shibutani 1966: 59). As Charles Oman (1922: 67) pointed out in his study of rumor in time of war, "the public always credited the Censorship with gratuitous stupidity." Fine (2007: 12f), in a similar vein, argues that, although democratic states with a tradition of individual free speech "easily permit rumor diffusion, these rumors may be less robust and consequential than those found in states in which the government forcefully attempts to direct what citizens have a right to know." Giving greater access to relevant factual—as well as procedural—knowledge would also allow independent actors to participate in rebuttal efforts, thereby avoiding any legitimation effect that might otherwise arise from official rebuttals.

Promoting conditions of publicity is important not only in order to ensure the uninhibited flow of reliable information, but also because it is only through individual participation in the free exchange of reasoned opinions between potentially unrestricted audiences that a person can arrive at an appropriate level of public trust. Often it is impossible, as a matter of principle, to check the reliability of one's sources—either because one lacks the expertise, or means, to acquire the requisite knowledge first-hand (as is the case with much of scientific knowledge), or because the information concerns

Rumor, gossip, and conspiracy theories 43

facts that are inaccessible in principle (as in reports of past events). Assessing the reliability of one's source directly—by checking reports against the facts, thereby gathering first-hand evidence of the source's track record—is rarely feasible in practice. Instead, we often rely on indirect evidence, such as agreement between reports from independent sources, coherence of reports with what we already take ourselves to know, and inferences concerning the motivation and interests of the speaker or source. When it comes to assessing sources that we have not previously encountered, we may also defer to those we have good reason to believe are in a better position than us to judge their reliability. If, for example, I am uncertain whether the product reviews on a particular technology website are reliable, I might solicit advice from a friend who I know to have extensive experience in buying gadgets from various technology websites. Much of the information required to make decisions about when, and whom, to trust depends on adequate background knowledge of the procedures, mechanisms, institutions, interests, and motivations that are prevalent in society. Such knowledge, however, can only be reliably acquired when the social mechanisms and processes are not shrouded in mystery; that is, under conditions of *publicity*. Publicity alone, of course, does not guarantee that the mechanisms and processes involved will *in fact* be reliable; however, it does ensure that, through interactions with others, exposure to opposing viewpoints, and inquisitive participation in public discourse, an individual reasoner, on average, will be able to arrive at an adequate representation of the social world around him or her and the level of public trust appropriate within it. In contrast, a climate of secrecy, in which reticence with respect to politically sensitive matters is encouraged, may result in a state of "pluralistic ignorance," in which individuals are unsure what other members of their community believe and, as a result, may pretend to go along with publicly supporting a position or norm, even though—like most people around them—they privately reject it. Using the collapse of Communism as his example, Timur Kuran (1997: 125) has argued that pluralistic ignorance is often a contributing factor in scenarios of social and political instability, as it may fuel "a pervasive sense of powerlessness," while at the same time making people more vulnerable to cognitive biases associated with the "mental shortcuts" that people—lacking publicly available evidence—resort to in order to estimate public opinion (Kuran 1997: 78).

Instead of a strategy of rebutting isolated rumors and conspiracy theories, which may have the paradoxical effect of conferring legitimacy to the claims thus singled out, a more promising approach—although one that requires considerably more patience and effort—would consist of encouraging, bringing about, and maintaining conditions that are conducive to free reasoned discourse between members of a potentially unrestricted audience. A merely formal endorsement of freedom of self-expression is unlikely to achieve this goal; at the very least, it must be complemented by a genuine concern for participation and actual communication. Maintaining conditions that meet the criterion of publicity takes considerable effort, as various social and

44   A. Gelfert

economic developments, such as concentration of commercial media owner-ship, increasing group polarization, a digital divide between users of new information technologies and digital "have-nots," etc., may have a detrimental effect on the scope and depth of public discourse—even if such trends are merely the collective outcome of individual autonomous decisions. However, such efforts may be richly rewarded, given that free reasoned debate conducted among a plurality of participants provides perhaps the best shot at counteracting unwarranted rumors and conspiracy theories—without the paradoxical consequences that may accompany "official" rebuttals.

Notes

1 For a survey article, see Gelfert (2008); for a comprehensive, although by now slightly dated, book-length treatment, see C.A.J. Coady (1992).
2 Partly because of this, Coady eventually concludes that gossip is not properly, although presumably still *prima facie*, a pathology of testimony; see C.A.J. Coady (2006: 256).
3 For a detailed Kantian discussion, see Gelfert (forthcoming).
4 The connection between gossip and familiarity might explain why celebrity magazines so often refer to actors and other stars by their first name.
5 Allport and Postman (1947: 33) did mention, although only in passing, that ambiguity might be induced "by some emotional tensions" on the part of the recipient.
6 See the papers collected in Goodman and Ben-Ze'ev (1994).
7 For a detailed discussion, see Phillips (2007), especially Chapter 4.
8 This, I believe, is one reason why it is rash of Sunstein (2008) to subsume gossip under rumor.
9 See, for example, the report by the Council of Europe (2007).
10 However, the difference in doxastic strength between beliefs based on rumor and those arising from conspiracy theorizing may simply be the result of different psychological processes that may be at work in each case; it should not be regarded as a demarcation criterion between rumors and conspiracy theories: both arguably arise as communal attempts at sense-making.
11 For a review of the literature on the "sleeper effect," see Pratkanis *et al.* (1988).
12 For a classic discussion of theoretical desiderata, see Hempel (1983).
13 That Coady is indeed committed to the possibility that justification can significantly accrue to rumors through the process of transmission is evident from the following remark: "It should be clear by now that the 'distance' of rumors from an original eyewitness account is not a general reason for skepticism about them. On the contrary, such distance may make belief in rumors more warranted" (D. Coady 2006a: 48).
14 The term "public sources of information" here includes, but is not limited to, government agencies, newspapers, broadcasters, and established news websites.
15 Edward Craig (1990) has argued that the notion of a "reliable testifier" is genealogically prior to the philosophical concept of (objective) knowledge.
16 Not all information "deficits" are avoidable, of course: accidents happen, official information is not perfect, unforeseen circumstances may arise. Some presence of rumor activity is thus to be expected and, indeed, may be necessary for the proper functioning of society.
17 All quotations are from O'Neill's (2009) lecture. I am grateful to Onora O'Neill for granting me permission to quote from her unpublished manuscript.

18 For a survey, see Gosseries (2008).
19 This is Kant's term in the Dohna-Wundlacken Logic, Volume XXIV.2, 740, of the Academy Edition. See Gelfert (2006: 644).
20 Hence Kant's injunction, discussed earlier, "not to pay attention to gossip."
21 For an eloquent discussion, see Sofsky (2008).

2 Have you heard?

The rumor as reliable

Matthew Dentith

Introduction

Rumors are often considered to be examples of unwarranted beliefs and the spreading of rumors is generally thought to be a pathological form of the otherwise reliable transmission process we associate with testimony. I wish to argue, in this chapter, that the transmission process of rumors is, contrary to what most people think, reliable. However, to do this requires that we distinguish between the act of *rumoring* and the problematic act of *rumor-mongering*, which is an unreliable and malicious transmission process. I will then compare and contrast rumors with conspiracy theories, which are sometimes thought to suffer from similar flaws.[1] In this chapter, I define a rumor as: *an unverified proposition that has been heard by one agent, which they then express to another agent.* This is a definition that I take as in line with how we commonly define a rumor.

Now, I think it is crucial to any definition of rumor that the hearer must have a belief that the rumor they are considering, which has been uttered by some speaker, is plausible: i.e., the hearer thinks that it might be true. I will work with a notion of plausibility here, rather than truth, when I am talking about the transmission of rumors, and I will combine it with an appeal to trust in order to characterize what I take to be a reliable transmission process. Plausibility, in this case, is a kind of coherence notion: a proposition conveyed by a speaker is plausible to some hearer when it does not contradict or is not defeated by the hearer's other beliefs. The transmission of a belief between the speaker of a rumor and the hearer of said rumor is successful when the hearer trusts the speaker and the content of the speaker's utterance coheres with the beliefs of the hearer.

It is important to contrast the act of testifying, which we normally take to be a reliable process of transmitting propositional beliefs, with the act of what I call "rumoring," the passing on of a rumor.

If a piece of testimony is to be properly treated as warranted by some hearer, it must, necessarily, be a proposition the speaker is justified in believing. This belief, if it is to be successfully transmitted to some hearer, must be one that is not contrary to the other beliefs the hearer holds and she must trust the speaker. If the hearer trusts the speaker and the speaker testifies some proposition p, then the hearer, should they have no defeater belief (a belief which, if

Have you heard? The rumor as reliable 47

the agent were aware of it, would be incompatible with some other belief the agent holds or, in this case, has just heard) with respect to the piece of testimony, should inherit belief that *p* (i.e., they should inherit, as a justified belief, the conveyed proposition); this is the trusting transmission of testimony.[2]

Here is an example that contrasts testifying with rumoring: Amanda and Ewan are discussing office politics. Amanda knows that Cindy, their boss, is dating Alice, who was recently fired. Amanda is curious to know when Cindy and Alice started dating; was it before or after she was dismissed from the workplace? As Amanda knows first-hand that Cindy and Alice are dating, she is able to pass this on to Ewan, who inherits the justified belief that Cindy and Alice are dating because Amanda has successfully testified to that fact.

Meanwhile, Ewan has heard that Cindy and Alice spent an inordinate amount of time in Cindy's bedroom at a party some five months ago so, when Amanda tells Ewan that Cindy and Alice started dating, he expresses what he has heard about Cindy, Alice, the bedroom, and the excessive amount of time they spent not engaging in the party all those months ago.

Ewan does not know this occurred; it is not a justified true belief that he holds but *merely* something he has heard. Furthermore, he is not claiming to have a justified belief with respect to this matter. Ewan, in this case, is spreading a rumor. The rumor is plausible to Ewan, because it fits with Ewan's other beliefs and is not inconsistent with Amanda's testimony (which he has recently come to believe).

I propose that what Ewan is doing here is a textbook case of the kind of thing that happens when we engage in rumoring: we express what we take to be plausible claims to other members of our community, effectively asking them whether what we have just said coheres with what they believe. Rumoring, I believe, is a kind of fact-checking mechanism.

So, should Ewan think that his claim about Cindy and Alice is plausible, but Amanda says, "No, that can't be the case; I know that Cindy and Errol were an item at the time, and Cindy is a serial monogamist!" then Ewan, if he trusts Amanda (say, as a reliable source of information about Cindy), should accept that the rumor is no longer plausible because it not only fails to cohere with Amanda's beliefs but it now fails to cohere with his beliefs (because, accepting Amanda's testimony to the contrary, Ewan now knows something more about Cindy, something that makes the rumor implausible). However, if Amanda says, "Yes, that makes sense: I saw Cindy and Alice kissing at that party five months ago," then what Ewan has heard will be all the more plausible to both Ewan and Amanda (because it now not only coheres with Ewan's other beliefs but it also coheres with those of Amanda). If Amanda has nothing to contribute in this matter, then Ewan or Amanda might go and ask someone else, to test out the plausibility of the rumor.

Rumoring vs. gossiping

Some people might object to the kind of story I am telling about rumoring here by saying something like "Surely what you have presented here is a case

48   *M. Dentith*

of gossiping?" because gossiping and rumoring might be thought to be the same kind of activity. I disagree, and here is why.

First, you could ask "Can gossip be rumor and rumor gossip?" It is not irrational to think that people are easily confused as to whether what they have heard is gossip or rumor. For one thing, people are not usually in the habit of expressly marking out whether they are gossiping or whether they are spreading a rumor. I might, for example, just assume that you know when I am gossiping or rumoring, or I might inadvertently use some ambiguous locution that confuses the issue. For another thing, I might deliberately misrepresent some piece of rumor as gossip; I overstate my case because the person I am rumor-mongering about, say, has done something to irritate me.

However, gossiping is a morally suspicious activity; when you gossip behind someone's back, you are asserting, as true, some belief about someone that they do not want spread, or would not be pleased to know you are spreading.

Now, in my example, Amanda knows that Cindy and Alice are dating, but she does not know when they started dating. Ewan has only heard that they spent an inordinate amount of time in Cindy's bedroom at a party some five months ago, but he believes this to be plausible (as it is not incoherent with his other beliefs about Cindy and Alice). He is not asserting that this is the case; rather, he is expressing what he takes to be a plausible belief about Cindy and Alice, and such expressions are not, typically, cases of gossiping. Gossip occurs when one person transmits what they know about someone to another: it is a kind of malicious testimony.

My second reason is this: even if Ewan knows that Cindy and Alice spent an inordinate amount of time in Cindy's bedroom at a party some five months ago, it is not obvious, in this case, that Cindy and Alice would object to him telling Amanda about this. Although Ewan is, on some level, talking behind the backs of Cindy and Alice, there is nothing inherently morally suspicious about what he is doing here; perhaps Ewan is too embarrassed to ask Cindy and Alice, which is why this conversation is going on without their input, or maybe Cindy is not at work today, and so forth.

This is an important point about rumors; while it is always morally suspect to gossip about someone behind their back (because gossiping requires you to assert information about someone who does not want said information asserted), it is not necessarily morally suspicious to engage in rumoring.[3] To engage in rumoring, I believe, is to engage in a process of assessing whether certain beliefs are plausible; it is a kind of fact-checking and, although the content of such rumors will sometimes be material the subjects of said rumor would object to being aired, this will not always be the case. Thus, there is nothing morally suspicious *per se* about rumoring, unlike in the case of gossiping.

C.A.J. Coady on rumors

A similar distinction between rumor and gossip can be found in the philosopher C.A.J. Coady's (2006) article "Pathologies of Testimony." In it, he argues that gossip is just a normal form of testimony, albeit a type that is restricted to the personal and can have malicious character. Gossip is reliable, according to C.A.J. Coady, because gossip is usually first-hand and is presented as being plausible. If you have a piece of gossip, then you have an example of a plausible belief that was formed by some immediate experience which you then passed on to a hearer like me in a single-step transmission process. If I trust you, as the speaker, then I will acquire the belief, the piece of gossip, which I will also regard as being plausible.

One way to see this is with the locution. Gossip, according to C.A.J. Coady, is usually prefaced with "Did you know?" (or some synonymous locution). When you gossip, you are testifying to that belief. If you believe that the testimony transmission process is reliable, then gossip, as a form of testimony, is a reliable source of justified beliefs.

Where C.A.J. Coady and I differ, however, is with respect to the characterization of rumor. He argues that the transmission of rumors is a misfire, or pathology, of the transmission process we associate with testimony. Coady (2006: 265) gives two reasons for this verdict:

> [R]umour can arise from the merest speculation. Furthermore, the speaker of rumor will often have no competence with regard to the "information" conveyed and may well be aware of that. If we think some degree of authority or competence, no matter how minimal, is a precondition for giving testimony then quite a lot of rumor will be disqualified as testimony.

Rumors, according to C.A.J. Coady, are not reliable—and this is evident in their locution. Rumors are introduced, he argues, with "Have you heard?"(Coady 2006: 262), which suggests that the speaker of rumor, unlike the speaker of gossip, does not believe the proposition they are expressing is plausible.[4]

I think presenting rumoring as testifying-gone-wrong is a slight mischaracterization of the act of rumoring. When someone says "Have you heard?", they are typically asking whether the rumor they have heard is something you, another epistemic agent, can either confirm or deny. When you testify, you assert some proposition; you convey that you take it to be justified. However, rumorers express what they take to be plausible propositions in order to see if others find them plausible. When you assert a rumor, you are making some claim that you have heard something you took to be plausible. As I will argue, this process of fact-finding or fact-checking is a reliable one. Its reliability is not the result of its being like the act of testifying, but rather because the longer a rumor survives the process of being audited by the hearers it is passed on to, the more likely it is to be considered plausible.

That being said, I think that C.A.J. Coady's criticism of rumor could be based on the locution "Rumor has it ...," which I think does signal that the speaker is *merely* transmitting a rumor they have heard without necessarily worrying about whether the rumor is plausible. The locution "Rumor has

50   *M. Dentith*

it ...," I think, carries with it no implication that the speaker thinks the belief being conveyed is plausible; it merely suggests that the speaker has heard a rumor and is passing it on.[5] Of course, not all rumors are clearly marked, and thus some instances of someone rumoring in a "Rumor has it ..." sense will be taken to be instances of "Have you heard ..." rumors.

C.A.J. Coady is concerned that the speaker of some rumor might even embellish their rumor, possibly to make a better story, add some detail, or simply because they can; this possibility makes it all the less likely that the transmission process of rumors can be considered reliable (Coady 2006: 263). This worry about the embellishment of rumors is interesting because I think this drives C.A.J. Coady's argument that the transmission of rumors is a pathological form of the transmission process of testimony. Although I think there are concerns that need to be addressed with respect to whether rumorers will embellish their rumors and what that means for the reliability of the transmission of rumors, I will argue that rumoring, as a kind of fact-finding or fact-checking, is a reliable act because the longer a rumor survives being audited, the more likely it is to be plausible or even true.

David Coady on rumors

David Coady (2006a: 41–42), in his article "Rumour Has It," argues that the transmission of rumors is a process that is more reliable than we might normally think, writing, "many rumours are credible (that is, it is rational to believe them), and that in general the fact that a proposition is rumored to be true is evidence in favour of it being true."

David Coady (2006a: 42) argues that rumors are expressed in a community of speakers and hearers, all of whom are able to check and analyze the content of the rumors they hear and, potentially, then pass them on:

> To begin with, for a communication to be a rumor, it must have "spread" through a number of informants (i.e., [rumorers]).[6] ... Furthermore, the number of informants through which a rumor has spread must be quite large. No second-hand account of an event can be a rumor, though it may be more of a rumor than a first-hand account. In general, the further a rumor has spread, the more fully it deserves the name.

David Coady (2006a: 47) thinks that the worry C.A.J. Coady has about rumors, that they will end up being embellished (or in the worst case scenario, be total fabrications), is reduced or even eliminated by the checks and balances of the transmission process:

> [A]ll else being equal, the greater the reliability of those who spread a rumor, the more likely it is to survive and spread. Hence, if you hear a rumor, it is not only *prima facie* evidence that it has been thought plausible by a large number of people, it is also *prima facie* evidence that it

has been thought plausible by a large number of reliable people. And that really is *prima facie* evidence that it is true.

David Coady is arguing that, if a rumor survives the checks and balances of its transmission process, then it is because at least some hearers in the community will be interested in either confirming or denying the rumors they hear and that this is a *prima facie* reason to think the rumor true.

The process of checks and balances in the process of rumoring assumes mutual trust: I, as a rumorer, express a rumor to you. You trust me to express it sincerely, and I trust you to either confirm or deny the rumor (or, at the very least, say whether you think it coheres with respect to your other beliefs).

If we take our community of agents to consist of mostly trustworthy speakers, then, I argue, it is the plausibility of a given rumor that we should be concerned with. As a rumor spreads, the plausibility of it to the community of speakers and hearers as a whole will take on more and more importance. A single hearer might well find that the belief coheres with her other beliefs, but that hearer might be anomalous. They may not be normal, with respect to the group, in the beliefs that they hold. As the rumor spreads further through the community, however, it will be checked and analyzed by more and more hearers and, should it not cohere with their beliefs, it is likely to stop being transmitted. This is, I admit, an empirical claim but one that I think is likely to be true.

A similar line of argument can be found in Cass Sunstein's book *On Rumors*. Sunstein (2009: 21) argues that a rumor can be countered by a defeater belief. As long as the hearer of some piece of rumor trusts the source of the defeater belief and the hearer does not have a strong commitment to the truth of the rumor, then the presence of a defeater belief should stop the transmission of a rumor from a speaker to a hearer (Sunstein 2009: 53–54). Sunstein's full model of rumor transmission is an example of what he calls a "social cascade." He has it that hearers will ignore defeater beliefs with regard to a certain rumor if most of their peers find the rumor plausible (Sunstein 2009: 22). Sunstein's argument seems to be that there are social as well as epistemic reasons that bear on the plausibility of rumors to hearers and that the pressure to conform to the beliefs of your peers will often trump epistemic reasons to consider a given rumor as implausible.

Therefore, with respect to David Coady's thesis about the likely truth of a rumor as it spreads further and further in a community, if a rumor spreads widely through a community without encountering defeater beliefs, then such a rumor could be considered to be superbly plausible to the community as a whole. As a rumor spreads it will inevitably encounter more in the way of interested hearers who will not pass on the proposition unless they consider it to be plausible, which is to say it coheres with their beliefs.

This is not to say that belief in rumors is always warranted, because the activity of what I will call "rumor-mongering" represents a pathology of the normally reliable transmission process of rumors. However, I will argue that

52 M. Dentith

there is a case to be made that belief in the substance of particular rumors is generally warranted, all things being equal.

Rumoring vs. rumor-mongering

The normal and, I claim, normally reliable transmission of rumors, rumoring, can be contrasted with rumor-mongering, which is the pathology of rumoring. Rumoring, as I have argued, is typically a kind of fact-finding: we hear something, think it sounds plausible, and then spread it on to someone else in the hope that they will confirm it, deny it, or pass it on so it can be confirmed or denied by someone else. Rumor-mongering, however, is not a fact-finding activity but rather the *mere* spreading of a rumor. I say "mere" here because, unlike rumoring, which, when all goes well, is the trustworthy transmission of plausible beliefs between speakers and hearers, rumor-mongering can result in the acquisition, by the hearer, of a belief in a rumor, even when the *speaker regards it as implausible.*

Now, it is true that many rumor-mongers have an interest in whether the rumors they are spreading are plausible. I might, for example, want to believe Cindy and Alice are engaging in an office affair because that belief pleases me, or because Cindy rejected my advances and thus Alice, who I hate and detest, is the kind of person I now think Cindy deserves (because I am ill-disposed towards her). However, the act of rumor-mongering can bring with it the act of embellishing upon a rumor, and I think that this could be the pathology of the transmission process that C.A.J. Coady is concerned about. Consider these two related worries about rumor-mongers and rumor-mongering.

The first worry is that rumor-mongers, because they are not sincere in their utterances, might be mistaken for being rumorers. The hearer might believe that the proposition they have just heard is one the speaker believed. If influential organizations engage in rumor-mongering, especially in situations where there is no official (and warranted) information available, then this is a serious problem as it could lead to the dissemination of disinformation.

The second worry about rumor-mongering is that hearers will not necessarily know whether the rumor they find to be plausible has been embellished, been tailored to look plausible to the hearer or so forth. If we assume (for the sake of argument) that most people express rumors without embellishments, then the fact that some people might not just embellish but even wholly fabricate the rumors they spread can lead to what is, otherwise, a generally reliable transmission process being perverted. Indeed, some charges of disinformation focus on how "those who are in power" spread tailored or fabricated rumors that appear plausible to the general populace in order to make certain conspiracy theories appear unwarranted.

This may explain part of the story as to why conspiracy theories and rumors are often confused; some of the evidence used to make the explanatory hypothesis of either an official theory or a conspiracy theory may be the result of rumor-mongering. Arguably, a lot of the evidence cited by 9/11

Have you heard? The rumor as reliable   53

Truthers consists of rumors that have been mongered, just as a lot of the evidence that was said to warrant the official theory that there were weapons of mass destruction being developed by the Hussein regime in Iraq was mongered as well.

Now, presumably embellished or totally fabricated rumors should not spread far because of the checks and balances of the community of speakers and hearers, but mongered rumors might persist in some cases.

Rumor-mongering, I think, shows that the normally reliable transmission process of rumors can be perverted. Now, the extent of this problem is really more a topic for sociologists, anthropologists, psychologists, and the like, who are better placed to tell us just how often people embellish or even fabricate rumors. Still, both the embellishment of rumors and the possibility that a speaker might spread rumors for the sake of spreading rumors are, I think, problems for my account of the generally reliable nature of the transmission of rumors.

Let us return to Ewan and his rumor.

Ewan has heard that Cindy and Alice spent an inordinate amount of time in Cindy's bedroom at a party five months ago. He then remembers that, at an office party some five months ago, he saw them in what can only be called a "compromising position" and infers that it is this particular party people have been talking about. He then starts a new rumor; he has heard that Cindy and Alice were already in a relationship five months ago. This is a kind of embellishment because Ewan is now adding content to the rumor. This move seems relatively unproblematic because Ewan's embellishment is simply a plausible addition as it is something that is consistent with the original rumor and may even confirm it. Ewan is not lying, although maybe he should, in this case, signpost his addition to the rumor.

Now, this embellishment of the rumor should end up being checked by those who hear it. If Amanda says "No, that can't be right; Alice and Jo started dating at that party," then Ewan's embellished rumor should not spread any further. If, however, Amanda goes "Hold on, now I think about it, I remember Cindy and Alice sharing a taxi after the party," then Ewan's embellished rumor may well end up spreading further because it coheres all the more with Amanda's beliefs about Cindy and Alice and now seems all the more plausible. This again suggests that plausibility is a key feature of rumors: an implausible rumor, one that does not cohere with the hearers' beliefs, is unlikely to spread far.[7]

The transmission of plausible propositions by trustworthy speakers, which seems to be what we have in the case of rumoring, should show us that the transmission of rumors is, by and large, reliable, and thus we have a case for treating rumors as *prima facie* warranted beliefs. The fact that we have to put up with some (perhaps even a lot of) elaboration and embellishment of rumors by rumor-mongers—just as we put up with the embellishments of historians, both written and oral, in our histories—is the price we should be willing to pay for a generally reliable process.

Rumors and conspiracy theories

The claim that conspiracy theories can be rumors is an interesting and recurring issue in the literature. Sunstein (2009: 7), for example, is of the opinion that conspiracy theories are spread by rumoring. However, it is important to distinguish carefully between conspiracy theories and rumors, so that, even if someone does not accept my argument about the reliability of rumors, they can still accept my argument that the transmission process associated with conspiracy theories is importantly different to that of rumors.

David Coady (2006a) draws an analogy between the lack of officialness of rumors and a similar lack of officialness with respect to conspiracy theories as a reason for finding rumors and conspiracy theories suspicious. He argues that, if a rumor is confirmed by some appropriate official source, then it will lose the status of being a rumor and that, in the same way, if a conspiracy theory is confirmed by some appropriate official source, then it loses the status of being a conspiracy theory. His thesis on the unofficial nature of rumors is as follows:

> [R]umours are essentially unofficial things. No public statement by a government or a government agency, for example, no matter how far removed it was from an original eyewitness account, could be a rumor (though, of course, it could confirm a pre-existing rumor or be responsible for starting another rumor).
>
> (D. Coady 2006a: 48)

This is a thesis that applies to conspiracy theories, as well:

> No official account of an event, no matter how conspiratorial it is, is likely to be characterised as a conspiracy theory. Both rumors and conspiracy theories seem by definition to lack official status.
>
> (D. Coady 2006a: 48)

Now, I agree that one of the reasons why we are often thought to be justified in our suspicion of conspiracy theories is because they lack a certain authority, to wit, official status. In the same respect, one of the reasons why we might find rumors suspicious is that they, too, lack authority.

Here is an example.

Amelia and Steffi are talking in the cafeteria. Both are concerned about the reasons behind the invasion of Iraq by the United States of America. Amelia is a conspiracy theorist with respect to this issue. She firmly believes that the official theory about the invasion, that the US government claimed that the Saddam Hussein-led regime in Iraq was developing weapons of mass destruction (WMDs), was not just a lie but that the real reason for the invasion of Iraq was that America secretly wanted to take control of the region's oil reserves. Amelia is asserting a conspiratorial explanation for the invasion of Iraq by American forces and is, thus, asserting a conspiracy theory.

Have you heard? The rumor as reliable 55

Steffi, on the other hand, believes that the government of the United States of America did mistakenly believe that the Iraqi government was developing WMDs (and thus she denies one of the conspiracy theories of the event). She has also heard that a motivating factor for the invasion was that, in addition to bringing down a government that was developing WMDs, it would also help America to take a controlling interest in the region's oil reserves, a proposition which she expresses to Amelia; Steffi is spreading a rumor.

Amelia, however, believes that her conspiracy theory is the actual explanation for America's invasion of Iraq; she is asserting that it is the case. Steffi, however, because she is simply spreading a rumor, is not asserting that her story is true but, rather, she is passing on something she has heard and found plausible. Should someone confirm Steffi's rumor with reference to some appropriately official source (say, leaked war documents), then not only would that make Steffi's rumor all the more plausible, it might stop any of her further communication of this information from being a rumor because she could now testify that it is the case.

I think it is reasonable to say that rumors lack any form of official status. If a rumor had been endorsed by an appropriate authority, then it would not be a rumor. Thus, I think David Coady's argument about rumors and official status is sound, provided that we appeal to some appropriate authority; if a rumor is endorsed by an epistemically suitable official source or influential institution, then the rumor will become a proposition that we are justified in believing. However, if the rumor is endorsed by an inappropriate authority, i.e., someone who lacks the right kind of credentials with respect to the content of the rumor, then it is not clear what that does to the status of the rumor. Herriman (2010), following Bubandt's (2008) research on leaflets in Maluku's conflict, makes a similar point, arguing that a rumor can be treated as having been officially endorsed, and thus plausible, when influential media institutions report it as fact. Herriman (2010: 726) writes:

> in North Maluku in 1999–2000, leaflets that contained oral rumors circulated. The information – conspiracy theories about Christian or Muslim "enemies" – was already hearsay, but gained authority through being written in the leaflets, and was a trigger for communal violence.

This kind of endorsement, I think, amounts to endorsing rumor-mongering, as the rumor has not been assessed to see whether it is plausible, but rather it is treated as being newsworthy and is transmitted on to hearers via a medium which (perhaps mistakenly) many hearers think is trustworthy. David Coady (2006a: 48–49) makes a similar point: in the right kind of society, rumors might be considered more reliable than official information.

However, part of the so-called "commonsense suspicion" about the *prima facie* unwarranted nature of conspiracy theories is precisely that they lack authority, to wit, they have no official status.

56　*M. Dentith*

Now, it is true that our suspicion of conspiracy theories is often based upon comparing them with their rivals, which are sometimes going to be official theories. In a case where we have an official theory, that is, a theory that has been endorsed, we might be tempted to consider the official theory to be the better explanation because the endorsement inherent in its official status implies that there is an appeal to authority that underpins the rival to the conspiracy theory. If this is the argument, then the lack of official status is a factor in the commonsense suspicion of conspiracy theories, but this commonsense suspicion is wrong: unless we know that the appeal to authority is legitimate, then a theory having official status tells us nothing about whether belief in it is warranted or unwarranted.

However, if this is a problem for conspiracy theories, then it is equally a problem for official theories because, arguably, we need to be able to assess how much trust to place in the sources of official theories before we can say that they trump their rivals.

Neil Levy (2007: 182) takes it that official theories are truth-conducive because they are transmitted between individuals and, if the official theory is to be considered plausible, then it must have been produced and preserved in an epistemically appropriate way. Levy's argument is that, if official theories survive in what we might call the "marketplace of ideas", it is because they are not just endorsed by official sources but also transmitted in a trusting fashion between speakers and hearers.

The problem with official theories is that, although they might well spread from speakers to hearers, such official sources are not necessarily going to be epistemically authoritative and may be an influential institution that is *merely* political in nature. In cases such as this, we need to ask questions about whether we have a case for trusting the utterances of said institution.

So, in the same way that the availability of an official theory could be said to provide a reason to doubt a conspiracy theory, a conspiracy theory could provide a good reason to doubt some official theory if the conspiracy theory gives us good reason to doubt either the appropriateness of the endorsing institution or their sincerity in that endorsement. Certainly, within certain communities conspiracy theories spread rapidly and widely and, I would hazard, this is because either the content of the conspiracy theory coheres well with the pre-existing beliefs of that group or the rival official theory is epistemically suspicious. This suggests that we can easily be fooled into accepting some proposition because of its plausibility or coherence with our other beliefs.

We need, then, to be able to appraise the trustworthiness of official sources before we can claim that official theories can trump conspiracy theories. This is precisely what some people, often pejoratively labeled "conspiracy theorists", are concerned with when they downplay the institutional endorsement of official theories. I think there is a perverse plausibility to this move. If you think "they" are out to get you, then you should expect that they will endorse false theories, expecting the public to treat such an endorsement as reason to think the theory has the right credentials.

Have you heard? The rumor as reliable 57

However, although rumors lack official status, this is not because rumors are denied by, or are in opposition to, some influential institution or authority. Rather, it is simply because rumoring is, as previously argued, a form of fact-finding or fact-checking. To engage in rumoring is to try to find out what is the most plausible thing to believe (often without asking the authorities directly).

Recall the example of Amelia, Steffi, and the real reason behind the invasion of Iraq. Amelia asserted a conspiracy theory to explain the invasion while Steffi expressed a rumor about why the invasion occurred. Conspiracy theorists regard the theories they assert as the most plausible explanation of the event; if there is a rival explanation to the conspiracy theories, then we need to assess both said rival (say, an official theory) and what this means for belief in the conspiracy theories.

This difference is crucial, I argue, to understanding why we should not conflate the spreading of rumors with the spreading of conspiracy theories; rumors are merely *mentioned* and conspiracy theories are *proposed* as the explanation. What makes the transmission process of rumoring a reliable one is that when a speaker transmits a rumor to a hearer we do not require the speaker or the hearer to believe the rumor is true, we only require that the hearer finds it plausible, which is to say it coheres with her other beliefs. Thus, when a speaker engages in rumoring and transmits a rumor to a hearer, the speaker should be prepared for the possibility that the rumor will be considered implausible by the hearer; a defeater belief might be asserted which shows that the rumor is implausible. This should not be a problem for rumorers or the process of rumoring as it is a process of fact-finding or fact-checking. A rumorer should not stand by their proposition *if it is defeated or becomes implausible to them.* Defeater propositions, which show that the rumor is implausible, will be something that, presumably, the rumorer should want to know. Indeed, the existence of a rival hypothesis with respect to a rumor may even be considered a good thing if it helps the rumorer to find out what is really going on.

Conspiracy theorists, however, will normally assert their conspiracy theories: the conspiracy theory presented by the conspiracy theorist is what they consider to be the best explanation of the event.[8]

There is, I admit, an obvious objection to my thesis that the spreading of rumors and conspiracy theories is importantly dissimilar, which goes like this: *Theorizing about conspiracies is surely also a form of fact-finding, just like rumoring. It is an activity undertaken by an agent who wants to find the best explanation for an event.*

I agree; theorizing about conspiracies can be a kind of fact-finding, but it is a different kind of activity to that of the spreading of conspiracy theories. The relationship between conspiracy theories and conspiracy theorizing is not analogous to the relationship between rumors and rumoring. Rumoring is a kind of fact-finding, fishing for information based upon agents testing propositions against what else they know, promoting plausible beliefs, and rejecting implausible ones. Theorizing about conspiracies might be similar (in that it is an activity where you seek to answer the question of whether some event could have occurred because of the existence of a conspiracy), but the spreading of conspiracy theories is not, typically, a fact-finding exercise *because conspiracy theories are proposed as the explanation for an event.* This is why the reliable transmission of conspiracy theories does not *merely* require that we trust speakers. It also requires that the speaker have a justified belief that some conspiracy theory is *the* explanation of the event in question. This task is not impossible, but it may well turn out to be difficult in many cases.

The reliability of the transmission process of rumors, however, is based on the plausibility of the rumored proposition to the hearer (and trusting that speakers will not embellish upon or fabricate rumors), whereas the transmission of conspiracy theories is reliable only when the speaker and the hearer are in a trusting relationship with one another such that the hearer inherits the asserted belief of the hearer.

Now, most people will say that this makes the transmission of conspiracy theories seem as though it is a reliable process and thus prone to producing justified beliefs. However, our commonsense suspicion about conspiracy theories has it that they are examples of unwarranted beliefs, so surely there must be something wrong with my analysis (because it goes against a view most of us regard as very plausible).

My response is that a transmission process is only as good as its inputs. If a speaker has a justified belief that a conspiracy existed and they pass that on successfully, then the hearer will also form a justified belief about said conspiracy. The question, then, is whether the speaker's belief in the existence of a conspiracy was itself warranted?

I think the answer to this question depends, in part, on whether conspiracy theories, as explanations, are formed in the right way. However, when it comes to assessing the transmission of a conspiracy theory for its reliability, it is not sufficient to *merely* say that, if a hearer trusts the speaker of some conspiracy theory, then the hearer is justified in taking onboard belief in said conspiracy theory. This is because we might trust the conspiracy theorist to be sincere in their assertion but not trust that they have arrived at their belief in an orthodox manner. We need to look at the inference to the existence of a conspiracy, which underpins the conspiracy theory itself, and ask whether the conspiracy theorist who originally proposed the conspiracy theory inferred the best explanation rather than just engaged in inferring any old explanation.

We might be tempted to think that a conspiracy theory must do a lot of work to be considered warranted. Conspiracy theories must not only be transmitted in a trusting fashion, but must also be the best possible explanation (out of a range of candidate explanations). The existence of competing explanatory hypotheses, as rivals to some conspiracy theory (or set of conspiracy theories), indicates that the conspiracy theory is controversial and, thus, must be backed up by an argument as to why the inference of the existence of a conspiracy, in this case, is the best explanation.

Conclusion

I have compared and contrasted the transmission processes of rumors and conspiracy theories, which are sometimes considered to be unwarranted for the same reasons. I argued that we should not confuse the issue of the reliability of rumors with that of the reliability of conspiracy theories because they typically have different transmission processes.

Rumoring is, typically, a form of fact-finding or checking, where propositions we have heard stated are tested against the beliefs of others. I argued that, when it comes to appraising rumors, what is important is whether the hearer trusts the rumorer to be sincere and finds the content of the rumored proposition plausible. If a rumor is implausible it is unlikely to spread far in the community of speakers and hearers because hearers, presumably, are interested in auditing the propositions that spread through their community. If a rumor is plausible to some hearer, then the hearer may well go and test the rumor out on some other hearer to see whether it is coherent with their beliefs. It is this set of conditions about the testing, or teasing out, of the plausibility of rumors that leads me to think that rumoring is a reliable process.

The activity of rumor-mongering, the insincere and pathological counterpart of rumoring, explains why we might think of rumoring as an unreliable process. An agent who engages in rumor-mongering may well embellish or even fabricate the rumors they spread. Rumor-mongering is an abuse of trust because rumor-mongering is the insincere transmission of a rumor. Now, the process of auditing, the checks and balances of the transmission process of rumors, will, I argue, mean that embellished and fabricated rumors will typically end up being implausible to hearers but, in some cases, such rumors may well persist in a community. This is a bullet we have to bite when it comes to the transmission of rumors: the reliability of the process means we cannot guarantee that all rumors will be plausible.

I also argued that the transmission process associated with conspiracy theories can be reliable but that there is an important difference between rumoring and the spreading of conspiracy theories. Conspiracy theories are asserted, rather than *merely* mentioned, as *the* explanation of an event. The conspiracy theorist does not *merely* believe their conspiracy theory is plausible, they believe it to be *the* explanation. It is in this way that rumors and conspiracy theories are different.

Or, at least, that's what I've heard. Rumor has it that people who say otherwise are conspiracy theorists.

Notes

1 I should like to acknowledge the feedback I received on this paper from Drs. Jonathan McKeown-Green and Justine Kingsbury, as well as a third person who does not want to be named. This unnamed person, along with Giovanni Tiso, Nathan Grange, and Paul Litterick, was instrumental in stripping out (hopefully) most of the many spelling and grammatical errors that were introduced to the text when I turned what was a chapter of my PhD dissertation into the chapter you are reading today.

60 *M. Dentith*

2 The definition of testimony I am using comes from Lackey in a recent survey volume which I take to be representative of the contemporary epistemological views of testimony. Lackey's (2006: 3) definition of the act of testifying is as follows: "T: S testifies that p by making an act of communication a if and only if (in part) in virtue of a's communicable content, (1) S reasonably intends to convey the information that p, or (2) a is reasonably taken as conveying the information that p."

3 I say "morally suspect" rather than "morally wrong" because, although gossiping is a morally suspicious activity, it need not be considered an activity that is actually morally wrong. For example: You might not like it that I gossiped to a police officer about your larcenous ways (thus I act in a morally suspicious manner with respect to our friendship), but my reporting on such suspicious behavior to a relevant authority is not itself an example of a *prima facie* immoral act on my part.

4 A recent paper by Cuonzo (2008) presents a slightly different view of gossip, focusing on the morally suspicious nature of gossiping.

5 Which might be explicable with respect to certain glosses on the etiquette of group communication, etc.

6 David Coady uses the term "rumor-monger" rather than "rumorer" but I have reserved that term to describe something different, as will become apparent later in the chapter.

7 The social media service Twitter (a micro-blogging platform) is a good example of how such a process works. Given the short nature of tweets, many messages on Twitter are either a URL or a quote with a corresponding request for confirmation of the content of said quote. If the quote or the content of the URL is plausible, the message will be retweeted by another Twitter user and, if the content of the quote or the URL is not plausible, either it will not be retweeted or the respondent will reply to the tweet with either a correction or a denial (Mendoza *et al.* 2010). Indeed, the rumor that President Obama was to announce the assassination of Osama bin Laden started spreading on Twitter almost an hour before the White House Press Conference on April 30, 2011, and the rumor, which became remarkably detailed in the minutes before the official announcement, was accurate; the rumor was plausible because it cohered with other information people had heard and no defeaters were presented during its spread (Stelter 2011).

8 As a purely psychological point, some conspiracy theorists are unlikely to be easily dissuaded that their explanation is incorrect just because some hearer finds it implausible, especially if the conspiracy theorist has questions about whether the defeater propositions presented by said hearer in response to a conspiracy theory are based on what the conspiracy theorist considers to be disinformation or an appeal to an official theory.

3 Triangle of death

Strategic communication, counterinsurgency operations, and the rumor mill

Daniel Bernardi and Scott W. Ruston

> Insurgent organizations like Al Qaeda use narratives very effectively in developing legitimating ideologies.
>
> (US Army and Marine Corps 2007: 25–26)

In 2005, Multi-National Forces-Iraqi (MNF-I), the military command overseeing US and coalition forces in the war-torn Arab nation began a bovine inoculation campaign to improve the health of cattle throughout Iraq.[1] Although the intent was to stabilize the food supply and increase return on investment for local cattle ranchers and dairy farmers, the inoculation program was also a key element in an information operation to counter insurgent violence and propaganda. At this stage of the war effort, the insurgents—comprised mostly of foreign jihadists, Ba'ath party loyalists, and disgruntled Iraqi soldiers—had severely degraded counterinsurgency communication efforts designed to paint US and coalition forces as liberators. The bovine vaccination campaign was a key pillar in what amounted to a narrative countermeasure attached to a civil affairs operation.

Yet, not too soon after the bovine campaign began, a rumor spread throughout Iraq that the Americans had embarked on a sinister plot to starve the Iraqi populace by poisoning livestock.[2] At a time when official news sources inside Iraq were either silent or lacked credibility, this conspiratorial charge—and the dramatic structure of the rumor—appealed more to imagination and fear than thoughtful reflection and questioning. Indeed, for farmers already wary of the US and coalition presence, wracked by societal and political instability, and suffering livestock losses to disease and a rapidly dwindling water supply, the bovine poisoning rumor explained the deaths of the herds, predicted future loss and gloom, while also linking the cause of their current woes to the US invasion and occupation. In turn, it provided a target for pent-up frustration, anxiety, and fear that led to some farmers turning a blind eye to insurgent activities and others to participate in violence. MNF-I's information operation and civil affairs mission backfired. The insurgents gained narrative ground at a critical juncture in the war effort.

All things being equal, the bovine poisoning rumor posed a local challenge for counterinsurgency and diplomatic forces in the area. It also dovetailed with three other rumors to form a kind of mosaic: (1) *American helicopters cause more and greater debilitating sandstorms by kicking up massive amounts of dust*; (2) *American forces and weapon systems contribute to the drought by using up water reserves and by helping create sandstorms*; and, most importantly, (3) *America invaded the country to steal Iraq's oil*. Linked to these others rumors, the bovine poisoning rumor advanced the widely held belief that the US invaded Iraq for its oil and had little to no regard for its people or their way of life. Seen in this light, it posed a geopolitical and, hence, strategic communication challenge for both the US and Iraqi governments.

Given the narrative landscape and everyday violence Iraqis experienced after the US invasion, the "nefarious" explanation implicit in the bovine inoculation campaign was—at least for many Iraqis—a rational one. With the country's infrastructure already decimated by the aftermath of "shock and awe," the story it told made sense: *US forces in Iraq are engaged in a crusade, destroying our land and livelihood, and something, even violence, has to be done to stop it lest our families go hungry and our country fall permanently in the hands of infidels*. Ground truth gave way to grounded lies, impeding reconstruction efforts in the battle to win the hearts and minds of contested populations such as rural farmers and the Iraqi people more generally. In other words, an otherwise local rumor, with relative plausibility, rushed into a knowledge gap during a period of extreme violence and political uncertainty, linked to an array of existing rumors about US forces and intentions; the rumor capitalized on a lack of official information and, in the end, provided a means to express and explain local, national, and regional fears.

Often dismissed as unimportant or even silly by many US commanders and government officials, rumors represent significant obstacles and raise several fundamental questions for counterinsurgency operations. In what ways do rumors indicate or predict rising social unrest and violence? In what ways are rumors and rumor mosaics susceptible to insurgent manipulation and propaganda? How do rumors that, on their face, seem too fantastic to be credible, nonetheless gain traction among a contested population and, in the process, lend credibility to insurgent propaganda? In short, how can strategic communicators achieve their tactical and strategic goals in a communication landscape besieged by rumors that appear rational to contested populations?

In this chapter, we offer an analysis of rumors and rumor mosaics, which we define as the interlocking system of related rumors that function to support broader cultural narratives. Our approach to studying rumors focuses on the context of counterinsurgency operations and the associated strategic communication campaigns. Rumors, we hope to show, are not unlike improvised explosive devices (IEDs)—the feared weapon of the insurgents in Iraq. Like their kinetic cousins, rumors are easily conjured up using local material; they are unpredictable; and, although most miss their targets, they are deadly under the right conditions. And, as we have seen with the MNF-I bovine inoculation effort, rumor IEDs can also slip past force protection measures and eviscerate carefully crafted and expensive strategic communication campaigns.

Triangle of death 63

Rumor networks

In this chapter, we focus on the impact of rumors during the US invasion and occupation of Iraq, a war-torn country where rumors have a long history of impacting popular perceptions and cultural sensibilities.[3] As Stephanie Kelley, an intelligence officer who tracked the spread of rumors in Iraq, notes: "Iraqis have long employed rumor as a credible information source and reflection of the mood on the street, suggesting that naturally occurring, readily available rumors are an ideal guide in the battle for hearts and minds in this conflict" (Kelley 2005). Kelley's approach to rumor positions them as a valuable open-source intelligence revealing the attitudes, anxieties, and morale of the Iraqi people during the height of the insurgency.

The Iraqi people, in fact, were softened by a bombardment of totalitarian-inspired rumors before the bovine poisoning rumor and its associated mosaic came on the scene. A well-established example is the rumors spread by Saddam Hussein that his country had stockpiles of weapons of mass destruction (WMDs). Hussein spread these rumors in an effort to intimidate his neighbors—especially Iran. After the Iran/Iraq war of the 1980s, which essentially resulted in a stalemate, Hussein remained wary of Iranian influence and intentions in Iraq, extending a historical tension between Persians and Arabs, and sounding a lot like the strategic communication milieu that defined the Cold War between the US and the former Soviet Union. Hussein used his so-called WMD program, largely decimated after the Gulf War, as a kind of "mutual annihilation" threat. Surprisingly, he continued this "whisper campaign" after the US announced its intention to invade the country in 2002 if the dictator did not divulge and destroy the WMD "stockpile."[4] Iro-nically, Hussein's rumor campaign backfired. The US posed the greatest threat to his rule, not the Iranian government.

Rumors of Iraq's WMD program formed a key communication strategy supporting the US's rationale for the invasion. The George W. Bush admin-istration found the rumors to be credible (or at least that is what it argued at the time) and used them as a platform for pre-emptive war. The "mushroom cloud" remark repeated by National Security Advisor Condoleezza Rice in various media engagements, a comment she in fact picked up from *The New York Times*, stands as one of many examples of how a rumor spread through the media by an apparently authoritative source high up in the US govern-ment to form a narrative justifying an invasion. The rumor of a WMD pro-gram and its threat was even artfully promoted by Secretary of State Colin Powell during his address to the United Nations Security Council on Feb-ruary 5, 2003. Drawing on the notion that Iraq's WMD program posed an imminent threat to the US and its allies, Powell argued for international sup-port for the war—an act that gave a clear aura of credibility to Hussein's whisper campaign. His evidence, all of which has since been proven to be false, rested on single-source reporting (we would argue rumor-mongering) from defectors with first-hand knowledge of Hussein's rumors rather than actual WMDs.[5] Like a Shakespearian tragedy, the Bush administration's narrative supporting the invasion also backfired.

An almost endless reserve of rumors in Iraq during Hussein's reign and prior to the invasion served to misinform the Iraqi and US people—while intimidating neighbors and allies alike. As the bovine poisoning and related rumors might suggest, the US invasion and mismanagement of the occupation had the effect of lighting those rumor reserves on fire.[6] With both US and Iraqi people softened up for the invasion, the result was a geopolitical informational disaster that subsequent counterinsurgency operators had to manage in an effort to quell rising social unrest and insurgent violence in the Arab country and beyond.

We offer this background not only because it is one of the defining events of the early history of the twenty-first century that continues today, but also because of the lasting lessons the study of rumors in Iraq brings to light for strategic communication, public diplomacy, and military operations. Rumors, we argue, have the greatest likeliness of impeding strategic communication efforts during times of collective anxiety, social upheaval, and political instability, driving wedges between constituent populations, between populations and their government, and between government institutions and their allies.[7] This is especially the case when insurgents work to keep rumors and rumor mosaics alive and focused on advancing their strategic messages.

Crucial to understanding the ideological function and effects of rumors is a recognition of their operation within narrative systems. Approaching rumors with a cultural and narrative-based approach not only aids in understanding what rumors do, but it helps identify how and why they circulate, repeat, and, most importantly, impede strategic communications. As we will show, although rumors circulate freely in society as credible stories, and in some ways are cross-cultural in that all cultures engage in rumor-mongering, rumors are a critical yet underestimated and understudied threat to counterinsurgency operations.

Rumors are not lone, discreditable ideas circulating aimlessly in a population. They are significant participants in the *narrative landscape*, the sense-making ordering of data and information that shapes an individual or community's viewpoint. They fit into this landscape both singly, but also in mosaics, further "clarifying" the picture for uninformed, suspicious, downtrodden, or fearful populations. These populations have a wealth of historical experiences, understood and remembered through narratives, to draw from—many of which end up sounding strikingly similar to what they are experiencing at the moment. A network of rumors informs this history and narrative landscape, making the job to "win hearts and minds" a particularly challenging one for counterinsurgency communicators.

Rumor minefields

> Propaganda through rumor has the further advantage of not being easily discernible as "propaganda."
>
> (Knapp 1944: 28)

Triangle of death 65

During counterinsurgency operations, rumors potentially undermine US strategic communication, diplomatic outreach, information operations, public affairs, and psychological operations. They are among the "weapons of the weak" (Scott 1985) and thus are the narrative equivalent of an IED—a discreet and seemingly ad hoc weapon that can radically disrupt carefully crafted and expensive operations because of their simplicity and the tendency of commanders to dismiss them as "merely" lies or gossip. At the same time, rumors are often indigenous and organic—arising within a population of their own accord— and, as such, can be taken as a strategic indicator of prevailing social anxieties and the shaping of worldviews. Insurgents are able to exploit the rumor mill, or the active propagation of multiple rumors, via multiple communication platforms, gaining a tactical and a strategic edge; this is especially so in environments of informational uncertainty where there is limited access to institutional media, where institutional media lack credibility, or when institutional media legitimize a rumor by presenting it as credible or fact.

The rampant spread of rumors during periods of upheaval and uncertainty and their cultural reverberation in the midst of national crises poses a particularly thorny problem for strategic planning and communication efforts. Broadly speaking, strategic communication is the production, transmission, and exchange of messages for the purpose of creating meaning (communication) in the service of a specific goal (strategic). For counterinsurgency operations, where the military partners with other government and non-governmental organizations to achieve political stability in the face of violent campaigns by non-state actors, strategic communication functions to allay public fears, keep citizens informed, and, in the end, facilitate broad support for and confidence in the host nation government while weakening support for adversaries.[8] As Sebastian Gorka and David Kilcullen (2009: 223) summarize:

> If a strategy is the plan by which a nation's goals are related to the means at its disposal to achieve those goals, strategic communications are the tools we use to garner support for that plan and the vision behind it, and the tools used to undermine an enemy's ability to obstruct us in achieving that vision.

Or they fail to do so. Strategic communication is not restricted to pro-government forces. Insurgent groups such as Al-Qaeda engage in highly effective communication strategies that include the dissemination of narratives that, as the epigraph to this chapter notes, "develop legitimating ideologies." For example, despite the fact that the vast majority of Muslims do not believe the Qu'ran permits terrorism, Islamic extremists are particularly adept at justifying violence against innocent people—including Muslims—by linking their cause to divine intervention. The killing is justified because the larger cause of jihad is based on highly selected passages from the Qu'ran and Hadith that extremists interpret as a divine sanction for violence under grave circumstances. Crusades against Islam justify extreme actions by Muslims.[9]

During the occupation of Iraq, insurgents were able to more easily entice contested populations into a kind of complacency, even tolerance, for kinetic IEDs targeting US and host-national forces by exploiting mass unrest and anxiety with highly explosive yet selective cultural narratives. For example, Abu Musab al-Zarqawi, the Jordanian terrorist who formed Al-Qaeda in Iraq (AQI), picked up on Bin Laden's 1998 Fatwa titled "Jihad Against Jews and Crusaders," which requires Muslims to kill Americans, both civilian and military.[10] And the bovine poisoning rumor, a particularly powerful narrative given the impact of the US invasion on the country's infrastructure and collective psyche, aided the insurgent cause while degrading the efficacy of the bovine inoculation campaign.

Not all rumors become "imminent threats" to counterinsurgency efforts. For a host of reasons, most fail to gain traction, die out, and thus do not stick with a contested population. For example, Kelley's study of 966 rumors circulating in Iraq between 2003 and 2004 included rumors ranging from the innocuous to the deadly. Few, however, were encountered during Daniel Bernardi's tour of duty in Iraq in 2009.[11] Nonetheless, despite the fact that many rumors end up being duds on the battlefield, during a particularly tense crisis, they can fast become a force multiplier for insurgents. This outcome is especially the case when rumors link up to form mosaics that complement or extend insurgent propaganda. When it comes to rumors and counterinsurgency operations, there is a lot at stake.

The bovine poisoning rumor illustrates the challenge that military personnel face when grappling with the myriad of rumors circulating on the battlefield of ideas. To begin with, the rumor's archetypes, plot, and ideological charge played to local Iraqi fears rather than rational thought and action. In this rumor, the US forces fill the archetypal villain role, one previously played by Crusaders, Mongols, and early twentieth century colonialists. The plot of the bovine poisoning rumor fits into the basic pattern of invasion, subjugation, oppression, and exploitation articulated by the Crusader master narrative. In the bovine poisoning rumor, the plot elements are simple: US forces administer medicine to cattle; cattle are observed to die in the region. There is no evidentiary basis for a causal connection but, by sharing similarities with existing narratives circulating in Iraqi culture (and Arab and Islamic cultures more broadly), the bovine poisoning rumor acquires a similar causal logic. In the Crusades, Westerners came, attacked, pillaged, and destroyed; in the contemporary situation, the bovine poisoning rumor implies, the US came, attacked, pillaged, and destroyed. This fits into a familiar pattern for local residents. It makes sense to them.

Also of note, there was no single source or provocateur promulgating the bovine poisoning rumor; rather, there were many "versions" or "retellings" of it in circulation. This aspect makes this rumor and other wartime rumors a particular challenge to track, assess, and thwart. As rumors fragment and cross various modes of expression—from word-of-mouth to mosque sermons to print and visual media—they gain legitimacy among contested

Triangle of death 67

populations. Understanding the formal complexity, cultural specificity, and spread, or transmediation, of rumors are the first steps toward assessing the threat they pose to counterinsurgency efforts.[12]

It is important to keep in mind that a rumor does not necessarily have to be a "lie" to be classified as a rumor; some rumors contain truthful, plausible, or even factual elements.[13] Indeed, some studies show that the more traction a rumor attains, the greater the possibility it will contain truthful elements (D. Coady 2006a).[14] This is mainly because people in general are less likely to repeat a rumor if they believe it to be untruthful. As David Coady (2006a: 45), extending Tomatsu Shibutani's use of natural selection as a metaphor to describe this phenomenon, explains:

> There is "competition" between different rumors (and different versions of the same rumor) in the sense that some will survive and spread while others will die out. Finally, which rumors (and which versions of rumors) survive and spread is not entirely arbitrary. In other words, there are selection pressures.

The notion that the survival and spread of a rumor indicates a truthful claim suggests that information operators and host nation public affairs should saturate contested terrains with accurate and timely information as often and as soon as possible. Doing so might not advance strategic messaging—as in the case of accurately reporting civilian, or collateral, casualties in a timely manner, for example—but it will act as an obstacle to the flow of rumors that occur in information vacuums.

Strategic communicators would also do well to remember that the narrative systems circulating in a culture define what is "truth" for local constituents far more than what is labeled as "truth" by counterinsurgency forces. Although Coady and Shibutani both offer insightful arguments about the relationship between rumors, traction, and ground truth, they miss a critical point essential to the study of rumors during counterinsurgency operations: in times of socio-political crisis replete with violence and existential threats to sovereignty, rumors survive and thrive on anxiety—which can lead to both truth-spreading and propaganda. Indeed, these kinds of threat rumors are often extended or initiated by rumor-mongers interested in facilitating greater anxiety and instability.

Insurgents, familiar with the culture and narrative ecosystem in which rumors evolve, actively spread rumors that they have concocted or that have arisen organically and serve their interests in order to advance their strategic messages. This does not mean that the content of the rumor is untrue, but it certainly also does not mean that, if it survives as in the case of the bovine poisoning rumor, it is likely to be true. This phenomenon is indicative of the relativity of truth; rather than black or white, true or untrue, fact or false-hood, plausibility, believability, and "truth" are all shifting and malleable concepts shaped in large part by cultural traditions and knowledge systems.

68 *D. Bernardi and S. W. Ruston*

The meaning of "truth" is often a key feature of hegemonic struggles such as that dominating radical Islam and the West today.

Rumor mosaics and the role of narratives

It is more useful to look at rumors as sharing the dual logic of a non-fictional narrative in that they have the "meaning" of the rumor and the "telling" of the rumor that align as "truth" until proven otherwise. This approach is consistent with narratology, which posits that a narrative consists of both content (the story, the "what happened") and telling (the discourse, the "how it was told"), and that both combine to create the narrative (Chatman 1978; Genette 1980). As narratives, rumors feature actors experiencing actions and events in specific settings at specific times. They go on to explain events through simple cause/effect strategies. In the process, they predict outcomes; in the context of counterinsurgency operations, outcomes that, if not averted, promise to bring on grave consequences for contested populations and the host nation more generally. Seen in this light, the "truth" of a rumor is almost irrelevant to the meaning it conveys and facilitates.

In counterinsurgency situations, rumors are particularly explosive when they coalesce across common themes to form a mosaic. As we suggested at the beginning of this chapter, rumor mosaics consist of a number of complementary rumors that repeat frequently within a given culture by appealing to local interests in a way that impacts regional and even national politics. In the bovine poisoning example, the rumor mosaic includes assertions that the US poisoned cattle, US helicopters create large dust storms, US technologies caused the drought, and the US invaded Iraq to pillage its oil fields; in other words, the US has little regard for the people or future of Iraq and is only interested in the country's natural resources. As rumor mosaics such as these gain momentum, they end up painting American forces and interests as an existential threat to the people the US is trying to protect and to the host nation it supports. Thus, these rumors contribute to a point of view that the Americans and the government of Iraq, not the insurgents, are the enemy that must be defeated.

When rumor mosaics draw upon master narratives, they run an even greater risk of spreading beyond national borders to become a geopolitical threat. Master narratives are systems of stories that circulate across historical and cultural boundaries, and express a desire to resolve archetypal conflicts through established literary and historical forms. Because master narratives are deeply embedded within a particular culture—and the fact that they are repeated in a labyrinth of cultural texts and contexts—master narratives are particularly powerful systems shaping opinions, perspectives, and ideological leanings.

The master narratives supporting Islamist extremism include stories of invasion and occupation, such as that of the Crusades or the Tatars; stories of martyrdom, such as the Battle of Karbala; a narrative conveying a reversion

Triangle of death 69

to primitive pagan barbarism called the *jahiliyyah*; as well as a narrative of pious opposition to an exploitative tyrant, the Pharaoh (Halverson *et al.* 2011).

The bovine poisoning mosaic implicitly invoked the Crusader master narrative in which non-Arab/non-Muslim invaders plunder Arab lands for their riches, all the while proclaiming allegiance to a higher power and a more righteous religion. This master narrative eventually framed the occupation across Iraq and—even more problematically—the Islamic world, undermining the US strategic messaging and, as a result, US strategic planning and vision. More importantly, the association that the bovine rumor mosaic has with this Crusader master narrative enhanced its threat: Muslims are likely to believe rumors such as these when they extend an historical, widely understood narrative about foreign invaders. And, conversely, belief in these rumors reinforces a prevailing narrative of invasion and exploitation. Hence, the rumor serves a circular logic: rational, seemingly truthful, given historical narratives and official information gaps; ahistorical and irrational upon scrutiny and further investigation.

The power of narratives such as these during counterinsurgency operations is, in fact, echoed by *The US Army and Marine Corps Counterinsurgency Field Manual*, which grew out of US military failures during the occupation stages of the Iraqi campaign:

> The central mechanism through which ideologies are expressed and absorbed is the narrative. ...Narratives are central to representing identity, particularly the collective identity of religious sects, ethnic groupings, and tribal elements.
>
> (US Army and Marine Corps 2007: 25)

The *Manual* goes on to emphasize the centrality of narratives in the struggle to "win hearts and minds," and makes clear that, despite insurgent lies and distortions, in this battle of ideas, the US military's best munitions are facts and "truth" (US Army and Marine Corps (2007: 5).

Depending on "truth" to deal with rumors, however, fundamentally misunderstands the nature of rumors and the politics of "truth."[15] Indeed, as narrative comprehension and adoption proceeds by individuals patterning available input data (stories, actions, etc.), flooding a communication landscape with information may overwhelm existing narrative patterns and generate new narratives (possibly to the advantage of counterinsurgents). Truth, as we have shown, is a malleable concept, influenced by prevailing narratives and worldviews as much as by facts in evidence. As Kapferer (1990: 229–231) describes, Procter & Gamble, a large US-based corporation, discovered that truth had little effect in combating rumors in the early 1980s about the company having satanic affiliations. Despite a telephone hotline and media campaign offering proof (or "truth") that debunked the rumor, public attention and negative publicity continued to plague the company to the extent they

70 D. Bernardi and S. W. Ruston

elected to remove their logo from their products in 1985. On the other hand, debunking the falsity of content and falsity of origins seems to be the primary effectiveness of World War II "rumor clinics" run by Allport and Knapp (Neubauer 1999: 133–39). The key, then, for strategic communicators is to understand the processes that create individual and cultural "truth perspectives" and recognize the role that rumors play in these perspectives.

Rumor politics

The power of insurgent rumors to disrupt or hinder counterinsurgency goals, and to create competing versions of "the truth," is seen in the case of US Special Forces (SF) operating in the southeast side of Al-Hillah, Iraq, the apex of the "Triangle of Death." The teams of SF soldiers, sailors, and airmen occupied a modest compound on the outskirts of this city of approximately 400,000 people. The compound is called Stack House in internal US documents and communications. Signifying the symbolic as well as the strategic value that the US SF place on the facility, it was named after Sergeant Major Michael B. Stack (US Army Special Forces), who was killed in the area on April 11, 2004. The Iraqis, on the other hand, call the compound *Beit Wazir*, which means the minister's house. It was originally built to house ministers from Saddam Hussein's Ba'ath party. It was abandoned after the US invasion, and it is now "owned" by the Ministry of Interior and contracted to the US military.

US SF teams lived and worked in the discretely fortified compound from 2004 until the US withdrawal from Iraq in 2011. Although capable of direct action, or killing insurgents in battle, their primary mission after the Iraq Security Agreement Act of 2009 was to train the Hillah Special Weapons and Tactics unit (SWAT), an elite Ministry of Interior police force under the regional leadership of Brigadier General No'aman Jawad. As is often the case with the SF mission, particularly the Green Berets who resided in the compound, the elite soldiers shared the risks associated with counterinsurgency missions with their elite Iraqi SWAT partners as they pursued insurgents and terrorists in an effort to stabilize the city. Yet, despite the strategic value of the facility and the US presence to Iraqi security forces, the US SF team was under constant threat of being "kicked out" by local politicians and business leaders so that the facility could be used for other purposes. Rumors played a significant part in a struggle to legitimize and thus maintain the US presence in the city.

According to the US Commander of Stack House in late 2009, Captain Ted Morton (US Army Special Forces), as well as Hillah SWAT constables, three rumors coalesced to threaten public support for the team: (1) *the compound is occupied by Israelis*; (2) *the compound is occupied by the US Central Intelligence Agency (CIA), which conducts water boarding and other torture techniques*; and (3) *Hillah SWAT is a puppet militia for the US forces residing in the compound*. These rumors were articulated in local papers, local radio programs, and local broadcast news coverage, not to mention conversations in

Triangle of death 71

mosques and other public places. In fact, this mosaic of rumors was pervasive throughout all strata of local Iraqi society; even the mayor of Hillah thought that Israelis occupied the compound.[16] Both Captain Morton and Brigadier General No'aman noted that the rumors disrupted civil affairs missions—including school refurbishment projects, park and recreational projects, and humanitarian assistance—designed to improve daily life for the local population while increasing public support for both US and Iraqi government forces. The SF teams described these civil and public affairs efforts as "working themselves out of a job" (i.e., leaving Hillah and Iraq secured from internal threats and with sufficient municipal, social, and political infrastructure). However, the rumor mill kept them and their SWAT trainees on the job under potential kinetic and ideological threat.

The SF team and their Iraqi SWAT partners responded to these rumors in concerted ways. In 2004 and 2005, when the "Israeli" rumor dominated the local rumor mill, Stack House experienced a high number of direct attacks from insurgents. US and Iraqi soldiers were killed and wounded in these assaults; the walls of the US Joint Special Operations-Arabian Peninsula in Balad, Iraq, and the Ministry of Interior base just outside Baghdad were populated by pictures of fallen US and Iraqi soldiers. The SF team at Stack House responded to those attacks with both lethal and non-lethal methods. With respect to non-lethal operations, they embarked on an information campaign, deploying civil affairs and public affairs units to engage in medical and media outreach programs, which, according to Captain Morton, "really worked to dispel that rumor." Over an eighteen month period there was not a single mortar attack on Stack House.[17] The lethality of the "Israelis in the compound" rumor was defused; however, the Israeli rumor did not completely dissipate and has meshed with the CIA and puppet rumors that continue to circulate in the Hillah area to create a non-lethal but nevertheless deleterious influence on counterinsurgency operations in the area.

Although Captain Morton and Brigadier General No'aman felt at times they were fighting an uphill battle against this complex of rumors, their constant efforts to engage the population through civil and public affairs activities—in short, through strategic communication—resulted in a kind of unstable equilibrium: "There is constant talk about evicting the team among the local population," the Commander told us, "but to date no legal course of action has been initiated." The team continued to train Hillah SWAT, which continued to grow as a force capable of securing the city from insurgent violence—but not propaganda. The SF team, its chain-of-command, and Brigadier General No'aman consistently negotiated with local politicians and Ministry of Interior officials to keep the US forces in the compound. The SF team continued to marshal its non-kinetic resources in support of that goal.

The Hillah Stack House rumor mosaic told a familiar story to the Iraqi people that worked to the ideological advantage of the insurgents: *American occupiers are interested only in Iraq's resources to the peril of its people; they engage in torture and support Israeli interests in keeping Iraq weak; and the*

72   D. Bernardi and S. W. Ruston

government of Iraq is ineffective in combating American interest or, worse, merely puppets.

And this story connects implicitly but in powerful ways to master narratives that define Iraq's history. In 1258, Hulagu Khan, for instance, led his Mongol army in the destruction of Babylon and the massacre of hundreds of thousands of Mesopotamian residents. "Hulagu" is an epithet still in circulation for invading leaders. In fact, it was even invoked by Osama bin Laden in 2002 referring to Chairman of the Joint Chiefs of Staff General Colin Powell and Defense Secretary Dick Cheney's role in the 1991 Gulf War invasion of Iraq. Furthering the support of the "puppet" rumors, the master narrative of Hulagu Khan concludes with Mongol governors ruling over Islamic lands. These governors converted to Islam, but still ruled in accordance with *Yasa*, the Mongol code, and thus were perceived not as proper Islamic rulers but as apostates and puppets of the Tatars.[18]

Zarqawi invoked this master narrative as a justification for killing Muslims in Iraq in an intercepted letter to Bin Laden:

The Qur'an has told us that the machinations of the hypocrites, the deceit of the fifth column, and the cunning of those of our fellow countrymen whose tongues speak honeyed words but whose hearts are those of devils in the bodies of men – these are where the disease lies, these are the secret of our distress, these are the rat of the dike. "They are the enemy. Beware of them." Shaykh al-Islam Ibn Taymiyya spoke with truth and honesty when he said – after he mentioned their (Shi'a) thinking toward the people of Islam – "For this reason, with their malice and cunning, they help the infidels against the Muslim mass[es], and they are one of the greatest reasons for the eruption of Genghis Khan, the king of the infidels, into the lands of Islam, for the arrival of Hulagu in the country of Iraq, for the taking of Aleppo and the pillage of al-Salihiyya, and for other things.[19]

Here, Zarqawi quotes a prominent imam to lend credibility to a master narrative that would speak directly to Osama bin Laden, thereby justifying the deaths of Iraqi Muslims in pursuit of the American Hulagu in the "lands of Islam."

The story of the Crusades, with an emphasis on Christian warriors attacking Muslim strongholds and extracting Muslim wealth, also reverberates to this day throughout the Islamic world, enhanced by the majority Christian status of US and coalition forces. Like the Hulagu master narrative, the Crusade narrative survived World War I and World War II in the form of the colonization and decolonization of what the British decided would be the territorial borders of Iraq; it is easily extended in narrative terrains such as the Iraq invasion and Hillah Stack House "occupation." The Stack House rumor mosaic builds upon these narratives, speaking to the local people in meaningful ways while also implicitly and explicitly aiding the insurgent information campaign: a campaign linked to bin Laden's global jihad via Zarqawi's

Triangle of death   73

deft use of powerful narratives justifying violence in a religion, the majority of whose members decry violence against the innocent and, especially, innocent Muslims.

Rumor gaps

As the Stack House case suggests, by invoking long-standing narratives the rumor mill can pose a significant impediment to effective economic, social, diplomatic, and military development—the pillars of counterinsurgency operations. Whether the goal is to develop cooperative relationships between non-governmental or government agencies or implementing counterinsurgent strategies, mobilizing popular support in today's media-saturated environment is nothing short of a communication challenge—made all the more complex when there are gaps in the flow of credible official information. In fact, the rumor mill is a particular challenge in the fight against terrorism and, more importantly, the spread of extremist ideology in places fraught with historic instability such as Hillah.

The rumor mill is made even more challenging when the intentions of the organization or government (and their accompanying justifications, explanations, and other strategic communication content) shift and change over a short period of time; especially so when their intentions are found to be based on erroneous facts or, worse, geopolitical distortions. With respect to Operation Iraq Freedom, counterinsurgents often come over tongue tied when countering rumors such as the bovine poisoning tale or the Israeli/torture story when their words, not their deeds, are juxtaposed with the shifting US narrative for the invasion and occupation of the Arab nation; from, in short, "weapons of mass destruction" to "establishing freedom and democracy in the Middle East" to "nation building." These shifts create gaps in narrative coherence explaining the US invasion and occupation. This lack of narrative cohesion interferes with comprehension, and the rumor mosaics fill the gap with culturally credible explanations.

Although we detail our approach to narrative theory elsewhere (Bernardi *et al.* 2012), and doing so here would distract from the thrust of our overarching thesis, it is important to stress that narrative is fundamentally a process of comprehension in which information fills patterns and relationships that then provide sense-making. Whether the input is scenes in a movie, sequences in a novel, events on the ground, or rumors, these narrative elements are fitted into comprehension patterns—or *schema*—by viewers, listeners, and community members. These patterns are constructed with an internal logic developed by the story, the audience expectations, and the narrator. When story elements violate this internal logic or the narrator lacks credibility and fails to perform to expectations, the narrative lacks cohesion, and either a new pattern must be applied or new story elements sought to complete the picture. This is the window of opportunity for rumors during counterinsurgency operations; they fill the gaps.[20]

This phenomenon is especially the case when contradictions appear in the dominant narrative. The gap between the rhetoric of civil rights support and the actuality of the Abu Ghraib torture case, for example, creates the space for other torture-related rumors to develop. In fact, the Abu Ghraib narrative frames many of the rumors circulating in Iraq, becoming a kind of master narrative in itself. Despite the open prosecution in the US Army of the perpetrators of the US-inflicted torture that occurred at the prison, the story—and particularly the images of torture, murder, and humiliation—still lingers in places like Hillah. This narrative cohesion gap still exists (the gap between a pattern fitting the US as liberator/protector and the events of Abu Ghraib) allowing for the plausibility of the "Stack House as CIA torture compound" rumor to grow; it ends up fitting nicely into the historical pattern of occupation and exploitation established by the historical record and the master narratives indigenous to the region. The believability of this rumor confers veracity on the others: *the compound inhabited by Israelis; Hillah SWAT is a puppet of the US, which is occupying precious Iraqi real estate and resources.* As a result, this mosaic of rumors supports the conclusion, at least rhetorically, that the US invaded Iraq for its natural resources. *Why else would the US perpetrate the Abu Ghraib and bovine-poisoning incidents? Why else does the US continue to occupy valuable property like Stack House inside key cities?* Where narrative coherence and alignment are lacking, rumors fly in to fill the gaps.

The shifting narratives around US involvement in Iraq (invasion justification, Abu Ghraib abuses vis-à-vis rhetoric of human rights) complicate efforts to combat rumors, as their inconsistency creates gaps and provides an opportunity for a semblance of narrative cohesion born of conspiracy theories and rumors offered up by insurgents and media pundits alike. The shifting narratives reveal contradictions and knowledge gaps, thereby introducing a high degree of contradiction (even hypocrisy) on the part of the US and Iraqi governments into an already complex and unstable information minefield. As a result, strategic communication practitioners working in government and non-governmental organizations, whose interests are not themselves always aligned, continually fight an uneven war of words against extremist campaigns of lies, distortions, and half-truths designed to undermine host nation officials and institutions—not to mention internal counterinsurgency missteps. With contradictions prevalent in the narrative landscape, community members have difficulty achieving a consistent understanding of political and military events around them. Rumors participate in the narrative system, filling in gaps and providing for a kind of explanatory cohesion that leads to comprehension.

Narrative provides a meaningful structure for these rumors to become politically powerful, and the narrative system in which they flow gives them popular credibility. This combination means narrative and the systems it supports are key to our understanding of rumor and the cultural context in which they arise and circulate. Rumors, then, are best understood as specific elements functioning in narrative landscapes, and they circulate both singly

Triangle of death 75

and as mosaics in specific cultural conditions. The greater is the unrest and public anxiety, the greater the threat of rumors spreading, invoking master narratives, and so threatening stability operations and development.

Toward a conclusion

Practitioners of strategic communication are forced to either grapple with or ignore, at their peril, the narratological and cultural dimensions of rumors (i.e., systems of stories that have a history of capturing and shaping public opinion, worldview, etc.). In times of cultural strife and social conflict, rumors have the greatest potential for influencing contested populations, threatening an already unstable social order, and challenging the legitimacy of a government regardless of their validity or even their plausibility. Although preliminary, we believe our study of rumors circulating in Iraq points to this conclusion and our theory predicts it.

It is important to note that we are far from the first to focus analytic energies on the Iraqi rumor mill. The circulation of rumors in Iraq was a potent source of frustration to diplomatic, military, and governmental efforts throughout the country during the US invasion and occupation, and the rumors have received sporadic attention from various organizations. The study closest to ours in terms of data set and application is a Master of Arts thesis completed at the Naval Postgraduate School by US Air Force Captain Stephanie Kelley (2004).

As we note at the beginning of this chapter, Kelley's study shows how rumors can be used as a method of identifying social anxieties and fear. Her approach to rumors first and foremost positions them as a valuable source of intelligence on the "attitudes, concerns, and anxieties of groups within a population" (Kelley 2004: 28). More specifically, Kelley categorizes rumors by way of two typologies (motivation and subject) in order to draw broad-based conclusions providing "general indications of Iraqi opinions and morale as well as highlighting specific concerns of the Iraqi people. Information operations and psychological operations units could use these findings to tailor campaigns that address many of these concerns" (Kelley 2004: 54). She also offers some counter-rumor suggestions, by combining rumor theory from sociology, psychology, and marketing with her study of Iraq rumors.

Kelley's study is insightful, and highly necessary at its time of publication, as no concentrated effort had yet been made to address the rumors rampant in Iraq hindering the coalition forces, US efforts at stabilizing the region, and the nascent Iraqi government. Nonetheless, the phenomenon of rumors deserves a great deal more attention—particularly in places such as Iraq, Afghanistan, Pakistan, the Philippines, and Indonesia where Islamic insurgencies coercively engage contested populations in an effort to win their consent to extremist rule. And these are also locales where rumors and rumor mosaics influence the prevailing narrative landscapes in which strategic communication professionals must operate.

76 *D. Bernardi and S. W. Ruston*

It is our belief that rumors are a particular type of story, one that—as has been widely agreed by most scholars from the landmark studies in the 1940s to present day inquiries—feeds on social anxieties, fears, hopes, and dreams and is fueled by gaps in information. Rumors are particularly impactful, indeed powerful, during counterinsurgencies. They get their political charge from the master narratives that give them cohesion and the ideologies that exploit existing culture and political fissures. When rumors coalesce to form a mosaic, the threat is even greater.

Notes

1 In late 2009, Multinational Forces-Iraq was changed to US Forces-Iraq.
2 This rumor first came to our attention in conversation with journalists embedded with US forces in Iraq and was confirmed by information operations officers who had been stationed in the country.
3 These rumors were collected in three ways: interviews with American military and press personnel upon return from patrols and information-gathering activities in Iraq; interviews with Iraqi military personnel familiar with the area; and face-to-face conversations with Iraqi citizens conducted by one of the authors.
4 In their seminal study, Gordon W. Allport and Leo Postman (1947) labeled the practice of using rumors to support propaganda "whispering campaigns." The label remains in use by scholars and US military personnel alike.
5 Several journalists have researched and written about the ways in which the Bush administration used the media to spread the story that Hussein's WMD program posed an imminent threat to the US. Much of their sourcing can be traced to US allies with a vested interest in seizing power in Iraq, including Ahmed Chalabai and other Iraqi defectors who needed US support to topple the dictator. See especially Isikoff and Corn (2007), Ricks (2007), and Hersh (2004).
6 For an account of the mismanagement of the occupation, particularly during the Coalition Provisional Authority period managed by Paul Bremer, see Chandrasekaran (2006).
7 This point is stressed throughout the literature on rumors. As DiFonzo (2008: 35) summarizes: "This is the famous law of rumor: Rumors abound in proportion to the ambiguity or uncertainty inherent in a situation, and the importance of the topic."
8 For an insightful study of how US strategic communication during the Iraq war amounted to information fratricide, see Paul *et al.* (2009).
9 Simon Cottee (2010: 331) makes a similar point: "Wherever the cause of terrorism may ultimately lie, the act of killing, maiming and terrorizing innocent people is enabled by a framework of justifying and mitigating narratives."
10 The Fatwa was also signed by Ayman al-Zawahiri, Abu-Yasir Rifa'i Ahmad Taha, Shaykh Mir Hamzah, and Fazlur Rahman. It can be found in its entirety at: www.fas.org/irp/world/para/docs/980223-fatwa.htm
11 A United States Navy Reservist, Bernardi served as the Public Affairs Officer for Special Operations Taskforce-Central from June 2009 to February 2010.
12 Transmediation refers to the reconfiguration and retransmission of messages into new media formats. Each change in medium involves alteration of both form and, subtly, meaning, a process affecting rumors as well as mainstream messages.
13 In some cases, a rumor might predict an event, such as a bank not being able to cover its deposits, which leads to a kind of panic that brings the event about or a run on the bank. For a broad overview of this and other arguments about the social psychology of rumors, see DiFonzo (2008).

14 Or as Knapp (1944: 47) suggests: "No rumor will travel far unless there is already a disposition among those who hear it to lend it credence. But once rumors are current, they have a way of carrying the public with them. Somehow, the more a rumor is told, the greater is its plausibility."
15 Which is not to suggest that "lies" are a legitimate or effective countermeasure.
16 Both the US Commander of Stack House as well as senior members in charge of Hillah SWAT reported this to us.
17 The decrease in lethal attacks on Iraqi and US forces in the region can also be linked to both the US surge as well as the increasing capabilities of Hillah SWAT.
18 See Halverson *et al.* (2011), Chapter 9, for a thorough discussion of Hulagu Khan and the Tatar master narrative.
19 Abu Musab al-Zarqawi. Letter to Osama Bin Laden (2004). Available online through Global Security: www.globalsecurity.org/wmd/library/news/iraq/2004/02/040212-al-zarqawi.htm
20 We elaborate on this theory of narrative in Bernardi *et al.* (2012). This chapter grew out of co-author Ruston's paper "Getting the Story Straight: Narrative Schema and Strategic Communication" presented at QRM 2010, University of New Mexico, April 2010, and adapts material published in Bernardi *et al.* (2012).

4 The politics of informal communication

Conspiracy theories and rumors
in the 2009 (post-)electoral Iranian
public sphere

Babak Rahimi

Most established forms of research on electoral politics pertain to patterns of voter behavior and institutional processes that either accommodate or dislodge an electoral outcome. Public opinion, based on either informed or uninformed knowledge, plays a critical role in elections, as political actors employ various linguistic strategies to effectively advance their positions or discredit opponents. Although it may be viewed as non-existent, as Pierre Bourdieu famously declared, or conceptualized as a social construct, public opinion is nevertheless a product of discourses that in many ways define the scope of political rationality under which official politics is normally recognized (Bourdieu 1979; Herbst 1993). Through rhetorical and symbolic statements, elites and electoral campaigners, as political actors, either express or communicate information, ideas, and images about themselves and their political competitors to configure perceptions and consequently maintain or increase their constituencies. In the context of democratic politics, formal communication such as formal speeches, sermons, slogans, and propaganda operate as strategies of persuasion with claims over public opinion that, in turn, shape or limit the boundaries of political discourse. The formal communicative boundaries of an electoral public are formed by how actors can use (or manipulate) the boundaries of discourses in various political settings and, ultimately, construct a "consensual majority" public (Carpini 1994).

The present analysis, however, looks at informal communication, and it does so in the context of an electoral process monitored and managed under authoritarian rule. The Iranian presidential elections of June, 2009 provide a case study in how political communication in the course of electoral politics can primarily produce informal discourses, articulated and mediated through unofficial channels of communication with the aim of influencing political behavior and outcomes. Although they may ultimately become official discourses, at times co-opted by the state, many of these informal discourses provide alternative strategies to either challenge or maintain power, carving out distinct (counter-)publics of interaction with an awareness, in the words of Michael Warner (2005: 56), of their "subordinate status."[1] By "informal communication," I am therefore referring to types of interpretative and strategic actions that, in the words of Mikhail Bakhtin (1981: 367), express the

The politics of informal communication 79

views of varied "social groups, professions and other cross-sections of everyday life." This multiplicity of views reveals the decentralized networks of communication through which narratives of information are disseminated, filtered, and made public for particular audiences (Gladwell 2000). Ultimately, what informal discourses such as conspiracy theories and rumors evoke is "plausibility" in social boundaries, creating a suspicious framework of experience that seeks to shape collective judgments (Fine 2007).

Rumors, in particular, serve as a type of discursive strategy that destabilizes power relations in an electoral setting by re-imagining existing politics and future possibilities of politics in alternative ways. Rumors—through varied network sites of everyday communication and used by various actors, including state actors—maintain their own rationality and expressive mode of inquiry. As Jacques Rancière (1999: 56–57) describes, rumors are formed by "linguistic acts that are at the same time rational arguments and 'poetic' metaphors." Far from chatter and "uninformed" noise, rumors identify an aesthetic of discoursing that, in both official and unofficial domains of regular interaction, seek out more information and, more importantly, maintain a level of distrust of knowledge endorsed by a perceived foreign enemy or a state undergoing a crisis of legitimacy (Kapferer 1990: 31). The performative dimension of rumors lies, as suggested by Veena Das (2005: 119), in its "perlocutionary force of words," the ability to force something by articulating and circulating a statement, an idea, an image, news, and so forcing a new way of looking at things. In short, rumors are a type of contentious performance of a discursive form that disrupts, and in the act of disruption, they seek to re-articulate the uncertainty of political circumstances and, ultimately, reconfigure it.

As elections under the Islamic Republic institutionally function to manage elite factionalism—inherent in the theocratic state in Iran since its inception in 1979—informal communication has continued to play a critical role in how collective judgments are formed within such a contentious political climate, in the course of which state power is legitimized through limited elections that ultimately reinforce authoritarian rule.[2] In many ways, conspiracy theories and rumors reflect deep skepticism about the political order and yet seek to provide a suitable expression for discontent about the status quo. In the post-election turmoil in Iran, the emerging political culture entailed the engagement of various strategies that aimed at increasing not only the mobilization of dissent, but also the scope of conflict and drawing the spotlight on to issues that could potentially delegitimize the state. These took the form of discourses of persuasion with the aim of changing views and sentiments on contentious political issues, although mostly revolving around the election results, which the supporters of anti-incumbent candidates strongly contested. The dynamics of such narratives emanated from a desire not just to make sense of an unpredictable situation that defined the post-election period, but also to build solidarity aimed at increasing mobilization and discontent. With distinct plot twists and unverifiable claims to truth, post-election rumors in

80 B. Rahimi

particular conveyed powerful narratives that entailed emotional commitment to perceiving political reality as suspect.

The following account highlights the socio-political implications of informal communications that signify distinct unofficial discourses during and after elections, and how such narratives in turn shaped new official and subversive publics. The study then focuses on the phenomena of political rumors and conspiracy theories and their discursive uses for political (non-state and state) actors as a way of carving out alternative spaces of contention. The main claim here is that rumors and conspiracies, as discourses of disbelief in an apparent reality, are disruptive performances through which political actors produce value-laden images of self and other in a complex set of network relations. It is primarily through the interpretative medium of rumors and conspiratorial languages produced in complex social networks that counterpublics shape the "collective text" of meaning (Geertz 1991: 267).

The chapter is divided into two sections. In the first part, the discussion revolves around the impact of informal communication in the pre-electoral phase (pre-June 2009), during which time gossip and rumors from anti-government actors created new spaces of dissent under the distinct strictures of electoral politics espoused by the Iranian government. Conspiratorial discourses too played a critical role for the pro-government hardliner factions in the construction of a public alarmism: a collective mood of xenophobic paranoia over a possible coup orchestrated by foreign elements against the nation. In the post-election period, however, the interactive yet porous field of informal communication became more intense, more agonistic with the anti-protest crackdowns and promotion of conspiracy theories (such as the "Velvet revolution" argument that depicted the protesters as foreign agents), along with the counterdiscourse of rumors in the idiom of state-sponsored acts of assassination, torture, and rape. In this second section, cyberspace and information technologies such as satellite and mobile phones provide alternative platforms for unofficial discourses, helping the dissident factions to launch a virtual attack on the state. Within these virtual spaces of interaction, rumors and conspiracies perpetuated new ways of thinking and doing politics in post-election Iran, forming new understandings of friend and adversary, self and other.

The Iranian presidential elections: a brief history

Although the Islamic Republic is an authoritarian theocracy, the changing tensions between society and state and, by extension, elite factionalism continue to shape the political realities of Iran. Much of the conflict goes back to the 1979 Islamic revolution that galvanized an overwhelming majority of Shi'i Iranians to rise up against the Pahlavi regime and install the only Islamic theocracy in modern history (Zubaida 1997). In many ways, the revolutionary movement that institutionalized the Islamist state was partly inspired by a culture of conspiracies and rumors that motivated the

The politics of informal communication 81

opposition to defeat the Pahlavi regime (Pliskin 1980). Rumors of state brutality and foreign conspiracies inspired many revolutionaries to risk death and engage in radical activism, some of which was inscribed with strong utopian inclinations and nationalistic calls for independence. The 1979 hostage crisis that followed the revolution was an indication of this expanding conspiratorial culture which saw as plausible the possibility of another foreign coup in the aftermath of a revolution that in many ways resembled the 1953 CIA-led coup that overthrew Mossadeq's nationalist government in 1953.[3]

The 1979 constitution, drafted mainly by militant clerics, institutionalized Ayatollah Ruhoallah Khomeini's political ideology of *velayat-e faqih* or the "guardianship of the jurist," which made Iran into a theocracy and established a nativist state with the objective of protecting the nation from foreign influence. Yet the Islamic Republic also brought to the fore a new interpretation of Shi'i Islamic government that assigned to *ulama* (clerics) the responsibility to rule on behalf of the Twelfth Imam, whose eventual return is believed to culminate in the establishment of divine justice on earth (Arjomad 1989). This new clerical oligarchy, along with ensuing tensions between unelected and elected institutions, set the basis for the rise of factional politics that followed the revolutionary upheaval when the "regime and its clerical vanguard gave vent to their charismatic aspiration" (Brumberg 2001: 100).

In this political context, elections served as one of the only republican features of the newly established theocratic state. Despite the presence of political factions, which could translate into meaningful political competition, both parliamentary and presidential elections under the Islamic Republic were limited to those who were loyal only to the official ideology of the state. By the early 1980s, the Council of Guardians, a clerical institution responsible for determining who could run for office, emerged to play an integral role in Iranian electoral politics, validating claims by the state to popular legitimacy. The presidential elections, in particular, came to reflect the obstacles to democratic politics in Iran, although a vibrant middle class gradually emerged to challenge such institutional strictures in the late 1990s.

The 1997 election of the reformist candidate, Mohammad Khatami, marked a major political event in post-revolutionary Iranian history. In a highly competitive contest, Khatami achieved an upset victory over a conservative candidate. The victory signified a political paradigm shift, mostly because the votes "were properly counted, the results publicly announced, and the voter's mandate accepted by the regime" (Bakhash 1998: 80). As the conservative establishment sought to manage informal factional alliances in the 2001 presidential elections, mainly by allowing the reformists to win another election, the emergence of multiple centers of power enhanced the conflict between elites and prolonged the process of factional politics. The election results confirmed the awareness of a counterpublic that was not recognized by the state and yet had won over the voting ballots.[4] At the societal level, Iran's civil society also grew in size and challenged the authority of the state over everyday social interactions; for instance, at political

82   *B. Rahimi*

gatherings, public events, religious ceremonies, parks, and shopping centers. Theocratic morality came under attack from an emerging younger generation, who were mostly born after the 1979 Revolution, as new norms of sociability, aesthetic tastes, and sensual practices replaced dominant publics and social behaviors endorsed by the state.

With the support of the Supreme Leader, Ayatollah Ali Khamenei, the 2005 presidential elections saw the ascendancy of a new political Islamic force: a coalition of new conservatives made up of groups such as the Abad-garan-e Iran-Eslami (Developers of the Islamic Iran, or DII). The new conservative movement was marked by a renewed call for revolutionary zeal and a pledge to Ayatollah Khomeini's original mission of establishing a just Islamic society in paving the way for the ultimate return of the promised Mahdi at the end of time. What distinguished the new conservatives from other political factions in the 2005 elections was an ideological emphasis on populist policies and a renewal of collective memory of the war years, a period marked by self-sacrifice, devotion to God, and piety in face of the inevitability of martyrdom on the frontlines of the conflict with Iraq. Mostly comprised of middle-aged hardliners of non-clerical background and veterans of the war, who had entered universities during the Rafsanjani period and maintained official positions in the state bureaucracy during the reform period, the new hardliners rejected liberalization of the country's domestic and international politics (Ehteshami and Zweiri 2007). Also, the new conservative political culture was deeply entrenched in conspiratorial views of the presence of a foreign enemy who cunningly continues to seek to overthrow the Islamic Republic using both hard and soft power. The new conservative candidate, Mahmood Ahmadinejad, a veteran of the Iran–Iraq war, represented a populist hardliner position with strong messianic tendencies and conspiratorial discontent with global organizations (Naji 2009).

With the launch of the 2005 election campaign and amid intense competition, the new conservative movement rallied around populist platforms with promises of social services and government assistance that appealed mostly to lower-class segments of the urban and rural population (Gheissari and Sanandaji 2009). In the first presidential run-off in the history of the Islamic Republic, the result was an upset victory for the hardliners' candidate, Mahmood Ahmadinejad, who, with 20 percent of the votes in the first round, had suddenly garnered 62 percent of the final votes, against 35 percent for Rafsanjani (Gheissari and Nasr 2006: 157). Although the 2005 elections saw no major signs of contestation, the result was not accepted by Ahmadinejad's rivals. Mehdi Karoubi, a leading reformist candidate, thought Ahmadinejad's victory reeked of fraud. Karoubi claimed that various state organizations, including the Revolutionary Guard Corps and the Basiji militia, had been mobilized to muster electoral support for Ahmadinejad. Rafsanjani also backed Karoubi's allegation and alluded to a paramilitary role in the elections (Wright 2008: 316–17). Others also highlighted a possible five million additional votes that were counted by the Guardian Council in favor of

The politics of informal communication   83

Ahmadinejad, including in Sunni-dominated provinces such as southern Khurasan (De Bellaigue 2007: 122). Meanwhile, rumors,[5] of an electoral coup circulated in the online media outlets, especially blogs.

The 2005 elections played a critical role in paving the way for the spread of rumors and conspiracy discourses about an electoral coup in the form of voter fraud and rigged elections. The proliferation of these discourses reflected a primary discursive attempt to make sense of the irregularity between electoral campaigning and the results. Rumors, in particular, served as a rational way to understand the discrepancies between perceptions about the elections and the official results announced by the state. Such views, possibly advanced first by political actors involved in the organization of electoral campaigns, put forward the notion that an electoral takeover of the executive office was engineered by the Supreme Leader and his supporters, including the Revolutionary Guard, along with the security–intelligence apparatus. Rumors of electoral fraud began to underline a deep political mistrust of authorities and institutional truths as narrated by the state media. In post-2005 elections, a new counterdiscourse of conspiracy and rumors shaped a strong commitment to the perception that the elections were no longer a secure means of displaying public opinion.

Pre-2009 presidential election: stories of a coup

The tenth presidential elections on June 12, 2009 were the most controversial in the history of the Islamic Republic. All opposing candidates built their platforms on themes that defied Ahmadinejad's populist and messianic politics. Meanwhile, the political ambiance of the electoral campaign set the stage for a highly competitive election with an assumption that the election results would be close and therefore would continue to a second round, just like in 2005. Ahmadinejad's drive to consolidate his power, with the support of the Supreme Leader, had met with resistance during his first term in the presidency, and now his opponents had a chance to challenge him.

Yet the lack of transparency during the previous elections fostered expressions of suspicion. Before Iranians went to the polls, two distinct kinds of rumors circulated in official media outlets and also everyday public spaces. The first set of rumors, disseminated by pro-government factions, identified a pre-orchestrated foreign plot to overthrow the Islamic establishment in the aftermath of elections (Evans and Dahl 2009; Press TV 2009a). According to national TV and other hardliner press such as *Keyhan*,[5] the upcoming elections had the potential to become a platform for the anti-government forces to launch a "velvet" coup against the Islamic Republic. By using leading reformist candidates such as Mehdi Karoubi and Mir-Hussain Mousavi, Great Britain and the US were prepared to support subversive activities such as organizing mass street protests to topple the regime. It was alleged that news channels such as BBC and VOA, as foreign-funded media agencies, would play a major role in provoking unrest and civil disobedience (Press TV

84   *B. Rahimi*

2009b). This set of rumors strategically purported to oppose the counter-discourses posed by Ahmadinejad opponents, who presumed a strong possibility of a hardliner manipulation of the elections as a way to maintain power.

For anti-incumbent groups, in this regard, rumors of a foreign-led coup spread by pro-government supporters appeared as a pre-emptive attack on the dissidents, heralding a possible offensive against the opposition during or after the elections. Rumors also circulated from the opposition, largely online and through mobile phones (text messaging), that a massive fraud would be under way if representatives of the opposition candidate failed to be present at the voting stations on the day of elections. One rumor described this massive fraud in terms of the use of sophisticated computerized electoral tactics by the Interior Ministry to increase the incumbent president's number of votes (*Fieldwork Observation*. Tehran. May 15–June 11, 2009). Others, however, were convinced that special pens with invisible ink would be provided by the authorities so as to discount numerous pro-Mousavi votes in certain parts of major cities around the country (*Fieldwork Observation*. Tehran. June 1–12, 2009). Days before the elections, pro-Mousavi campaigners predicated major crackdowns immediately after the election results were announced (*Fieldwork Observation*. Tehran. June 1–12, 2009). Rumors of fraud and repression had set the scene for a new experience of political activism with a demand to change the circumstances in such a way as to prevent defeat and exclusion from politics.

Rumors therefore entailed calls for action. For anti-Ahmadinejad campaigners, including the supporters of the conservative candidate Mohsen Rezai's camp, the best way to tackle possible fraud was to forcefully set up inspectors and representatives at voting ballets and stations, monitoring the activities of those in charge of transporting and counting votes. As a hardliner victory could ultimately be realized with the support of the Interior Ministry, the best strategy would be to participate in the elections on a massive scale in order to counterbalance possible vote rigging.

More rumors circulated in the days before the elections about possible attacks by the state and counterattacks from the opposition. As rumors of a government coup became a staple of an electoral political culture, an ambiguous political milieu was formed with the question of who would instigate the first attack, and how acts of violence could force the government to either undermine or acknowledge the opposition's demands. The most talked about story of a possible coup involved the Revolutionary Guard and the intelligence forces with previous plans to consolidate power in 2008, when the Supreme Leader, in one of his sermons, had given his public consent to the re-election of Ahmadinejad (*Fieldwork Observation*. Tehran. May 15–June 11 2009). Another popular rumor described how the hardliners sought to identify the opposition by encouraging them to openly participate in election campaigns organized in visible urban or virtual spaces, permitted by the regime before the elections (*Fieldwork Observation*. Tehran. May 15–June 11,

2009). When Facebook was finally unblocked in February 2009, and as many anti-government individuals and groups began to create sites to voice their opposition, rumors of state agents identifying dissidents online became a topic of everyday discussion (Gheytanchi and Rahimi 2009; see also Morozov 2009). Central to such rumors was the extent to which the regime could be genuine in permitting would-be voters to freely express themselves and whether such social openings could be trusted as a sign of progress or merely as an attempt to stifle dissent once the elections were over.

When the election results were announced—declaring Ahmadinejad as the winner with a huge margin of votes (more than 60 percent) over his competitors—even with many of the votes still not accounted for, Mousavi supporters and other disgruntled voters took to the streets of major Iranian cities. The state immediately responded with a brutal crackdown on the protesters, leading to the arrests and deaths of a number of demonstrators in the days following the election. In the weeks following the election, the new political movement known as the "Green Movement," a coalition of opposition groups and factions led by Karoubi and Mousavi, forged ahead with demonstrations and mass rallies protesting about the election. More importantly, the increasing crackdowns by the security forces and the Supreme Leader's support for the repression opened a wider conflict, a fissure that raised questions about the legitimacy of the Islamic Republic thirty years after its establishment. The ambiguous and conflict-ridden situation played a catalytic role in the consolidation of political discourse of conspiracies and rumors. The post-election rumors challenged not merely the election results but the lack of transparency and accountability under a theocratic state that had become increasingly dependent on the paramilitary Revolutionary Guard forces to maintain power. Although various narratives circulated in the public domain about how acts of fraud took place, rumors of a coup had now developed into conspiracies around the electoral scheme. Rumors as repertoires of discontent not only cast doubt and hence rejected official accounts of the elections, but also sought to capture public discourse on the results.

Post-election narratives of suspense: rumors of violence and violence of rumors

A crisis of legitimacy over the parameters of theocratic governance came into full swing just days after the elections. First, a number of reports, especially from the Karoubi and Mousavi camps, surfaced about a list of fraudulent activities in both provincial and urban areas. One of the most popular rumors described how the government had forged millions of votes of non-existing individuals or deceased persons (*Fieldwork Observation*. Tehran. June 13, 2009). There were also reports of millions of pro-Mousavi votes that were lost or destroyed on the day of the elections.[6] Another popular account described the role of the Electoral Commission in electoral irregularities. The commission is legally expected to wait three days before confirming the results of

86   *B. Rahimi*

elections, a process that will ultimately be approved by the Supreme Leader. But, in an unprecedented move, Ayatollah Khamenei in fact congratulated Ahmadinejad immediately after the election results were announced on June 13. This move is consistent with the Supreme Leader's pre-election support for the president, a fact that complements his conflict with Mousavi during the 1980s.

The most well-known account, however, came from two prominent Iranian filmmakers in France, Mohsen Makhbalbaf and Marjane Satrapi, who made public an alleged letter from the Interior Ministry to the Supreme Leader about the true electoral result, which was overwhelmingly in favor of Mousavi (Reals 2009). The letter was later posted online where it continues to be circulated on anti-government websites. The letter joined the thousands of documents that shaped Iran's post-election culture of rumors and conspiracies.

At street level, the post-election demonstrations became a breeding ground for the circulation of conspiracies and tales of state brutality. The sort of rumors that surfaced in the course of anti-government marches reveal a sense of paranoia over arrests, attacks, and claims of rape and torture in prisons. Footage of anti-government demonstrations, and their subsequent crackdown by the security forces, shot by cell phones and spread via the internet, depict scenes of intense emotion and displays of dissent unprecedented since the 1979 revolution. SMS and social networking sites such as Facebook provided near-instantaneous platforms of communication for the protesters to transmit information about future political rallies or patterns of state brutality on a street-by-street basis. Protesters, both inside and outside the country, disseminated statements, slogans, or news mostly through social networking sites such as Persian-language Balatarin, Facebook, or, to a much lesser extent, Twitter notes (or #hashtags) on where the state police would gather up forces and how best to escape or fight.[7]

In the weeks after the elections, the internet became a virtual battle zone between state and non-state adversaries. In what Lee Rainie and Barry Wellman (2012) have called "networked individualism," each political activist would participate in networking structures that run on operating systems which enable individuals to connect and exchange information and ideas that provide them with the autonomy to shape their social environment. Various social media such as Facebook and YouTube sites enhanced individual networking practices, especially in the way political actors would take part in the dissemination of conspiracy and rumor and stylize accounts and narratives according to the rapidly shifting situations offline. Such forms of activism built around personalized communication practices, operating through a system of "networked individualism," would decentralize the idea of authorship and attest to the unsettling validity of public information, as propagated by the state in politically volatile situations. Although blogs had provided glimpses into such individuated social networking processes in previous years, the 2009 elections saw the launch of a new generation of Facebook or

The politics of informal communication 87

Balatarin activists with the skills and knowledge to disseminate and spread unofficial news, statements, or interpretations about the political situation, together with new practices of communicating, narrating, and inserting meaning to the unfolding events (Manoukian 2010; Rahimi 2011; Sreberny and Khiabany 2010).

It was also in cyberspace where the post-election culture of rumors and conspiracies was advanced by networked individuals who spotlighted police brutality to underscore state repression and hence its illegitimate claim to power. Numerous footages of security forces' assaults on protesters circulated online, first posted on Facebook or YouTube by computer-savvy protesters; these clips and videos would later appear on mainstream satellite TV channels such as *Al Jazeera* and *CNN International*. The framing practices advanced by the networked activists entailed a full-fledged symbolic strategy to define the state as brutal and tyrannical. One popular rumor that first appeared on Twitter was that, in the early period after the election crackdown, police helicopters poured acid and boiling water over the demonstrators (Esfandiari 2010b). Another rumor depicted state security forces as non-Iranian in origin, namely Iraqi or Lebanese Arabs trained and prepared by the Revolutionary Guard to suppress street demonstrations (Bahrampour 2009). These rumors sought to frame the Islamic Republic as a transgressor and a conspiratorial entity with foreign interests. Among other rumors were assertions that the regime had infiltrated various anti-government websites, including Facebook and Twitter, in order to manipulate information and interrupt the opposition's channels of communication (Grossman 2009; Morozov 2009). This latter type of rumor reflected both perceptions on the conspiratorial nature of the state and also the element of distrust within the opposition movement that produced such discourses of discontent.

Yet such informal discourses carved new spaces of hope with a promise of redemption through suffering caused by repression. It was in the rumors of rape, torture, and violence during the street protests and at prisons that new understandings of self, new interpretations of political action were articulated in symbols of protest and narratives of heroic triumph through sacrifice. The life of post-election protesters, as narrated and perceived in the medium of conspiratorial narratives of state repression, became less about the formalities of politics (i.e., political rallies) and more about the unknown, unpredictable events that in their eruption could either signify state involvement in various aspects of everyday life or resistance by subtle acts of subversion. Emotions play a critical role here as well. Sunstein (2009: 7) refers to this as "biased assimilation," a cognitive process that pushes people to assimilate received information in a preconceived way that only confirms the strong emotions those individuals may have about a perceived malevolent entity. For Sunstein, such cognitive experiences gain social currency through "group polarization" by enabling like-minded people to affirm commitment to a rumor after it is shared and circulated among the actors in the group. Rumors, in other words, become real in the social processes of an intensely emotive nature.

88   *B. Rahimi*

Jokes about those in power, too, were no longer mere depictions of incompetent characters caught in funny situations (e.g., Ahmadinejad mistakenly thinking that the protesters' cry of "death to the dictator" is meant as a compliment for recognizing him as the head of the state and not the Supreme Leader), but a reversal of values of official culture endorsed by the state. Rumors about possible backdoor negotiations between prominent clerics such as Hashemi Rafsanjani and the Supreme Leader, with plans to remove Ahmadinejad from the office of presidency, raised suspicion about the perceived flow of events and cemented a view of the state as a conspiratorial actor in a struggle for survival. All in all, such informal discourses against the background of the street protests revealed a type of collectivity of perceptions that essentially viewed the apparent reality as problematic and, in the words of Mark Fenster (1999: 123), "posit a new world order."

Rumors of a death: the case of Neda

The case of Neda Agha Soltan serves as a prime example of how the post-election culture of conspiracies and rumors developed with the growing repressive measures adopted by the state. Neda's assassination by an unknown gunman gained worldwide attention once it was posted on Facebook and later YouTube on June 20 (for an account of her death, see Assmann and Assmann 2010). The symbolism of a bloody image of a female body, breathlessly lying on the pavement of a chaotic street, provided more than a propaganda device for the opposition to attack the regime; it became an emotional rallying cry, bolstering solidarity in the ethos of martyrdom that sustained the protestors' momentum. While footage of Neda circulated online and later on mainstream media (e.g., *Al Jazeera* and *CNN*), the computer-savvy protesters began to circulate the identification card of Neda's alleged assassin, a member of the feared Basij.[8] The photo of the killer fueled more rumors as to how and why Neda was killed, and the whereabouts of the assassin. Reports related to Neda's death also involved her burial procession (apparently banned by the state) and how, it was rumored, her family was forced to keep silent.

Immediately after footage appeared on major international news channels, the Iranian government fought back with a series of counternarratives of Neda's murder. In an apparent attempt to spin the story, a number of state officials quickly went public with the claim that foreign forces—including the CIA—were behind the assassination. Shortly afterwards, a second narrative then emerged on Iranian national TV, which described Neda Agha-Soltan as someone who was actually still alive and not killed as the video suggested. The report showed interviews with the "real" Neda and claimed that the video of the murdered female was a fake. The third narrative, however, appeared in the form of a documentary and provided a more adventurous explanation. The girl on the video is actually the deceased Neda Agha-Soltan, but her murder was a mere performance. In reality, the documentary claimed,

The politics of informal communication 89

Neda acted out her death in order to discredit the regime. While she was transported to hospital in an ambulance, Neda was murdered by two male assailants, one of whom was a medical doctor working as an intelligence agent for Britain in Iran. According to this final narrative, Neda was unaware of her ultimate fate at the time she appeared on the video, but the masterminds behind the operation had plans to sacrifice her in order to blame the government.[9]

In many ways, the state's propagation of various conspiracies around Neda's assassination served as a strategic discursive attempt to produce a counterdiscourse in order to discredit anti-government allegations and rumors of state brutality. But in doing so, those counternarratives also became part and parcel of a growing post-election culture of conspiracies that shaped an ambience of trepidation and disbelief in the apparent everyday state of affairs. State-endorsed rumors of foreign involvement in fanning the flames of the protestors' rage aimed to recognize the prestige of the regime and justify further violence by the security forces. As an entity in charge of protecting the nation and its citizens, the state saw its job as protecting its citizens from misinformation created by foreign states and the seemingly demonic ferocity of anti-government factions inside the country. In addition, such reports generated a sense of solidarity among the pro-government factions against those who questioned the state's legitimate right to rule. Counternarratives such as Neda's documentary, which were made official in the state media, also transpired a theatrical performance that successfully manifested a latent story of a battle between good (us) and evil (them), with the regime identified as the victim and the opposition as the perpetrator.

Who killed Ali-Mohammadi?

Within the battle of vying narratives articled through rumors and counter-rumors, the opposition managed to strategically (although temporarily) reverse the narratives of Neda, as endorsed by the state. Dissidents were able to make victims of post-election crackdowns into symbols of martyrdom and pose their narratives of self-sacrifice as a moral language of resistance for a nation undergoing a major political transformation. In idioms and symbols of martyrdom, the opposition also managed to make rumors into rhetorical strategies of political solidarity through which new meanings and sentiments of discontent were shared and felt, enabling actors to feel incorporated into a collective based on a shared interest for action. Yet, for the opposition, the narrative of martyrdom that embodied the ethos of struggle against injustice was less about the instrumentality and more about the public display of moral claims of a movement facing tyranny from an unjust state. Rumor is the vehicle of collective integration, which shapes the perceptions and emotions of collective activism.

In this light, the death of Masoud Ali-Mohammadi, a professor of physics at the University of Tehran, killed by a bomb blast in northern Tehran on

90   *B. Rahimi*

January 12, 2010 provides another case of a post-election strategy of rumor for enhancing distrust in a political terrain dominated by authoritarianism. The news of the assassination came as Tehran faced the possibility of new sanctions imposed by the UN Security Council, following a deadline for Tehran to respond to economic and technological incentives in return for cooperation over its nuclear program.

Who killed a nuclear scientist and why? From the perspective of the Iranian regime, the murder of Ali-Mohammadi, a "staunch" supporter of the Islamic Republic who was involved in Iran's nuclear program, reeks of foreign involvement. Shortly after the explosion, Iran's foreign ministry blamed Israel and the US for carrying out the operation with the help of a pro-royalist group, who sought to re-establish monarchy in Iran. Meanwhile, the assassination was described on state media as a desperate act by Western powers to hold back the country's nuclear research program. As the Supreme Leader praised Ali-Mohammadi as a "martyr," the hardliners in power described the culprits as those who sought to inhibit Iran's scientific progress and prevent the country from achieving nuclear technology. A number of conservative online news sites also compared the terrorist act with Israel's earlier attacks on Egyptian nuclear scientists and Iraqi and Syrian nuclear facilities. Hardliner analysts were also quick to compare the bombing with the case of Shahram Amiri, a nuclear scientist, whom Iran accused Saudi Arabia of kidnapping on behalf of the US.

To what extent Israel and the US were involved remains unknown. For the most part, Israel refused to comment on the assassination and other possible covert operations to eliminate key human elements in Iran's nuclear program. Although there has been speculation of increasing covert activities as a result of Washington's new diplomatic outreach to Iran, which has prevented Israel from engaging in military action, the US State Department publicly ruled out the possibility of American involvement, calling Iran's accusations "absurd" (*BBC News* 2010). In many ways, the assassination left a puzzling mix of questions as to why an academic at a research university, with no political links to the state, should be the target of assassination. The opposition stepped in to advance its own theory.

First, according to dissident websites, and as the Iranian Atomic Energy Agency publicly explained, Ali-Mohammadi had no associations with the state's nuclear program.[10] In fact, Ali-Mohammadi's main research mostly included participation in a scientific project led by an academic association based in Jordan (SESAME), which conducted experimental science with other leading academics in the Middle East, including Israeli researchers. Not only had he no relations with Iran's secretive nuclear program, run by the Revolutionary Guard, but he also had little expertise in nuclear physics.

Second, the opposition argued, Ali-Mohammadi was not a supporter of the regime. In fact, Ali-Mohammadi had increasingly become politically involved in the opposition movement since the disputed 2009 elections. On his website, *Kaleme*, Mir-Hussain Mousavi, the defeated 2009 presidential candidate and

The politics of informal communication 91

the current leader of the opposition, had described Ali-Mohammadi as one of his staunch supporters and a prominent supporter of the Green Movement. Mousavi also publicly described the murder as "part of an extensive plan" to stifle dissent. To many reformists, the murder of Ali-Mohammadi, who was also known to have participated in the post-election street demonstrations, serves as a warning to other opposition figures, heralding a campaign of assassinations very much reminiscent of the 1999 wave of murders charged to the intelligence security forces. Yet the attack was also meant to shift attention from Iran's domestic turmoil to an external enemy, an attempt seen by the opposition to stoke nationalist sentiment to legitimize a state that had lost considerable credibility since the elections.

What both the Neda and the Ali-Mohammadi cases demonstrate is how rumors of victimhood and conspiracies of murder can generate new conceptions of good and bad, false and truth, as "interrogative" statements about the status quo (Fine 2007: 6). The strategic aim is more revealing than the truth behind a reality that has been obscured by the adversary, but primarily shapes memories of how a crisis event can be recalled and re-narrated in the future. This aspect precisely underlines the performative force of informal communication, particularly rumors. In the form of competing narratives, rumors and conspiracies about Neda's and Ali-Mohammadi's assassinations are tied to assumptions of how political reality maintains a depth, which is difficult to access but ready to be uncovered by involving certain acts of "epistemic risks" or suspension of what seems self-evident (D. Coady 2007: 196).

Dramas of suspense: why conspiracies and rumors?

In the above discussion, I have argued how discourses of conspiracies and rumors can be used to legitimize both civic opposition and state power. However, these informal communication provided more than legitimizing strategic attempts to discredit or reinforce the power of one group or entity against another. Rather, informal communicative actions are types of discursive performances in which social realities are mediated through specific genres and performances that demand a change in reality through creating strong emotional bonds between political actors. Especially in emerging mediums of communication such as the internet, where subaltern voices gain the opportunity to articulate and, through networking, interactively define a world upside-down, a world of mistrust and plausibility is constructed in the form of disruptive activities that question authority and the claims to the authenticity of a political order. Such interactive processes involve dramaturgical frameworks through which actors produce meaningful social dramas of self and other, dramas as discourses of suspense that produce cognitive framing and communicative performances that display commitment and solidarity, which ultimately blur the boundaries between audiences and activists in shaping a social movement with a distinct collective memory. In short, informal discourses are not about validity claims, but social action.

92 B. Rahimi

In the case of the post-election Iranian conspiracies and rumors, both society and state actors engaged in various discursive strategies and dramaturgical processes with the aim of creating experiences as convincing and as authentic as possible. The state-endorsed documentary of Neda's death, for instance, was produced in order to delegitimize the authenticity of the video, allegedly recorded and posted online by an anti-government protester. The opposition's public display of a letter from the Interior Ministry marked a theatrical performance of suspense that brought the entire electoral process into question.

Social drama, therefore, lies at the heart of a public culture of informal communication. What the emerging new information technologies such as the internet create is the virtualization of such dramas of action through which rumors and conspiracies spread to re-examine official claims of social significance. Rumors thrive in virtual space, mostly because they couple and decouple from their source in ways unknown in cybernetworks of interaction. For the most part, such discourses spread as living narratives of alternative realities that are now under threat. Narratives of rumors, as dramas of suspense, seek to destabilize the official understandings and re-reinterpret the world in other meaningful complex terms. Although the extent of their diffusion varies from one social context to another, what produces these informal communications is the creative ability of human agency to reconfigure reality. In certain situations, such as under authoritarian rule, conspiracy theories or rumors can in fact serve to mediate trust in society, making claims to truth accountable to further scrutiny. It is the vibrancy of rumors that reveals the underlying crisis of legitimacy in the state.

Notes

1 I borrow the notion of "counterpublics" from Nancy Fraser's (1990) influential definition, in which she defines the public sphere as a social field of tension between dominant and marginal publics.
2 For a history of electoral politics in Iran, see Gheissari and Nasr (2006). On the function of electoral politics under authoritarian rule, see Brownlee (2007).
3 The revolutionary students who took the American diplomats and embassy personnel hostage saw this ultimately as a strategic way to discredit and circumvent a possible US attack (see Brumberg 2001: 118).
4 For a detailed study of counterpublics and polling strategies in Iranian elections, see Shahrokni (2012).
5 *Keyhan*, which means universe, is the most hardline newspaper in Iran and is believed to be under the direct supervision of the Supreme Leader, Ayatollah Khamenei. *Keyhan* is also rumored to articulate the views of the state intelligence agency, largely responsible for the crackdowns on unrest after the elections. The interaction between rumor culture and state-funded media systems is a complex issue which requires further research.
6 According to one rumor, a group of men were waving those missing votes during an anti-government demonstration.
7 Some analysts have described the post-election unrest as the "Twitter revolution." But in reality, Twitter is a recent phenomenon in Iran, and its impact is less than

that of cell phones and social networking sites. See Morozov (2011: 14–19) and *The Washington Times* (2009).

8 The Basij is a volunteer state militia. Since 2008, the Basij unit has been incorporated into the Revolutionary Guard's central command and plays a significant role in security operations at street level.

9 For an interesting analysis of the state media's account of the Neda video, see Esfandiari (2010a) and Mackey (2010).

10 See Dr. Ahmad Shirzad's blog online: shirzad.ir/2010/01/post_164.html (accessed January 10, 2010). This blog appears to be offline now. A cached copy can be found at: web.archive.org/web/20100115130329/http://shirzad.ir/2010/01/post_164.html (accessed March 14, 2013). Ali-Mohammadi was a professor of particular physics who had published numerous articles in international journals. Shirzad was a friend and colleague of Ali-Mohammadi.

5 Rumors, religion, and political mobilization

Indonesian cases, 1965–98

Mark Woodward

> All societies live by fictions taken as real. What distinguishes cultures of terror is that the epistemological, ontological and otherwise philosophical problems of representation – reality and illusion, certainty and doubt becomes infinitely more than 'merely' philosophical problems. ... It becomes a high-powered medium of domination.
>
> (Taussig 1986)

This chapter concerns the role of rumor in Indonesian political discourse. It draws on theoretical studies in cultural anthropology and sociology that view rumor as being both a form of "social cognition" as well as "political strategy" (Bordia and DiFonzo 2004). Rumor is rather much like pornography, easy to recognize but hard to define. A generally accepted definition of "rumor" is that it is a more or less plausible account of events that can be neither verified nor falsified. The uncertainty and ambiguous status of rumor distinguishes it from "information." At the same time, rumor is socially and politically salient because of its plausibility. Non-verifiable and non-falsifiable, it constitutes and occupies a liminal space between fantasy and fact. One need not be a radical post-modernist to accept the view that "truth" is often contested and that power relations figure significantly in these contestations.

In an early study that focused on understanding and controlling rumors during World War II, Knapp (1944) suggested that rumors serve to relieve anxiety and provide plausible explanations for phenomena that cannot otherwise be explained during periods of danger and uncertainty. He pointed towards, but did not develop, the thesis that rumor and myth have common features. The "basic law of rumor" of Allport and Postman (1947) asserts that rumor strength varies with thematic importance and ambiguity, most commonly employed to delegitimize public persons and, in the case of conflict situations, to precipitate or justify violence by demonizing "enemy others." Another type of rumor, more commonly referred to in the academic literature as "prophecy" and characteristic of revitalization movement centers, tells of the immanent emergence of a religiously exemplary leader (in Indonesia, a *Ratu Adil* or Just King) who will restore society to its sacred, pristine condition.[1] In cases such as these the insights of religious studies scholarship, and especially those of Mircea Eliade (1954), can add an important dimension to the existing theoretical literature.

Linking the analysis of rumor with that of myth aids in an understanding of both the appeal of rumors and their political significance; Eliade's (1954: 39) observation that mythological narratives often emerge from an interpretive process in which events are re-interpreted and retold from the perspective of symbolic structures he refers to as "celestial archetypes" is especially useful. In both instances, stories of actual persons, places, and events are reworked through a process that Dan Sperber (1975) terms *symbolization*. For Sperber, symbolization is the cognitive process through which representations of events (encyclopedic knowledge) are brought into correspondence with the conceptual categories (symbolic knowledge) of particular cultures. The result is that what he later referred to as "apparently irrational beliefs" are plausible, if not verifiable, because they are formulated in terms of cultural or religious assumptions that are *in principle* non-falsifiable (Sperber 1985). This approach is especially useful in understanding the persistence of rumors even in the face of what would appear to be overwhelming evidence to the contrary of the claims that they make.

Eliade (1954), Levi-Strauss (1966), and other students of mythology are cognizant of the ways in which history becomes myth, but suggest that it is something less than a conscious process that occurs gradually over time. The speed and deliberate way in which the myths of the New Order described later in this chapter were constructed suggest that a more cynical Foucaultian and even Orwellian mode of analysis would be appropriate. I have argued elsewhere that this process is remarkably fast and that archetypes of good, evil, suffering, and victimhood play important roles in the emergences of politically salient myths and rumors (Woodward 2006). Given Sperber's understanding of symbolization as a basic cognitive process, it is logical to suggest that the transformations on which rumors are based can be nearly instantaneous. One of the points that I want to make in this chapter is that rumors can become "facts" very quickly and endure over long periods of time if a strong hegemonic power controls the production and reproduction of knowledge. Counterhegemonic rumors and "facts" can be equally persistent unless opposition forces are silenced.[2]

There is an enormous literature concerning rumor and politics, especially with regard to ethnic, religious, and racial violence. The ways in which rumor is understood is, in part, a function of the political location of the analyst. Rumors can be one of what James Scott (1985) calls the "weapons of the weak," especially in the context of colonialism or other hegemonic information environments. They can also be among the discursive tools that political entrepreneurs use to incite violence. Tambiah (1996) has shown that governments are often complicit in the construction and dissemination of narratives that would be considered "rumor" if they circulated in non-official circles, and for analytic purposes must be treated similarly.

96   M. Woodward

The study of rumor can also be linked to anthropological and other scholarly debates concerning orality and literacy (Stewart and Strathern 2003). Rumor is most frequently understood as oral communication. However, as Bubandt has observed, rumors also circulate in written and increasingly electronic formats. The symbolic power of print is such that, when they are published, or posted online, rumors often become facts, or at least they enter into a different domain of discourse in which their "factuality" can be publicly contested (Bubandt 2008). At the same time, fax machines, the internet, and text messaging have increased the speed with which rumors spread and the size of the communities in which they circulate enormously. These unofficial media play critical roles in involving diasporas in the social and political lives of their communities of origin. The boundary between orality and literacy is increasingly blurred in these discourse systems.

Indonesian cases

The cases examined in this chapter are political rumors that have circulated in the Javanese city (and Sultanate) of Yogyakarta, and elsewhere in Indonesia, since the mid-1960s. They are based on ethnographic fieldwork conducted between 1978 and 2009 and on the analysis of oral, written, and internet texts.

I will be concerned with two very different but complementary sets of rumors. The first are those formulated and enshrined as history by the New Order (1965–98), depicting the Indonesian Communist Party (PKI) and especially GERWANI, the Communist women's organization, as archetypes of evil deserving of death. The purpose of these rumors was to legitimize first politicide and then the establishment of authoritarian military rule. The second are varying counter-hegemonic rumors concerning the religiously and culturally inappropriate conduct of President Suharto. These reflect both Javanist and Islamist modalities of symbolic and narrative resistance.[3] As long as the New Order endured, they were very much "weapons of the weak." They circulated for decades as oral tradition, but have since emerged in print as "historical fact." In assessing the political saliency of these rumors, their "truth value" is irrelevant.

Narratives in the first case are lies (or false rumors) that become facts and continue to inflict enormous psychic pain on victims and their families. Many Indonesians continue to believe them. The second case reflects the collective problem solving of a significant portion of the population of Yogyakarta, which have now emerged as triumphalist narratives. In both cases, rumors, in both oral and written form, contributed significantly to social and political mobilization. Rumors concerning the immoral character of Communist women provoked and justified the mass killings of 1965 and 1966. Those concerning Suharto's immoral behavior galvanized support for mass demonstrations that contributed to the fall of the New Order in 1998.

Case one: rumor, myth, history and the origins of Indonesia's New Order

In this section, I will be concerned with the ways in which rumor can become mythology and history. It is argued that rumors initially intended to promote and justify political violence were subsequently used as myth to legitimize authoritarian rule and, by virtue of the fact that they were recorded in history textbooks, acquired an aura of factuality that could not be questioned or debated. Indonesia's New Order came to power in the wake of an abortive coup and subsequent politicide in which hundreds of thousands of members and supporters of the Communist Party (PKI) were killed.[4] Almost immediately after the September 30, 1965 coup attempt, government-sponsored rumors concerning the moral depravity of the alleged perpetrators began to circulate by word of mouth and in the press. Newspapers ran fictionalized stories describing the brutal atrocities and sexual depravity of GERWANI cadres (Stanley 1999; Wieringa 2003). The mildest described them as prostitutes. Tales of them dancing naked, participating in orgies with male party members, and desecrating the corpses of their victims by gouging out their eyes and biting off their genitals were repeated so often that many Indonesians now believe them to be true. In the chaotic days following the attempted coup, there were also rumors that the PKI had planned to kill all who were not party members or supporters, or that they planned to kill Muslim leaders and establish Communism as Indonesia's official "religion." In Yogyakarta, there were rumors that they had killed, or tried to kill, the Sultan or, alternatively, that the Sultan had thwarted these attempts with his spiritual powers. Many of these rumors came to be accepted as fact, especially by younger generations of Indonesians who do not remember the events. Even today, there are persistent rumors about "Communist" ghosts that are "immune" to Qur'an recitation and other traditional Muslim means of controlling ghosts and evil spirits.

The purpose of these rumors was to create a climate of fear and loathing sufficient to motivate and justify mass slaughter in retaliation. The rumors subsequently became myth and official "history." Related myths concerning the possible resurgence of the Communist Party legitimized military domination of Indonesian life until its collapse in 1998. These myths depict the forces of Indonesian nationalism, including the armed forces, and the ideology of *Panca Sila* as engaged in a nearly eternal Cosmic War against atheist Communism.[5] The Cosmic War was pushed into the past by describing Communist uprisings in the 1920s and 1940s as precursors to the attempted coup of 1965, and by cultivating fears that the PKI might somehow rise from the ashes of politicide. To guard against this absurdly remote possibility, and preserve anti-Communism as a legitimizing ideology, the government cultivated fear and vigilance about the "extreme left" and took steps to ensure that the struggle continued. Communist prisoners were occasionally executed, and suspects continued to be arrested well into the 1970s. "Leftist"

98   *M. Woodward*

publications and even those suspected of being "Leftist" were banned. These rumors—morphing into mythology—then became history. They were taught as fact in schools throughout the nation.

Perhaps the most insidious aspect of this imagined "Cosmic War" was the restrictions placed on the civil liberties of those labeled as ex-Communists, or "X PKI." They were denied public employment and education and were under constant suspicion. Their identification cards indicated what level of suspicion they were under. These restrictions applied not only to former PKI members but to their descendants for a period of seven generations. For the duration of this period, entire families were to be denied basic civil rights including public education and employment. This is significant as seven generations is the limits of Javanese kinship reckoning.[6] Through these acts, the New Order suggested that the Cosmic War against Communism was a permanent feature of Indonesian life and nationalism—and that only military rule could hold the forces of evil at bay.

Rumors that justified the mass killing of 1965 were enshrined in monuments throughout Indonesia and served as the basis of the official "history" of the New Order. Monuments to the "martyrs" of the coup were erected in Jakarta, Yogyakarta, and elsewhere. The most significant Jakarta monument is called *Monumen Panca Sila Sakti* (Monument of the Power of *Panca Sila*). Here, rumors/myths/history of GERWANI atrocities are depicted in dioramas. In Yogyakarta, the old Dutch Fort Vredeburg, located just outside the *Kraton* (palace) walls, was used by the Indonesian armed forces during the revolutionary and early Republican periods and as a prison for suspected Communists from 1965 until 1971; it was then abandoned and allowed to fall into ruins. In 1991, it was restored to house a museum of the Indonesian Revolution. Today, it is a representation of the cosmogonic myth of Indonesian nationalism. It includes several hundred dioramas depicting critical episodes in the nationalist movement and the struggle against Dutch and Japanese colonialism. The last series of dioramas draws the myth of the destruction of the PKI and the founding of the New Order into this larger narrative. It begins with a series of dioramas commemorating the killing of military officers by PKI members in Yogyakarta and anti-Communist rallies. It also includes lifelike statues of the officers dressed in uniforms similar to those they were wearing when they were killed and a glass case containing replicas of the weapons used to kill them. It concludes with a diorama depicting President Suharto revealing plans for the propaganda/indoctrination program P-4, which identified the national ideology *Panca Sila* with the military regime, to grateful, enthralled-looking students and faculty members at Gadjah Mada University. Seen as a whole, this mythic narrative is teleological. It states that the New Order was the divinely ordained destiny of the Indonesian people and, quite literally, that the institution of P-4 was what Francis Fukuyama (1992) was later to call "the end of history" in Indonesia.

This narrative was repeated in other media. The propaganda film *G30S-PKI* depicted the "atrocities" of the PKI in gruesome detail. It was shown

Rumors, religion, and political mobilization 99

annually to school children and on television. The martyrdom of the generals and victory over Communism was celebrated as a national holiday known as *Hari Kesaktian Panca Sila* on October 1. They are also honored on Heroes Day. It was also among the central elements of the official history curriculum at levels ranging from primary schools to universities.

This campaign of myth construction was at least as systematic as that conducted against the PKI. It created a coherent narrative describing the chaos and violence of 1965 and 1966 as a virtuous struggle between good and evil. This campaign of mythic representation, blaming and demonizing the victims of politicide, was remarkably successful. It was especially successful with generations that had little, if any, personal memory of the events. Today, many people in their twenties and thirties remember referring to President Suharto as *"Bapak Pembanguanan, Jeneral Besar!"* (Father of Development and Great General!) in primary school. This was a mythologization of the discursive and programmatic shift from economic nationalism and class struggle to the neoliberal, development-oriented economics of the New Order. It carries the processes of blaming, discrediting, and demonizing the victims far beyond what psychologist Judith Herman (1997) describes as being characteristic of perpetrators of violence. It is at the same level as Nazi demonization of Jews in the 1930s and 1940s. De-humanization is a psychological process that defines "enemy others" as lacking basic human personality traits (Bernard *et al.* 2002 [1965]). Demonization is a variety of de-humanization that operates in religious or quasi-religious contexts. It defines the other as not only less than human but also the embodiment of evil. The "other" comes to be what "we" hate and fear most.

The New Order—rumors as counter-hegemonic discourse

The processes described in the preceding section are examples of the ways in which the construction of rumors and their transformation into myth and history can be used by a brilliant and ruthless state apparatus to establish and maintain its legitimacy. From 1966 until 1998, the power of the state was unchallengeable. As New Order lies, rumors, and historiography came to dominate public discourse, counter-rumors concerning Suharto's moral laxity and culturally inappropriate behavior and aspirations emerged as counter-hegemonic discourse. In Yogyakarta, they were often linked to prophetic rumors concerning the coming of a *Ratu Adil* who would restore moral order and justice.[7] Many believed that Sultan Hamengkubuwono IX was this just king. The strength and persistence of these two sets of rumors contributed to the mobilization of support for the *reformasi* movement of 1998 and the later emergence of Hamengkubuwono X as a national political figure.

From the first time I visited Indonesia in 1978 until the fall of the New Order in 1998, harsh criticism of the regime circulated in the form of rumors. There was no other way for it to circulate because the media were either state controlled or engaged in a high degree of self-censorship. One of the most

100 *M. Woodward*

extreme rumors was that Suharto and his family were secretly Christian and were conspiring with Chinese Roman Catholics to "Christianize" Indonesia. Another was that he planned to proclaim himself king.

Another rumor that circulated widely after the death of Suharto's wife Siti Hartinah in 1996 was that people did not want to visit her grave because they could hear her crying—a sure sign that she was already suffering the pains of hell. The same is now said of Suharto. One friend told me that he knew someone who had video-taped the grave site and that, although he heard nothing at the time, when he played the tape back he could hear the former president screaming *Tolong! Tolong!* (help! help!), which suggests that he too was suffering the pains of hell.

In 1997, freedom of speech and the press came to Indonesia in ways that they never had before. Nowhere was this more apparent than in accounts of the former president and his family. Much that had long been spoken in private began to appear in print. The rumors discussed below are those that circulated during the crisis that precipitated the fall of the New Order. Their publication indicated that, once again, rumor is slowly becoming history.

One of the rumors circulating is a vitriolic Islamist critique of Suharto's "sins." Others explain his rise and fall in the language of Javanese Islamic mysticism. The fact that what were formerly rumors now appear in print increases their credibility. Some of these accounts include photographs, which further enhances their credibility. Here, I refer to published versions, which correspond very closely with the oral texts that I have heard for many years.

Islamist Indonesians attributed the economic and political crisis of the late 1990s to Suharto's moral failings. Many believe that the collusion, corruption, and nepotism of which Suharto was routinely accused were not simply political crimes but also sins for which God punished the entire nation. They argued that the crisis could only be "overcome" and prosperity restored with the emergence of a leader whose moral character and commitment to *Shari'ah* (Islamic law) would re-establish the flow of divine blessing on which the well-being of the nation depends. Some *Kejawen* (Javanist) Muslims offered an even more esoteric interpretation, according to which Suharto had sought and acquired sources of power associated with Javanese kings and *dukun* (Javanese spiritual healers and practitioners of the magical arts) and that his wife, Siti Hartinah, or Bu Tien as she was commonly known, held the "*wansit keprabon*" (Javanese divine appointment) that enabled Suharto to hold on to power for so long. These sources state that, with her death on April 28, 1996, his mystical power began to slip away.

Both explanations circulated widely as rumors throughout the crisis. They began to appear in print shortly after Suharto's resignation and remain extremely popular more than a decade later. These works merit discussion here because they provide insight into the ways in which religious concepts of authority and leadership shaped the discourse surrounding the crisis of 1997–98 and the ways in which they contributed to political action in the closing days of the New Order.

15 Dalil Mengapa Suharto Masuk Neraka (*15 Religious Proofs that Suharto will Go to Hell*) by Khairil Ghazali al-Husni (1999) is an Islamist critique of the New Order. The text is located within a larger Islamist discourse system that seeks to explain Indonesian history in terms of anti-Islamic and anti-Indonesian conspiracy theories.[8] It is also an example of how critiques of the Suharto regime shared by many Indonesians of all religious persuasions are viewed through an Islamist lens. In a broader sense, it is a contemporary example of a classical discourse which speaks of denouncing the transgressions of rulers as being among the greatest of Muslim virtues. In an analysis of the place of "forbidding the wrong" in Muslim discourse, Cook mentions the following *Hadith*:

> The finest form of *jihad* is speaking out in the presence of an unjust ruler and getting killed for it.
>
> (Cook 2003: 75)

By publishing this work, al-Husni clearly spoke in the virtual presence of the ruler he denounced. He did not risk "getting killed" because his book was published after Suharto's fall, but then most versions of the *Hadith* omit the concluding phrase (Cook 2003: 75).

The alleged "sins" of President Suharto described reflect the concerns of Muslims associated with *Dewan Dakwah Islamiyah Indonesia* and other Indonesian Islamist organizations. The text is also what Azyurmardi Azra (2003), the former rector of Jakarta's State Islamic University, calls a "death *fatwa.*" It states explicitly that Suharto should be killed. "Death to Suharto!" was one of the rallying cries of the *Reformasi* movement. Attempts to bring him to trial continued until his death in 2007. In this respect, al-Husni's critique does not differ significantly from those of other Indonesians. He simply locates it within an Islamist framework.

The introduction of the book summarizes Suharto's "sins" including restricting the power of the *ulama*, paralyzing the economy, encouraging family planning, manipulating history, jailing political opponents, bringing about a decline in social values, looting natural resources, and installing himself as a dictatorial tyrant. In the following chapters, al-Husni summarizes common Islamist complaints about the New Order and others that are shared with non-Islamists. These include complicity with the US Central Intelligence Agency in masterminding the 1965 coup, enriching himself and his family, and suppressing dissent. He also exposes more explicitly religious sins: links with the Anti-Christ, child abusers, and sorcerers, forsaking Islam, and persecuting Muslims.

In Indonesia, and especially in Java, there is a broad consensus that political stability and economic well-being are linked to the moral qualities of leaders. For those Indonesians oriented towards scripturally-based Islam, the characterization of Suharto as an unredeemable sinner did much to explain what came to be known as the "multidimensional crisis" and to justify his removal from office.

102 *M. Woodward*

The *Kejawen* literature is more nuanced than the Islamist literature because the concept of power, unlike sin, is morally ambiguous. Accounts of the *gawat* (Javanese: 'powerful but dangerous') character of Suharto's regime began to appear in the tabloid press shortly after his fall from power. There is now an extensive literature on the subject (Artha 2007a and 2007b; Pamungkas 2007; Mubarok and Rasyidin 2008; Shoelhi 2008; Soempeno 2008). These books are enormously popular and are sold in most major bookstores. They focus on both the ways in which Suharto acquired the power, in the Javanese sense, to rule Indonesia for more than thirty years, and how he lost it. This literature is almost exclusively concerned with the mystical and religious foundations of the New Order and the crisis that brought it to a close. Very little, if any, mention is made of the currency crisis and outside factors contributing to it or about Western notions of power and politics.

The epistemologies used in their diagnoses of the crisis are almost exclusively Javanese. Artha, at least, is clearly aware of this distinction. He argues that there are two "doors" to understanding Suharto and the New Order. The first is that of politics. He finds this approach deficient because, even though it is open and transparent, it focuses on the strategies employed by "particular groups" to advance their own interests. He characterizes these as rotten, scheming, and manipulative even if true.[9] The second door is that of *kebatinan* (mysticism) which, in his view, provides a more holistic understanding that all Javanese can appreciate. His view is that *kebatinan* provides a more profound, although often less direct, explanation of political events. In Artha's and other works of this genre, there are four basic themes.

1. Suharto's origins as a "child from a village."
2. His quest for "magical power" through asceticism by the acquisition of *pusaka*.
3. His relationships with *dukun* and *paranormals*.
4. The importance of his wife, Siti Hartinah (Bu Tien), as the *wangsit keprabon* or spiritual power behind the throne.

Suharto's fall is attributed to a combination of Bu Tien's death and the subsequent withdrawal of divine authority and the inappropriate, if not evil, intentions motivating his quests for *kesekten* or power in the Javanese sense.

Suharto was proud of the fact that he was a "child of the village" (*anak desa*). He and Bu Tien were often photographed standing in rice fields wearing the cone-shaped straw hats favored by Javanese farmers (Mubarok and Rasyidin 2008: 124). And yet, for many Javanese, it was more than something of a mystery that an *anak desa* managed to become president, let alone remain in power for more than thirty years. Suharto had none of the characteristics that, from a Javanese perspective, would have prepared him for leadership. He was from a poor family and not particularly well educated in either modern or Islamic tradition.[10] As Artha (2007a: 14) puts it, he was "not an important person." Suharto did have one personal characteristic that could have contributed to his accomplishments, and it was a particularly Javanese one. He was born on the day *kliwon* of the five-day Javanese market week.[11] People born on this day are believed to have hearts that are as hard as stone. These factors led many to search for mystical explanations. Rumors concerning Suharto's quest for magical power had circulated for decades, but were spoken of openly only as power slipped from his grasp and appeared in print only after he resigned.

Suharto is often said to have employed a variety of strategies in a systematic quest for "magical" (Indonesian *magis*) power. These included "fasting, not eating, not drinking and not abandoning the customs of the ancestors such as conducting *Slametan* for his family" (Artha 2007b: 14). He also practiced another form of asceticism that is believed to be particularly potent and associated with the great kings of the past. This is *Kungkum*, a form of meditation practiced while sitting nearly submerged in a river (Artha 2007b: 179).[12] These are entirely normal mystical practices. But Suharto also engaged in others that are known as *klenik*. These are mystical practices motivated by a selfish desire for power, which sometimes border on sorcery. Suharto is said to have consulted as many as 1,000 *dukun*, and *kyai* (Javanese for *ulama*) with similar abilities, from various parts of Indonesia. According to some accounts, he had at least one from every province. Even a report that refuted this allegation claimed that, at most, he had 200 who "actively helped him" (Pamungkas 2007: 8–9). In either case, it is an astounding number.

He is also said to have acquired at least 2,000 *pusaka* (heirlooms imbued with supernatural powers), also from every part of Indonesia. His acquisition of *pusaka* from the Javanese court of Surakarta was possible because its survival depended almost entirely on his personal financial support. He is rumored to have tried, but failed, to "borrow" *pusaka* from Yogyakarta. It is not surprising that Bu Tien plays an important role in oral traditions concerning the "first family" and Yogyakarta *pusaka*. It was Bu Tien, not Suharto, who is said to have asked to "borrow" some of the most important Yogyakarta *pusaka*. Hamengkubuwana IX is said to have remained straight-faced and silent, as was his practice when he disagreed with a proposal, and escorted her to the room where they are kept. She promptly fainted and had to be carried from the room. Suharto is said never to have asked to "borrow" a Yogya *pusaka* again.

It is widely known that Suharto regularly visited graves and other holy places associated with Javanese royalty, particularly those where kings are said to have performed asceticism. Among these is the stone seat in Kota Gede where the founder of the Mataram dynasty, Panembahan Senopati, is said to have performed austerities. Some speculate that Suharto tried to make up for his humble origins by these pilgrimages to royal holy sites. An alternative explanation is that, by "seizing" the regalia of kingship, including both heirlooms and holy places, Suharto attempted to seize the mantle, if not the titles, of kingship.

104   *M. Woodward*

Heine-Geldern has suggested that, in pre-modern Malay cultures, seizing the royal heirlooms was the equivalent of seizing the throne (Heine-Geldern 1942). It would seem that this is exactly what Suharto tried to do. Actually, he attempted to seize the heirlooms of many traditional states without claiming to be king of any of them. It is not possible to determine how many of these rumors are true,

Conclusions

Rumors were an important part of Indonesian political discourse throughout the New Order period. The manipulation of current and historical events in ways that started as rumors and moved in the directions of myth and history figured significantly in the formation of the New Order, resistance to its hegemonic truth claims, and to its ultimate demise.

This shift from hegemonic to resistance discourse in the Indonesian culture of rumors demonstrates that most or all of the theoretical works of rumors capture something of their importance. They are mechanisms for coping with uncertainty and anxiety *and* for constructing mythological narratives, regardless of the political contexts in which they are located. The analysis and deconstruction of rumors can reveal a great deal about the complexities of political discourse. They are just below the surface of "history" and are often the lenses through which more "respectable" narratives, such as those appearing in the press, are understood and interpreted. For purposes of understanding the dynamics of state society relationships, the veracity of rumors is of limited significance.

The study of rumors is important because it provides insight into the ways in which political actors and the general public understand and interpret political events. Rumors are also among the elements of the knowledge base on which political action is based. They can motivate political action because they are, despite sometimes obvious (to detached observers) irrationality, presumed to be true. This is especially true in socio-political contexts in which the elements of symbolic knowledge on which the interpretation of political events is based are religious assumptions concerning the limits of human agency and the instrumentality of things besides human beings and forces. This is where the methods of cultural anthropology and religious studies can aid in the analysis of rumors in political discourse and praxis in the many societies in which politics continues to be understood in religious terms.

Notes

1 On revitalization movements, see Wallace (1956). Probably the most widely discussed revitalization movement is the "Ghost Dance" that swept across the great plains of the United States in 1889 and 1890. It was fueled by prophecies/rumors that European settlers would soon disappear and that American Indian people would regain their lands and honor (Lebarre 1972). On revitalization movements in Indonesia, see Van der Kroef (1959).

Rumors, religion, and political mobilization 105

2 My analysis resembles Gramsci's (1971: 475) understanding of the politically motivated manipulation of knowledge, with the caveat that it is as characteristic of counter-hegemonic as well as hegemonic communities.

3 The term Javanist refers to a particularly Javanese form of Islam, which emphasizes mystical practice and rituals including pilgrimage to holy graves and prayer realms (*slametan*), while placing less emphasis on rituals prescribed by Islamic law, including the five daily prayers and fasting during Ramadan. See Woodward (1989).

4 On the mass killings of 1965 and 1966, see Cribb (1990).

5 *Panca Sila* (The Five Principles) is Indonesia's national ideology. *Panca Sila* could not be debated or questioned publicly during the New Order period. The five components of *Panca Sila* are: (1) *Ketuhanan Maha Esa*—Devotion to the principle of divine oneness; (2) *Kemanusiaan yand adil dan berahad*—Human society which is just and characterized by mutual respect; (3) *Persatuan Indonesia*—The unity of Indonesia; (4) *Kerakyatan yang dipimpin oleh hikmat kebijaksanaan dalam bermusyawararan/perwakilan*—Society governed with wise justice in the context of mutual consultation and assistance; (5) *Keadilan social bagi seluruh rakyat Indonesia*—Social justice for all of the people of Indonesia.

6 The ban was rescinded by President Abdurahman Wahid after the fall of the New Order. He also lifted the ban on the publication and public discussion of books written by Karl Marx and Marxist thinkers.

7 On the *Ratu Adil*, see Van der Kroef (1959).

8 In this respect, its discourse style resembles that of the popular Islamist periodicals *Media Dakwah* and *Sabali*.

9 Artha (2007) mentions Luhulima's work as an example of this style of analysis.

10 This is true not only in an absolute sense but also in comparison with other nationalist leaders, many of who were educated in Dutch schools.

11 The Javanese calendar is extremely complex. It includes five-day and seven-day weeks and Islamic and international months. This yields a large number of unique days, each of which is said to have its own mystical association.

12 Hamengkubuwana I's practice of this form of meditation is depicted in the reliefs and the *Pagelaran* wall of the Yogyakarta *kraton*.

6 Rumors of terrorism

Social cognitive structures, collective sense-making, and the emergence of rumor

Greg Dalziel

Introduction[1]

On February 27, 2008, Mas Selamat bin Kastari (hereafter "Mas Selamat")—accused of being the leader of Southeast Asian terrorist group Jemaah Islamiyah's Singapore branch—escaped from a secretive detention facility run by Singapore's internal security services.[2] A large and extensive manhunt failed to find him. It was over a year later in June 2009 that he was re-arrested in Malaysia, where he had managed to escape to. Mas Selamat's ability to escape, disappear, and elude capture by the authorities was an incredulous situation to those living in Singapore. It did not cohere with a narrative that typically framed the Singapore state as an efficient authority with a strong security identity. Whitley Road Detention Centre, the detention facility Mas Selamat had escaped from, was well known to Singaporeans as a place where enemies of the state were confined without charge and interrogated. The Internal Security Department, who ran the facility and maintained internal state security, had a reputation as a secretive yet efficient and knowledgeable organization. Assigned to guard the facility were Gurkhas, outsourced Nepalese soldiers famed for their fearlessness and good soldiering.

The incoherence, or dissonance, that the escape created among the various elements of the Singapore state's overarching security narrative engendered a situation requiring definition via collective sense-making. It necessitated sorting out the immediate drama while trying to understand what it meant for the future: Would Mas Selamat now attempt to fulfill the plots he was detained for allegedly planning? Would terrorism come to Singapore immediately, or would he meet up with his colleagues in Jemaah Islamiyah to plan spectacular acts of violence later? What did this mean for how others saw Singapore?

In this chapter, we offer a preliminary account of how Singaporeans, in the context of the state's narrative of security and terrorism, engaged in a process of collective sense-making. We understand the state's security narrative in terms of a social cognitive structure (Hopf 2002)—a collection of shared schema, beliefs, worldviews, images, and collective identities—that create symbolic and discursive boundaries within which Singaporeans make meaning.

Rumors of terrorism 107

The individual-level cognitive structural elements of rumor have been noted in previous work (DiFonzo and Bordia 2007: 115), and the social-level cultural context of rumor is an element of classic rumor and folklore studies (Fine and Turner 2001; Knapp 1944; Prasad 1935). Largely unexplored in this context is looking relatively freely at people's collective communication interactions to examine aspects of the sense-making process that may not involve the production of rumors, but are still vital to the production of meaning. By looking in detail at elements of the social cognitive structure in operation during the pre-crisis period and at the immediate communication interactions at the beginning of the crisis, we gain a better understanding of the collective sense-making process, the production of meaning, the impact of state communication practices, and so the subsequent emergence of rumors. Studying this emergence allows us to "watch how people deal with ...inconceivable events [and] pay close attention to ways people notice, extract cues, and embellish that which they extract" (Weick 1995: 49).

In this chapter, we are less interested in examining the circulation of particular rumor stories or people's attempts to interrogate the validity of particular items of information categorized as rumor. Instead, we follow Shibutani's concept of rumors being the product of an active process in which people experiencing ambiguous events *attempt* to form a definition of the situation. It is the various elements of the process we are interested in and, in this sense, rumors are but one outcome of the collective sense-making process. The emergence of rumors can be typified as being towards the end of this process, representing a period in which meaning (or definition) has been brought to a situation, however tentative. Other outcomes include the production of shared narrative themes—collective schema—through which future events are viewed. In attending to a close examination of this process, we show how collective sense-making is contextual and relational, situated within a broad shared cognitive structure, and consisting of a number of stages that have multiple outcomes that unfurl over time.

To examine the context out of which this collective sense-making process took place, we first explore the collective sense-making process and the construction of shared narratives, looking at how this process is shaped by a social cognitive structure. We then move to a discussion of one social cognitive structure at work in Singapore and look at how the state understands and communicates security and threats to its citizens. In doing so, we provide an account of the "narrative terrain" (Corman and Dooley 2008) that Singaporeans found themselves in after the escape and highlight the impact that social cognitive structures—and state communicative practices—can have on collective sense-making and the emergence of rumors.

Shared narrative communities, rumors, and collective sense-making

Situations of pervasive ambiguity (Ball-Rokeach 1973) where narratives are disrupted and meaning must be established find people forming what Gary

108   *G. Dalziel*

Alan Fine terms a "shared narrative community" (Fine 1992: 18). This concept highlights the importance of narrative in social cognition and the collective, interactive nature of the process of meaning-making.

Over the coming hours, days, weeks, and months after the escape, Singaporeans attempted to make sense of what was happening. This sense-making took place in a variety of locations: at home, in the workplace, in *kopitiams* (coffee shops) over large bottles of *Tiger* beer or *kopi* (coffee), or online in blogs and message boards. Some of these shared narrative communities were fleeting and impermanent, existing only for a moment. Perhaps a quick chat in passing with a cook while ordering noodles in the hawker center (food court) or during a ride with a gregarious taxi driver. Other shared narrative communities, however, were more intentional, persistent, and iterative in nature. This characterizes those formed online, which required participants to seek them out, and where sense-making takes place among a large group over an extended period of time.

In the intervening period between his escape and capture, a variety of rumors circulated about how Mas Selamat managed to escape, where he was at that moment in time, and speculation about what all of this meant for Singapore and Singaporeans. Although not an exhaustive chronicle by any stretch, some of the rumors circulating at the time included: (1) that he had died in detention (either naturally or accidentally from torture) and the escape was faked as a cover-up; (2) that he had secretly been given over to US custody and sent to Guantanamo, the escape a cover to assuage outrage from Muslims in the region at such an action; (3) that the escape was a sting operation and Mas Selamat was intentionally released to "flush out" other Jemaah Islamiyah operatives; or (4) that he had used mystical powers (*bomoh*) to escape and disappear.

These are all examples of fairly well-defined narratives that posit an explanation for an event that Singaporeans lacked an explanation for. Studies of rumor and related forms of social communication (e.g., urban legends) often examine the diffusion of well-travelled tales or discrete, particular items of communication that circulate within a community and may tell us something about the boundaries of collective identity and the often unstated hopes and fears circulating socially (e.g., Adams 1999; Dodoo *et al.* 2007; Langlois 2005). This can involve content analysis of online discussions about the validity of particular rumors (Bordia and DiFonzo 2004), testing statements and seeing how respondents classify them (as rumor, gossip, news, etc.), or asking individuals to give a questioner some examples of information statements of uncertain provenance they had heard recently (DiFonzo and Bordia 2007). Such approaches, however, have the tendency to treat communication as relatively static (Shibutani 1966: 8).

If we take Shibutani's definition of rumor as a collective process of sense-making, then the sort of relatively well-defined rumor stories one often finds in rumor research typify the end of the sense-making process. Rumor stories represent plausible alternative or contested knowledge claims about a situation that has already gained some semblance of meaning or definition to a public.

They are aspects of a broader collective system of meaning, in which we see narrative as a "coherent system of stories" (Halverson *et al.* 2011: 23) within a particular thought community or cognitive subculture (Zerubaval 1999). Such plausible knowledge claims are categorized as "rumor" to allow members of a thought community to differentiate between various types of knowledge claims. The category of rumor differentiates it from that categorized as "true" or "fact"; or, indeed, the normative acceptance of information may mean it is not overtly categorized, remaining unmarked (Brekhus 1998). The category may be applied to temporal claims of either prior events or expected future events that may or may not turn out to be true in hindsight, or for which the veracity of the claim can be checked against later information. As products of a collective sense-making process that fit into a broader system of narrative meaning, these rumor stories represent plausible claims related to events, sequence, plot, or gaps therein (Maines 2000).

Before these knowledge claims can emerge, however, there is the messy process of sifting, sorting, and making sense of available (and unavailable) information. This process is dynamic and evolving. The beginning of an experience of ambiguity, a crisis, may mark a period when the conventional narrative of everyday life is overturned and information gaps are pronounced.

In the immediate period of a crisis, one finds a process relying on shared cognitive schemas, frames, and prior experiences through which people begin to try and understand what is happening, and why. Much of this communication could be labeled "rumor" in that it is unverified information; yet we find such a label is inadequate in this case as these posited explanations of the whys and wherefores—the elements of plot and structure that are missing in a period of uncertainty—lack the sort of addition of claims to epistemic authority that one often finds in information categorized as rumor (Bangerter and Heath 2004; Fragale and Heath 2004). These early sense-making elements, however, often find their way into subsequent rumor stories.

Themes that emerge and are selected during this process can also have an affective dimension. Attitudes towards the uncertainty begin to be formed, and it is here one finds the *creation* of schema that can be relied upon to help understand future (perhaps overtly unrelated) events. This process of schema creation is similar to what Bormann (1972) calls a shared "rhetorical vision" involving the selection and testing of "values and attitudes." This therefore also involves the production and reproduction of collective identity; such expressions of identity involve the crafting of distinctions and the formation or reformation of the boundaries of a particular thought community in which rumor stories will circulate and for whom future events will be viewed through the lens of these shared rhetorical visions.

The process of collective sense-making, then, involves the production of three elements: (1) the selection of themes for possible rumor stories; (2) the creation of new schema; and (3) the marking of the boundaries of a thought community. These do not operate sequentially; although the first two categories have a temporal location, they are bounded by the thought community.

110   *G. Dalziel*

Rumor stories will fit into narrative systems that attempt to explain the event to which they relate and are sustained as long as the pervasive uncertainty lasts, i.e., until meaning (however tentative) is collectively defined. In this sense, rumors represent but one outcome of the collective sense-making process and are linked to the situation within which they emerge. The shared cognitive schema generated (akin to rhetorical vision) are far more persistent, however, and are used to understand *future* events unrelated to the particular periods in which they were crafted.

As previously discussed, we do not examine the later circulation of rumor stories; nor do we do discuss the ways in which newly created shared schema were utilized to understand later events. Instead, we pay close attention to how Singaporeans were situated within a broader social cognitive structure in order to improve our understanding of plausibility and credibility and the variety of influences on the outcomes of the collective sense-making process.

The social cognitive structure and collective sense-making

The concept of a social cognitive structure is used by Ted Hopf to explore the impact of identity formations on foreign policy decisions. For Hopf (2002: 22), the social cognitive structure is constituted by "discursive formations," and it is through this structure of discursive formations—of the shared discourse of a group—that shared meanings and beliefs circulate and groups understand themselves and others. In addition, Hopf (2002: 6) posits that the predominant social cognitive structure "establishes the boundaries of discourse within a society" and, in that sense, may also constitute the boundaries of credibility and plausibility in knowledge claims.

This concept of a social cognitive structure is similar in nature at the individual level to concepts in cognitive and social psychology such as "cognitive structures" (Sedikides and Anderson 1992), "knowledge structures" (DiFonzo and Bordia 2007: 115), or "schemas" (D'Andrade 1995; Ross 2004). In this case, however, we are not examining the cognitive structures held in the individual but those that are a "shared stock of knowledge" (Cerulo 2010: 115).

DiFonzo and Bordia (2007: 115) note that rumors themselves can activate schemas or cognitive structures at an individual level and that these structures "determine the course of explanation throughout the process" of sense-making. We start with the activation of these structures through an *event*— the escape of Mas Selamat—and the sense-making that occurs before the production of rumor. To understand this emergence and how people make sense of inconceivable events, we now look at how the state understands terrorism, security, and identity, and how this meaning was communicated to the public through discourse and symbols. We then give a brief outline of the escape of Mas Selamat and how the state communicated this escape to the public. In doing this work, we begin to map out the social cognitive structure—the narrative landscape—in which Singaporeans found themselves when the escape happened.

National identity, security culture, and the discourse of crisis: terrorism and strategic communication

Discovering terrorism: Jemaah Islamiyah in Singapore

The rather unexpected nature of Singapore's birth as an independent state in 1965 after its abrupt departure from the Federation of Malaysia created an immediate need to craft a "Singaporean" national identity. This awkward situation, with the birth of a state preceding that of a "nation," led to an elite-driven, top-down, nation-building program aimed at forging a national identity (Velayutham 2007). Surveys taken as early as 1969 and 1970, however, point to a remarkably cohesive predominant identity as "Singaporean" among its multicultural population (Chin 2010; MacDougall 1976). However, state-driven efforts aimed at inculcating a particular set of values and, in turn, a Singaporean national identity acceptable to the state still persists today.[3]

At the same time, the nature of its independence also drove the formation of a predominant security culture through which Singapore state leaders viewed, and continue to view, one could argue, the international environment.[4] This includes the idea of Singapore as a small state without a hinterland, without strategic depth, and lacking natural resources. The perception of security and threat is therefore driven by a predominant security culture, or narrative, of vulnerability (Leifer 2000; Vasu and Loo 2010). These two factors, of a state-driven national identity project and a security culture typified by vulnerability, frame what some argue is a utilization of discourse as a means of producing social cohesion through unifying crises (Birch 1992).

Previous violence linked to Islamist groups in Southeast Asia could have been characterized as violence "over there" and not threatening the internal security of Singapore. However, between December 2001 and August 2002, the Singapore authorities detained a total of thirty-six people under the Internal Security Act (ISA), all alleged to have links to either Jemaah Islamiyah[5] or the Moro Islamic Liberation Front (MILF).[6] These individuals were accused of being part of a number of plots to attack both locals and foreigners in Singapore, although perhaps only one of the plots had made it past the reconnaissance stage (Ministry of Home Affairs [MHA] 2003: 11).

The Jemaah Islamiyah detentions in Singapore were initiated after reconnaissance videos were apparently found by coalition forces in Afghanistan and subsequently passed to the Singaporean authorities (MHA 2003: 12). This linked the perceived global character of the Al-Qaeda organization, the 9/11 attacks, and the subsequent actions in Afghanistan to Singapore. Even more shocking for the Singaporean government was that there seemed to be "Singaporeans who [were] prepared to sacrifice innocent lives for their cause" (Ibrahim 2003). Then-Minister for Home Affairs Wong Kan Seng (2004) noted in a speech that "terrorism ...posed the single most critical threat to Singapore's national security."

The threat of terrorist attacks in Singapore after 9/11, then, was not only conceived of in terms of physically destructive effects that must be guarded

112 G. Dalziel

against but also as one that was a threat to the unity of the Singaporean nation and, ostensibly, the state's national identity project. The security discourse in Singapore with regard to potential terrorist attacks took on the form of a discourse of crisis used in an attempt to bolster the unity of the nation and to move forward the state's national identity-building project. As such, security in Singapore is often viewed through the prism of national identity.

This can be seen in state discourse on security and terrorism, which often assumes that the goal of Jemaah Islamiyah and other groups is to pit Singapore's neatly bounded racial communities against each other. One government publication states, "We must ensure that terrorists' attempts to create distrust and divisions between the different races in Singapore do not succeed" (National Security Coordination Secretariat [NSCS] 2006: 91). Former Prime Minister Goh Chok Tong said in an interview about the terrorism threat,

> ... can you imagine what harm it would do in Singapore? The non-Muslims will begin to doubt Muslims. Muslims will also begin to feel that they are singled out by other races ... It would have undone all the good work that we have built up over the years.
>
> (Chia 2004)

The Ministry of Home Affairs' white paper entitled *The Jemaah Islamiyah Arrests and the Threat of Terrorism* stated that terrorism threatened both "the safety of Singaporeans and the cohesion of Singapore society" (MHA 2003: 2). That is, beyond any physical damage to life or property, terrorism threatened the very social fabric of the Singaporean nation.

This is not to say, however, that the threat of terrorist attacks in Singapore was fabricated by a government needing a new unifying narrative for national identity. Nor does this imply that a real threat was consciously overplayed in the strategic service of the state's need for a new unifying national narrative; rather, it is simply that we can take these statements as public communications that are expressions of the state's security culture and its nation-building national identity project. In concert, these two factors are critical to how the state understands and communicates threat to the wider population.

Communicating terrorism in Singapore

The state's reliance on crisis as a unifying discourse focused government efforts towards extensive strategic communication campaigns with the stated goals of improving what they called "public security awareness" (NSCS 2006: 79). Violence caused by a terrorist group was communicated to the public as being inevitable (Vasu and Ramakrishna 2006: 150) and targeted at "anyone, anywhere, anytime" (NSCS 2006: 12). In addition, the government campaigns communicated that the goals of "terrorism" in general, as well as the effects of a violent incident, were targeted at undermining Singapore's inherently fragile (as perceived by the state) multicultural and multiracial make-up.

Rumors of terrorism   113

These communication efforts were carried out via a number of means using a variety of methods, including community meetings with names such as the *Community Engagement Program* and *Inter-Racial Confidence Circles*, school programs, and public exhibitions (Vasu and Ramakrishna 2006). Additional, and extensive, visual campaigns were (and continue to be) conducted on public transportation as well as on television, including a 2002 drama series, *Frontline*, and one in 2006, *Without Warning*.

The government even produced an educational comic book aimed at children entitled *Fight Terrorism? Don't Joke!* (NSCS 2008). This was apparently commissioned because "comics are more effective in conveying our National Security messages as content can be conveyed in a more visually appealing and less cognitively demanding manner" (NSCS 2009). Highlighting the unifying role that such crisis discourse was geared towards, teaching materials associated with this project noted that one of the comic book's objectives was "to have students understand their role in the battle against terrorism ... [e.g.] upholding the values of racial harmony and social resilience as part of Singapore's counter-terrorism efforts" (NSCS 2009).

A public service video produced by a government agency makes an even starker case for how such "national security awareness" campaigns were shaped by a narrative of vulnerability and the use of crisis discourse in the service of the state's attempt at forging, or maintaining, a national identity. Entitled "Be as one,"[7] the thirty-second spot aired on national television in Singapore starting in 2009. A baritone and serious man tell us that each Singaporean has "an important role to play" in guarding against the threat of terrorism. A large and appropriately multicultural cast of Singaporeans are featured, along with shots of "vulnerable" targets such as the mass rapid transport (MRT) system and the airport. Some of the cast are soldiers, policemen, or emergency response employees, tasked with ensuring Singapore's safety and security. Others are everyday Singaporeans, young and old, all enjoying the "good life" these government employees provide. Each person in the video is holding a single stick, painted red or white. At the end of the video, these red and white sticks are arranged in a fashion that reveals, when the camera pans upwards—just in case you weren't paying attention to the message of the video—a single Singapore state flag. The full text of the voiceover is illustrative of the collective identity-building goals of such campaigns:

> Terrorism is real and evolving. Each and every one of us has an important role to play in ensuring our peace and security, and in protecting all that is dear to us. A single stick may be weak. But together, a bunch is strong. Let us be vigilant, resilient, and stand united against terrorism.

Communicating terrorism: security symbols

Previously secretive organizations such as the Internal Security Department (ISD) also "embarked on an extensive security education and outreach

114 *G. Dalziel*

programme to sensitise audiences ... to the various security threats the country faces today."[8] The Internal Security Act (ISA)—which allows for preventative detention without charge—was also the subject of a campaign, publicizing it as being integral to keeping Singapore as "a safe place to live, work and play in ... because we are careful and are able to stop harmful activities before they happen" (MHA 2002). Wong Kan Seng (2003) stated in a speech to Internal Security Department employees that,

> Some people continue to be critical about the Internal Security Act. But for most Singaporeans today, they now know the value of the ISA. For the skeptics, I would tell them that without the ISA and ISD ... they would not have enjoyed this sense of safety and security today.

The use of the ISA by Singaporean authorities—beyond any practical or ethical questions—signaled to the public that people held under this law were threats to the national security of Singapore, and to the way of life of ordinary citizens; the ISA, in this sense, is not only a coercive tool of the state but a security symbol (see Chua 1995: 180–82).

The ISA, as characterized in the above speech by Wong, was critical in that sense not as a means of protecting the security of the state but one geared towards protecting the nation, of ensuring that the "good life" Singaporeans enjoyed was maintained. Now, whether or not Mas Selamat was indeed the fanatically violent man he was characterized as being, the mere fact of his detention in ISD custody under the ISA signaled his real threat to all Singaporeans. The ISA, being a law used only against those who purportedly threatened the safety of Singaporeans and national security, and therefore a key security symbol in Singapore, placed Mas Selamat in a category separate from and above that of "normal" criminals.

The escape

Mas Selamat, who apparently took over as head of the Singapore branch of Jemaah Islamiyah in 1999 (MHA 2003: 10), managed to escape the dragnet in 2001/2 and fled, first to Thailand and then to Indonesia (MHA 2002). The Singapore authorities accused him of planning to crash hijacked planes into Changi airport; all available information suggests that this "planning" had not advanced beyond the discussion stage, and the plot may have been abandoned after the crackdown by Singapore's security agencies (Singh 2002).

Mas Selamat was then arrested in Batam, an Indonesian island near Singapore, in 2003 (US Department of State 2004a: 28). He managed to escape from an Indonesian prison cell, breaking his leg in the process, before being recaptured by the Indonesians in 2006 (Hussain 2008). In February 2006, he was transferred from Indonesia to Singapore, where he was held under the Internal Security Act at Whitley Road Detention Centre (US Department of State 2007: 44). Regardless of how far away he was from fulfilling his plans, Mas Selamat was characterized in the press as, perhaps the most dangerous member of the Jemaah Islamiyah's (JI) Singapore cell at large—till yesterday. Hot-headed, elusive and on the run since Singapore authorities foiled a plan to blow up American, Israeli and other targets here in December 2001, he was bent on revenge.

(*The Straits Times* 2003)

Scheduled for a regular visit from his family on Wednesday February 27, 2008, Mas Selamat—as he always did before such a visit—was allowed by his guards to use a bathroom in the Whitley Road Detention Centre to change and have a shave beforehand.[9] He went into a stall in the bathroom while a guard and minder stood outside the doorway. Sometime between 3:54pm and 4:05pm, he managed to squeeze through a small window in the bathroom and, using a pipe on the outside of the wall, climbed down, hopped across a fence, and disappeared (Committee of Inquiry [COI] 2008: 2). It was later announced that not only was the window not properly locked, but the closed-circuit television (CCTV) cameras for that particular area were in the process of being upgraded and were not functioning properly (Wong 2008b: 9).

The authorities did not alert the public for a period of four hours, instead putting out a number of police officers and security forces in a sweep of the immediate neighborhood, setting up roadblocks and increasing security at immigration checkpoints (Skadian 2008a). Those stopped at roadblocks were told it was a "routine check" (Quek 2008). *The Straits Times* (Singapore) reported getting calls to their newsroom from locals curious about the increased police activity in the area and trying to find out what exactly was going on (Skadian 2008b). Indeed, this initial security operation—launched before any public statement or press release from the government—can be seen to have been the initial communication of the government to the community as "the huge uniformed presence signalled [sic] immediately to residents of the affected areas that something big was going on" (Skadian 2008b).

On the evening of Wednesday February 27, Singapore's Ministry of Home Affairs (2008) issued a press release with two pictures of Mas Selamat, one with a goatee and one shaved. The statement read:

> Jemaah Islamiyah (JI) detainee Mas Selamat bin Kastari escaped from the Whitley Road Detention Centre at 4:05pm on 27 Feb 2008.
> The public is advised to immediately contact the Police at 999 if they know of his whereabouts.
> Mas Selamat was the leader of the Singapore JI network. He walks with a limp and is presently at large. He is not known to be armed. Extensive police resources have been deployed to track him down.

Further information, however, would prove to be sparse; the authorities did not release information on the clothing he was wearing until Tuesday March 4, fully seven days after his escape (Nadarajan and Teh 2008).

116 *G. Dalziel*

The day after his escape, then-Minister for Home Affairs Wong Kan Seng made a statement in the Singapore Parliament, which served as the initial government explanation of the event. In it, he noted that Mas Selamat had escaped when using the toilet, but does not state how he actually managed to escape (e.g., through a window, or the toilet drain, or a hole in the wall). In addition, Wong said that, while Mas Selamat was in ISD custody as a "security threat," they had "no information that he has any plans that threaten public safety." However, even though he was both, on the one hand, deemed a security threat but, on the other, did not threaten public safety, Wong noted "Nevertheless, we are not taking any chances," which certainly raises the possibility of a threat to safety in the imagination.

The full text is included below:

> There has been a security lapse at the Whitley Road Detention Centre, which allowed Mas Selamat to escape. He was taken out of his cell to go to the family visitation room to wait for his family. He requested to go to the toilet and escaped. This should never have happened. I am sorry that it has. An independent investigation is under way. We should not speculate now. Security at the centre has been stepped up. Mas Selamat is a security threat which is why he was placed under preventive detention. However, there is no information that he has any plans that threaten public safety. Nevertheless, we are not taking any chances. Our security agencies assessed that he was of no imminent danger to the public. The focus then was to lockdown the immediate vicinity of the detention centre and start a systematic search. The priority is to find and arrest Mas Selamat.
>
> (Wong 2008a)

Many of the earlier rumor theories made a distinction between rumoring by publics and "authoritative" news sources (government, news media, and trusted experts), which were considered more epistemologically sound or "verified" (Allport and Postman 1946; Knapp 1944).

In this case, however, traditionally authoritative sources were also engaged in their own (very public) sense-making on the subject. Indeed, an editorial in *The Straits Times* echoed some of the sentiments being expressed by Singaporeans online, saying, "It stretches credulity to imagine this was an opportunistic solo effort, sprung when he was about to receive a family visit. The escape was too easy, too neat" (*The Straits Times* 2008a).

Newspaper articles speculated on where he was or where he might be trying to flee to (often Indonesia in general, and Sumatra specifically), or whether he was still in Singapore—"I don't think he has left Singapore because the situation is too hot right now. He's probably trying to hide until things have cooled down" (*The Straits Times* 2008b). Whereas one "expert" agreed that he was "waiting for the right time to flee to Indonesia" (*The Straits Times* 2008b), another editorial in *The Straits Times* suggested that "With the terror operative Mas Selamat Kastari still not caught three days after his escape, it is probable he has slipped out to either Malaysia or a nearby Indonesian island. From these places, the cocoon of the southern Philippines beckons" (*The Straits Times* 2008a). Some "experts" speculated with great specificity that he was most likely heading through the Riau islands to reach Sumatra, whereupon he would definitely attempt to link up with his Jemaah Islamiyah associates in order to assuredly continue plotting violence against Singapore (Rekhi 2008), while another rumored, in hindsight quite correctly, "He's definitely not going to leave by conventional means, so maybe he would swim across or hijack a boat ... he would want to wait until the time is ripe" (*The Straits Times* 2008b). Other articles consisted of minute updates of the search or by what means he was surviving in his assumed hiding place in the few wild spaces left in Singapore.

Just like the expressions of fear that predominated in many of the early discussions of the escape, Mas Selamat himself was portrayed as a real threat to the security of Singapore, notwithstanding Wong Kan Seng's statement that he was no "imminent danger to the public." One self-proclaimed terrorism expert stated with certainty that Mas Selamat—even though he had never actually been able to successfully undertake a terrorist attack—"[He is] like Al-Qaeda, he goes for mass casualty and suicide-type attacks" (Boey 2008). This same "expert" then went on to state that the risk of a terrorist attack had changed "dramatically" and breathlessly characterized Mas Selamat in the following manner:

> He's ... the most ruthless of the Singapore JI members ... he presents an immediate and real threat to Singapore and the region. I cannot think of a Singapore terrorist who is as ruthless as he is ... The probability of a terrorist attack in Singapore is very low but the escape of Mas Selamat Kastari changes that equation dramatically.
>
> (Boey 2008)

After the escape: the evolution of a shared narrative community

Online shared narrative communities

Persistent online shared narrative communities formed within hours of the escape, and developed over time with Singaporeans attempting to make sense of the situation based on information released (or not released), using activated schemas, relying on local knowledge, history, and extant narratives to help explain how and why such a thing could happen, and what it meant. In addition, much of the sense-making at work was done directly in response to the lack of information provided by state authorities or the manner and timeliness with which it was released.

In examining the themes that emerge in the first two weeks of online message boards at just one particular website in Singapore, *Stomp.com.sg*,[10] regarding the Mas Selamat escape, we can group them into four broad categories of sense-making: (1) how Mas Selamat managed to escape; (2) where he was now; (3) what would happen next—often expressed in terms of fear; and (4) what this meant for Singapore as a nation. The first two types of statements one could characterize as situational sense-making, trying to fill in the gaps in the narrative concerning the action of the main story of Mas Selamat's escape. Cognitively, concepts used here included perceptions of the size of Singapore and previous events and knowledge that were thought to be comparable and would provide some manner of framing the escape. The second and third types, however, utilize extant narratives, culture, and collective identity to aid in framing what meaning this event had for people. This was often expressed in relation to fears of terrorism or to collective identity. In all four categories, however, we can see people making use of cognitive schema and various information sources, relying on past experiences and broader narratives to make sense of a situation typified by pervasive ambiguity (Ball-Rokeach 1973: 378–89).

The first message on *Stomp* came shortly after it was announced on the news with a simple call for more information, "Jeez! How did it happen?" The content of the initial messages can be seen to be shaped by a desire for information ("Until now [12:22pm, 28–02–2008] there is still no news how he escaped! How come? We need answers!") and the paucity of precise information released by the government ("I mean come on, we're not idiots. He can't have just escape from the toilets ... this 'slipped thru the toilet' excuse could be just a cover up"). In this environment, many attempted to reach conclusions just on how (and by what means) Mas Selamat managed to escape. Knowledge claims began to circulate. One posting stated: "[the] toilet is a lame excuse. It must be something else." Whereas another wrote, "Prolly a mole somewhere in the prison guard." These themes of government malfeasance in the escape, whether as a cover-up of their own mistake or as cover for some sort of operation, were quick to take root and persist, highlighting both the implausibility of a man's escape from the control of the Singapore state along with the plausibility that the ever-competent Singapore state did not make mistakes.

Singapore is not a large island geographically; cognitively, the manner in which space is thought about affected how Singaporeans attempted to make sense of the escape. The detention facility in which he was held, Whitley Road, is not located in some *ulu* (far away) isolated part of the Singaporean "heartland" but sits on a rise in between the busy Pan-Island Expressway (PIE) and Bukit Timah Road, close to the upscale neighborhoods of Bukit Timah and Goldhill as well as the Orchard Road shopping district. The perception of the size of Singapore entailed for many that he would be caught soon ("Singapore is so small ... Where can he hide?"). As the days turned into weeks, and then months, this sense of space would play a major part in the meaning this event had for people.

Narratives about the government's competence, state power, and a strong security force made the situation even more incredulous for many. Here, we see the influence of state security symbols on Singaporeans' sense-making practices in terms of understanding how the escape was possible. Given the secrecy surrounding the ISD and the Whitley Road Detention Centre, Singaporeans did their best to fill in the blanks: "Whitley Detention Centre is a high security centre, [whose] cells are built underground and to escape from [sic] is almost impossible." The idea that someone could escape from a high-security facility without help was outlandish to many. On the other hand, having accomplices may also mean that the existence of undiscovered active supporters of Jemaah Islamiyah within Singapore was a plausible proposition for some people.

Experience and understanding of previous events in Singapore were activated to make sense of this situation; a prominent one repeated in many of the early postings was the 2004 Huang Na murder case (Nadarajan 2004; Vijayan 2004). A Malaysian national suspected of the killing of a young girl escaped across the border to Malaysia, without a passport (Fong 2005). One commenter on the message board wrote: "If Tok in the Huang Na's case can just breezed through the checkpoint without any detection I don't see why this JI leader cannot do the same."

Anything can happen: responding to uncertainty

The first message expressing fear and uncertainty was posted within an hour of the start of the thread, with a user simply writing "now anything can happen." The language used in these postings shares a remarkable similarity to state security discourse; Mas Selamat was repeatedly characterized as being "ruthless" and "dangerous" and, as he had escaped the confines of government detention, he presented an "immediate and real threat to Singapore" (Boey 2008).

In its use by the authorities to detain those under the ISA from the 1960s onwards, Whitley Road stood as a potent symbol of what happened to those deemed a threat to the sanctity of the state. Karl Weick's notion of enactment during sense-making is discussed in terms similar to that of intersubjectivity or social constructionism, namely that "enactment [means] ... people often produce part of the environment they face" (Weick 1995: 30). In this sense, the ISA and Whitley Road as security symbols ensured that the Singapore state enacted their role in how people responded to the escape. Between 1989 and 2008, there were reportedly seven successful or attempted escapes from custody—none from Whitley Road and all with far less hullabaloo than the Mas Selamat incident (Luo 2008).

During the sense-making process, meaning is created by people in relation to the state's discursive and symbolic practices; the manner in which the state communicated terrorism resonates in the expressions of fear and danger by Singaporeans. One individual wrote, "As long as he is still outside, we civilians, have our lives highly endangered!" Someone else posted "anything can happen which can be very very scary for us." The escape provided, for many

120   *G. Dalziel*

Singaporeans, a public recognition or reminder that a terrorism threat was present, however distant or unlikely. The narrative and symbols surrounding Mas Selamat provided such cues. However improbable or unlikely a terrorist attack was in the immediate period after the escape, the story provided a reminder for the public of the existence of terrorism, a rehearsal for an imagined future functioning as a story of what might have been (Weick 1995: 130).

This was a process that was not only discussed online, but in the real world too. *The Straits Times* reported that some parents in the vicinity of the detention facility withdrew their children from school the day after the escape. Nearby schools also increased security guards, implicitly communicating the direct threat to public safety that Mas Selamat posed. One parent said, "I can't bear leaving my daughter here when such a dangerous man is on the loose" (Tan *et al.* 2008), while another said, "I have told my daughter not to play in isolated spots of the school ... You never know what might happen" (Quek 2008).

Shifting sense-making: image and identity

By March 1, three days after the escape, the bulk of the conversations on the message board turned to the production and reproduction of a collective Singaporean identity that was concerned with how others viewed Singapore as a country. A Singaporean identity is actively being used and constructed in this event, by people examining what it means for Singapore as a whole, not simply for what it means for Chinese, Malay, Indian, or "other" Singaporeans, as the state might expect, given their reliance on fairly rigid social categorization by race. We do not see in this particular case the production of racial and religious identity that the state perhaps expected.

Many were concerned less with the safety implications of terrorism here than the impact the escape would have on the Singapore nation's international reputation and on upcoming prestige events such as the 2008 Singapore Grand Prix scheduled for later that year, or the 2010 Youth Olympics; typifying this theme are statements such as "How will the world view Singapore now" and "Failing at recapturing him is very bad for our reputation." Another wrote,

> We are lucky we clinched the rights to host [the] Youth Olympics 2010 before he managed to escape ... Such security lapses could bring great [disrepute] to our country ... Just imagine if his escape were to be during [the] F1 [race] in Singapore, the spotlight on the world will not be on the beautiful skyline of our city ... Such impact on our status in the world would be irreparable.

The influence of the state's social cognitive structure, including the boundary effects of its discursive practices and the influence of security symbols in how the escape was understood, can be seen in the variety of themes and discourse expressed in Singaporeans' online sense-making in this particular context. Just as the state saw terrorism in terms of identity and culture, so did Singaporeans. However, although some early statements could be characterized as racial in nature, they were a distinct minority. The production and reproduction of collective identity in this sense-making episode did not see Singaporeans expressing racial or religious identities but a collective "Singaporean" identity. The perceived fragility of race and religion by the state exemplified in its communicative practices with regard to terrorism and security did not show up in this case. This could mean either that the strategic communication campaigns encouraging Singaporeans to "Be as One" in the face of terrorism were successful, or that the lens through which the Singaporean state understands national identity is flawed; that is, the racial and religious boundaries constructed by the state do not correspond with the boundaries of collective identity in Singapore.

Conclusion

In this chapter, we have offered one account of the work Singaporeans did in making sense of Mas Selamat's escape and disappearance. By examining part of one social cognitive structure that circulated before the escape, we hoped to demonstrate the effect of the narrative terrain on people's sense-making work and the later emergence of rumors. The selection and emergence of themes during this initial period became the basis for later rumor stories when some semblance of narrative was produced to make sense of the meaning of the escape. In addition, this work done in the early crisis stages involved the crafting of collective schemas through which Singaporeans would analyze later events. This sense-making, or meaning-making, work did not operate in a vacuum, nor was it bounded solely by the beginning of the crisis period. Instead, we find that this collective sense-making process operates in relation to the state's discursive practices, to the manner in which the state itself understands security, threat, and terrorism. Thought communities, may be distinct in certain regards, but they do interact with each other, even if the boundaries of plausibility differ. Understandings of the master narrative of state security practices influenced the level of ambiguity in this case; previous frames, knowledge, and experience were used to make sense of the situation, while people relied on schema related to cognitive understandings of the geography of Singapore and risks and threats associated with terrorism to aid in the sense-making process.

In his initial statement to parliament on the escape, Wong (2008a) said, "We should not speculate now" as to what had happened. However, the lack of information about his escape (and, to be fair, the government itself may not have had conclusive information about the escape), Mas Selamat's custody by ISD under ISA law, and the pervasive and very public threat perception of terrorism ensured that, naturally, people would speculate in order to make sense of such a novel situation. It also demonstrates the effect secretive state

122   G. Dalziel

communication practices can have both in pre-crisis and crisis communication efforts; the reticence or disorganization in the release of information such as Mas Selamat's clothing or appearance certainly increased ambiguity during this period.

What this initial account of the work Singaporeans did to make sense of the Mas Selamat escape highlights is the influence that social cognitive structures—the shared schema, beliefs, worldviews, images, and collective identities—have on the collective sense-making process. As we can see in how people in inter-action attempted to make sense out of this event and to create a cohesive narrative for the event, the communication between state and society is not a simple sender–receiver relationship; in fact, there may be multiple senders involved in the way people make meaning in interaction, whether it is state organizations, traditional media outlets, "experts," or regular citizens inter-acting on- or offline, all constituted by social cognitive structures. The char-acterization by Wong (2008b) of the escape as an "episode [which] made good creative material for cynical humour" highlights the state's view of people as passive recipients of information rather than as people with agency who come together in shared narrative communities to collectively help one another in understanding situations where meaning is yet to be established.

Notes

1 Versions of this chapter were presented at the 2009 ISA-ABRI Conference in Rio de Janeiro and at the 2010 ICA Annual Conference in Singapore. Much of the research for and writing of this chapter took place while the author was employed by the Centre of Excellence for National Security (CENS), Singapore. I gratefully acknowledge their support. Special thanks must go to Christ Lundry, Paul T. Mitchell, and the anonymous reviewers for their comments, which greatly improved this piece.
2 This organization is called the Internal Security Department (ISD), organization-ally located within the Ministry of Home Affairs (MHA).
3 The full scope of the meaning to the state of such persistent efforts is outside the bounds of this chapter but, for a succinct summary, see Chin (2010).
4 Our use of the term "security culture" here is an extension of the concept of "strategic culture" (Gray 1999; Johnston 1995) combined with insights from the security identity literature (Baldwin 1997; McSweeney 1999; Mitzen 2006). Strate-gic culture generally refers to (rather thin) culturally bound explanations of varia-tions in state attitudes and behaviors with regard to the use of force and violence, limited organizationally to state militaries. Given the broader state meanings of security that persist in Asia, especially in Singapore, security culture here therefore combines internal and external perceptions of security and moves beyond the organizational boundaries of the military. Such a move is necessary to better explain state policies, discourses, and—most importantly—practices in relation to security, threat, and risk.
5 For more on Jemaah Islamiyah, see Ramakrishna (2009a).
6 For more on MILF, see Liow (2006) and Tan (2003).
7 "Be as One" available online at: www.youtube.com/watch?v=zcB0WYcMzAk (accessed 30 August 2010).

8 See Internal Security Department (ISD) website, "Security Education," at: www.mha.gov.sg/isd/se.htm (accessed 20 June 2009).
9 These regular visits from family members were part of a broader "rehabilitation" or "deradicalization" program that detainees at Whitley Road underwent. For more, see Ramakrishna (2009b).
10 *Stomp* is a popular message board and "citizen-journalism website" operated by Singapore Press Holdings, which publishes *The Straits Times*, among other newspapers. The website can be found at: www.stomp.com.sg/index.html

7 Rumor, culture, and strategic communication across old and new media in Southeast Asia

The case of terrorist Noordin Top

Chris Lundry and Pauline Hope Cheong

Introduction

Studies in terrorism and conflict have recently shown renewed interest in the notion of "soft power" and the spread of extremist views as a key component in the global ideational battle for hearts and minds. Governments worldwide are turning to "smart power" (Nye 2004) and the creation of persuasive rhetorical policies involving the vigilant building of public diplomacy campaigns and "nation branding" to improve strategic communication performance (Dinnie 2007). Accompanying this rejuvenated interest in the informational realm of terrorism and security is an inquiry into rumors as a form of strategic communication. Given that rumors may communicate provocative content and instigate extremist actions, they have strategic implications for terrorism and counterterrorism efforts. Indeed, prior literature in the fields of sociology, political science, and cultural studies has noted the role that false rumor plays in engendering fear as a "prosthetic of violence" to reinforce stereotypes and further social divisions (Feldman 1997; Fine and Turner 2001; Sunstein 2009). Yet less attention has been paid to the cultural and socio-technical conditions in which rumors are discursively created, propagated, and received in today's multimodal environment.

This chapter examines the communicative behaviors undergirding the spread of rumor as it functions as a "cultural meme" within its social and mediated milieu. A meme is an idea, instruction, behavior, or story that replicates and spreads via informational networks (Blackmore 2000). Memes generate virus-like imitations and reproductions that do not have to be exact in order to reinforce beliefs and spur thought contagion to influence a society's agenda. Cultural memes in the form of rumors can spread via multiple face-to-face and mediated channels.

A contemporary development in what Henry Jenkins (2006) has dubbed "media convergence" points to the "transmediation" of stories or narratives where they are created, remediated, and disseminated across multiple digital media platforms (Bolter and Grusin 2000). Unlike the traditional top-down dissemination of information, transmediation involves additive and iterative forms of consumption and integration of multiple media forms when audiences or fans engage with media and with each other to create new texts. According to Meikle (2008), these creative possibilities of digitalization and social web practices are facilitating different kinds of representations and constructions of "truth." In light of the emergence and increasing adoption of web-based applications, we propose that the production and dissemination of terrorist-related rumors may function as memes, accelerating the intensity of their spread and the rate at which rumors gain traction in a mediated social system. Some consumers are also acting as producers or what Axel Bruns (2008) terms as "produsers" (producer/users) when they recycle and reproduce rumors and make connections among dispersed media content. Specifically, our chapter examines the fascinating case of rumors surrounding the demise of Southeast Asia's most wanted terrorist, Noordin Mohammad Top.

On the morning of September 17, 2009, the life of Noordin Mohammad Top came to a violent and bloody end at the hands of Indonesia's anti-terrorist police squad, Densus 88 (Detachment 88).[1] A leader of the organization Jemaah Islamiyah, and recently suspected of having established a violent splinter group named Tandzim al-Qo'idah Indonesia, Noordin was implicated in a number of major terrorist attacks in Indonesia, including the July 17, 2009 suicide bombings at the J.W. Marriott and Ritz-Carlton hotels in Jakarta. His death is a notable success for anti-terrorism efforts in Indonesia.

Following the shoot-out in which Noordin was killed, his corpse was sent to Jakarta in order to verify his identification (a repetition of the process following the killing of a terrorist falsely identified as Noordin the previous month). Nearly two weeks after his death, Indonesian police spokesman Nanan Sukarna announced that, during the autopsy, the examiner found that Noordin had an infundibuliform (funnel-shaped) anus, and asserted that he therefore engaged in passive sodomy. This information was verified by Mun'im Idris, a forensics expert from the University of Indonesia.

Although Nanan stated that the findings were of a personal nature and were to be kept secret, the following day, mainstream Indonesian print and broadcast media reported the story, despite acknowledging the "private" nature of the disclosure.[2] By the following day, the story had disappeared from the mainstream media, partly as a result of the tragedy of the Padang, Sumatra, earthquake taking precedence in terms of media coverage, but it was picked up and disseminated by online "produsers," who appropriated the words and images associated with the story and changed them to reflect their views.

As the role of rumor has historically served as a mobilizing agent in communal violence to fuel the "politics of paranoia" in Indonesia (Bubandt 2008), this chapter responds to the official rumor following Noordin Top's autopsy and examines the veracity of its claims. We then describe the broadcast and transmediation of the rumors about Noordin Top. The chapter analyzes how new media are appropriated to construct unofficial rumors for further social inquiry into the life and mission of Noordin Top, as well as to contest nationalist identities. Finally, we examine this state-sanctioned rumor in the context of strategic communication to discuss the role of rumors and

126　*C. Lundry and P.H. Cheong*

their efficacy in counterterrorism efforts. In particular, as in the case study discussed below, we suggest that the official creation and dissemination of rumors about Noordin Top's peculiar physicality may be especially compelling given its congruence with the extant "cultural logic" which views homosexuality as taboo and deviant (Fine and Turner 2001).

During times of heightened attention to key terrorist leaders—who are sometimes promoted as heroes and celebrities—political propaganda in the form of culturally taboo rumors may help chill the laudatory discourse and eulogies to quell the legacy and impact of a terrorist's death. In this case, the rumors concerning Noordin Top may have had a chilling effect on communication lauding him among Southeast Asian extremists following the results of the autopsy. Compared with those who acted as suicide bombers in the July 2009 bombings and those killed alongside him on September 17, and given Noordin's comparative status, the absence of martyrdom and eulogical discourse is startling.[3] In comments on jihadist sites where it was discussed, such as *Ar Rahmah*, respondents argued over the truth of the rumor as well as what it meant about Noordin Top.[4]

To provide context to this case, we now turn to a brief background of Noordin Top, including his rise in the ranks of Jemaah Islamiyah and his death at the hands of Densus 88.

Rumor creation: history and background

Noordin Mohammad Top was born in Kluang, Johor, Malaysia, on August 11, 1968. He turned towards terrorism in 1995 while a Master's student at Universiti Teknologi Malaysia, attending lectures at the Lukmanul Hakiem pesantren (Islamic boarding school) run by Abdullah Sungkar, the co-founder (along with Abu Bakar Basyir) of the terrorist network Jemaah Islamiyah (JI). He joined JI in 1998, and became the Director of Lukmanul Hakiem. As the Malaysian government cracked down on JI in 2002, the school closed and Noordin left for Indonesia (International Crisis Group 2006).

JI's campaign of violence in Indonesia reached a new height that year with the first Bali bombing on October 12, 2002, which killed over 200 people. Noordin was thought to be the mastermind behind the Bali bombing and subsequent attacks. According to the International Crisis Group (ICG), by the following year, Noordin was operating more autonomously, although he continued to identify himself as a JI member (International Crisis Group 2006). The ICG speculated that Noordin perceived himself as representing the "true JI," willing to carry out bomb attacks despite the context of heightened security following the Bali bombing and subsequent attacks; Abu Bakar Basyir's rhetoric justifying violence became significantly toned down following his two stints in prison (International Crisis Group 2006). Noordin is thought to have coordinated the July 17, 2009 attacks on the Ritz-Carlton and J.W. Marriott hotels in Jakarta. Following the bombing, an announcement attributed to Noordin was posted on the internet describing a new JI offshoot—Tandzim al Qo'idah Indonesia (Lundry 2009a).

The case of terrorist Noordin Top   127

Following the July 17, 2009 Jakarta bombings, Indonesian police—including the anti-terror force Densus 88—ratcheted up their operations in search of Noordin Top and other terrorists. On August 8, 2009, Densus 88 surrounded a house in Temanggung, Central Java, and, after a seventeen-hour siege and firefight, local media announced that police were 80 percent certain that Noordin top had been killed in the raid (there were no indications as to how such a figure was calculated). The following several days were fraught with speculation, but a DNA test determined that the man killed was not Noordin Top but rather another person associated with the July 17 bombings, a man called Ibrohim.

On September 17, however, Densus 88 conducted another raid in Central Java, this time killing Noordin Top and four others and taking three captives. Southeast Asia's most wanted terrorist was finally dead.

In a September 30, press conference, police spokesman Nanan Sukarna said that investigators had discovered evidence that the corpse of Noordin Top showed signs of anal trauma consistent with sodomy, leading to speculation that he might have been bisexual. The same day, Universitas Indonesia forensics expert Mun'im Idris told reporters that there were "irregularities" with Noordin's corpse, and he later verified that they pointed to sodomy.

Although the announcement was made in front of reporters, Nanan stated,

> This is the doctor's secret. Indeed I do not know who was stating this. It has to be kept secret, it cannot be announced. There is a code of ethics, it is a problem of visum etrepesum [sic: repertum].
>
> (Hermawan 2009)

Yet for whom was the announcement, which reported details of the investigation, intended if not the public? How many nods and winks were shared between reporter and spokesman, the understanding that this "news" would of course be disseminated?

And disseminated it was, with slight variations. *Kompas* [online] was discreet in its coverage, but quoted Mun'im as saying there were "peculiarities" (*Kompas* 2009b). The flagship paper of eastern Indonesia, *Pos Kupang*, also quoted Mu'nim but more directly: "Yes, there is damage to Noordin's anus" (Seko 2009). Perhaps the best example of the nod-and-wink game is the reporting from *Kompas*, Indonesia's most respected national newspaper: "Nanan: The Matter of Noordin's Anus has to be Kept Secret" the headline blared in an unattributed story (*Kompas* 2009a). The story, by its very nature, was irresistible to the Indonesian mass media. It was titillating and maligned a notorious terrorist (the mainstream Indonesian press has been supportive of Indonesia's anti-terrorism efforts, reflecting similar support among the Indonesian population at large). By the following day, however, the story had mostly disappeared from mainstream media, displaced by stories about the Padang earthquake.

128   *C. Lundry and P.H. Cheong*

Rumor examination: autopsy of an autopsy

The source for connecting a funnel-shaped anus with anal sex originates in nineteenth-century France. Auguste Ambroise Tardieu (1818—1879) was a prominent forensic medical scientist who was the "leading medical expert on pederasty in France" (although his advocacy work on behalf of children was mostly downplayed or disregarded at the time).[5] In describing the physical harm associated with active and passive sodomy, he noted that complementary physical deformities manifest in the sodomites' sex organs:

> In the case of the passive sodomite, Tardieu claimed to have found evidence that the anus had become severely damaged. "The characteristic signs of passive pederasty," he wrote, "are the excessive development of the buttocks, the infundibuliform deformation of the anus, the relaxation of the sphincter, the effacement of the folds [of the anus], the crests and caroncules around the circumference of the anus, and the extreme dilation of the anal orifice.
>
> (Peniston 2004: 54)[6]

Tardieu's claims about identifying sodomites extended to their outward appearance as well.[7] The identification of sodomites was important because sodomy allegedly showed moral and intellectual deficiencies, which led to criminal behavior.[8] Tardieu had access to prisoners in French jails, which is where he conducted most of his research, hence begging the question: "finding" cases of sodomy among criminals (convicted of both sodomy and other crimes) and then arguing that sodomy led to crime.

Despite Tardieu's reputation, his conclusions were by no means universally accepted. Peniston notes, for example, that contemporary German medical experts believed homosexuality was an inborn trait in some and a choice for others. Later, others challenged his conclusions about the physical manifestations of sodomy, including Paul Brouardel, who succeeded Tardieu in the Faculty of Medicine in Paris (Peniston 2004: 57). American Charles B. Kelsey wrote in his 1883 medical text *Diseases of the Rectum and Anus, Their Pathology, Diagnosis and Treatment*:

> A condition of weakness causing a patulous anus is a very common symptom of grave disease of the rectum; and the same patuous condition is considered by the French writers as a proof of the constant practice of passive paederasty, but without sufficient grounds. The muscle is adapted for frequent contraction and expansion, and there is no reason for believing that the frequent introduction of the male organ should cause its paralysis any more than the equally frequent passage of fæces. However it may be in warmer climates, I know that it would not do in America to infer the practice of unnatural vice from a relaxed and funnel-shaped anus, as seems to be the case in France.
>
> (Kelsey 1893: 13)

The case of terrorist Noordin Top   129

Not all Americans concurred, however. Thirteen years after the publication of Kelsey's book, Samuel Goodwin Gant's _Diseases of the Rectum and Anus_ argued that a funnel-shaped anus was indeed the result of sodomy (Gant 1906: 303).

Whether or not there was physical evidence associated with anal sex, the drive to identify homosexuals was in the context of identifying criminals. Tardieu's position was such that it was primarily doctors trained in his techniques who were employed in criminal cases to identify pederasts (Peniston 2004: 58–59). Tardieu's ideas remain in circulation, despite evidence—and medical experts' conclusions—to the contrary.

Ironically, sodomy was also linked to Islam during the period in which Tardieu was writing; there were widespread European perceptions of Muslims as homosexuals (Perry 1989: 76). Victims of homosexual rape were thought to be on the first step of a path that would lead them to greater evils:

> Piracy and sodomy were construed as closely related transgressions from the early modern period onward. Both were seen as particularly infectious forms of behavior. Accounts of "white slavery" at the hands of the barbary pirates of the North African coast spun out of trajectory: homosexual rape, conversion to Islam, and, ultimately, a career of piracy against Christian Europe. Like piracy, sodomy was seen as more than a personal failing; it was a transgression against national character.
>
> (Land 2006: 97)

Vernon Rosario (1999) notes a shift in thinking about homosexuality in the early twentieth century among psychiatrists including Sigmund Freud and Abraham Brill; the latter argued that open-mindedness on the part of the family was the best reaction to homosexuality. This shift also represented a shift in focus from the body to the mind. At the dawn of World War II, however, Rosario notes a "turn for the worse," as Freud was challenged and homosexuality was linked to a wide range of psychopathological conditions. Although still widely persecuted, homosexuality became increasingly debated, and—after the Stonewall Riots of 1969—eventually declassified as a pathology by the American Psychiatric Association (1973) and the American Psychological Association (1975).

In what Human Rights Watch (2004) calls a "fully technologized violation of the subject's integrity, dignity and privacy," Egyptian doctors continue to test the anuses of suspected sodomites using techniques that build on Tardieu's methods, but incorporate manometry (to determine pressure in the anal cavity) and electromyography to determine whether someone is a passive sodomite:

> (Egyptian Deputy Minister of Justice Dr. Ayman) Fouda was at pains to stress that these technological methods did not supersede the antiquated standards of Tardieu, merely elaborated on them: "We don't discard

130   *C. Lundry and P.H. Cheong*

Tardieu's criteria, and I do not mean that the funnel-shaped anus is not a sign of habitual use. I mean that electromyography is more exact ..." In response to this article, Professor (Robert) Nye told Human Rights Watch "I have never heard of such a wild notion" as mapping the electrical conductivity of anal tissue.

(*Human Rights Watch* 2004: 111n.408)

Scott Long, author of the Human Rights Watch Report, found an Arabic-language World Health Organization report entitled *Forensic Medicine and Toxicology* (1993) that echoed Tardieu's criteria save for the funnel-shaped anus claims. "See how the WHO ... condones categorizing consensual sodomy as a 'crime,' and calls for tortuous expeditions around the anus to prove it. Tardieu endures" (Long 2004: 127).

Other experts have noted the baseless nature of Tardieu's claims. Professor Lorna Martin, a forensic pathologist at the University of Cape Town, calls Tardieu's conclusions "bizarre and antiquated ... rubbish ... It is impossible to detect chronic anal penetration" except in cases of injury resulting from non-consensual sex (*Human Rights Watch* 2004: 109). Robert Nye, a historian of sexology at Oregon State University, referred to Tardieu as "utterly discredited," and the Egyptian examinations "horrific in the extreme" (*Human Rights Watch* 2004: 109).

This is not to claim that the condition known as funnel anus does not exist— it certainly does—but rather that it is not caused by sodomy. The condition is congenital and makes up 3.5 percent of all low anorectal anomalies. It leads to constipation and a condition called megacolon, which requires surgery. Soumalainen *et al.* suggest that there is a connection between funnel anus and embryologic and genetic etiology (Soumalainen *et al.* 2007).

Although the connection between the physical condition of funnel anus and sodomy is spurious, the question remains as to whether Noordin Top truly did have a funnel-shaped anus. On this, the authors remain agnostic; there were no reports of subsequent forensic examinations either in Indonesia before Noordin's corpse was repatriated or after its arrival in Malaysia. Consistent with Islamic tradition, he was buried quickly after arrival.

Regardless of the truth as to Noordin's physical condition and the spurious connections between funnel-shaped anus and sodomy, the accusation was made publicly by both a police spokesman and the forensics expert. Apparently no mainstream media outlet publicly challenged the assertion that funnel anus is caused by sodomy (although some speculated that a funnel-shaped anus could be the result of an attempt to hide explosives) (*The Star Online* [Malaysia] 2009).

Rumor spread: transmediation of official and unofficial stories

According to Yahoo, the term "Noordin M. Top" was the most searched term in Indonesia for 2009 (Althaf 2009). Although we are not asserting that

The case of terrorist Noordin Top   131

the rumors following his autopsy are what caused his name to be the most popular search term, the rumor certainly contributed to its popularity. Other reasons include, for example, the July 17 J. W. Marriott and Ritz Carlton bombings, for which he was blamed, the online announcement attributed to him in which he claimed responsibility and announced the formation of a new extremist group, the reports—which turned out to be false—about his supposed death in August, and of course the reports concerning his actual death in September. Despite the spurious science on which the claim was based, the story was picked up and broadcast by blogs and other online sources, including those outside Indonesia. Although it is impossible to pinpoint the effect of the rumors on the popularity of the search term, it is highly plausible that rumors about Top fueled the popularity of online searches related to him.

The transmediation of the Noordin Top story began through re-postings of the original news stories, often with additional commentary. The day after the announcement, Malaysia's *Topix.com*[9] (2009) screamed "Fact! Noordin was Frequently Sodomized." Comments multiplied rapidly, with respondents choosing sides. "Character assassination!" screamed one supporter, as though being gay (or sexually deviant) was worse than being a murdering terrorist, and implying that Noordin had any character left to assassinate. One supporter speculated that the damage to Noordin's anus could have been done sometime after his death or during the autopsy.[10] Although skeptics—primarily those sympathetic to Noordin Top but others such as terrorism expert Al Chaidar[11]—raised doubts about the police announcement, these were vastly overshadowed by commentators who took the announcement at face value. None questioned the validity of the forensic science on which the claim was based.

On October 1, the *al-Yaasin* website posted sections of the news articles about the rumor, but added to its content unattributed comments allegedly made by psychologists at Surabaya's Universitas Airlangga speculating on Noordin's psychological condition. His heterosexual relations with women were described as "torture," and his alleged homosexuality was blamed on his "psychopathic" condition (Gus Rachmat 2009).

Given the nature of the rumor, the online commentaries quickly turned to parody and crude jokes, many of which were disseminated in the form of striking graphic memes. "Produsers" began to acquire and manipulate official images of Noordin Top (from, for example, his wanted posters), changing them to feminize Noordin in order to reflect the accusations of bisexuality. These "produsers" added a *jilbab*, or a woman's long hair, or rouge to his cheeks (Figure 7.1). Others made multiple images of Noordin, some feminized, others simply for humor, for example Noordin Top as robocop, Michael Jackson, Axl Rose, a pirate, a clown, and as reflecting various musical styles (emo, rock "n" roll, punk, and *dangdut*, an indigenous Indonesian pop music influenced by Indian and Middle Eastern music) (see Figure 7.2).

Interestingly, memetic isomorphism[12] or similar representational forms that were mapped upon graphic memes was evident in postings that copied text and images used by Singaporean bloggers in reference to the February 2008

Figure 7.1 A *produser*'s manipulated images of Noordin Top's "wanted" photo

escape of fellow JI terrorist Mas Selamat. The similarity in the photoshopped responses illustrates how rumors utilizing similar frames of references may spread within culturally close contexts and related mediated spaces online. From this example, it is clear that Indonesians were aware of the Mas Selamat case from 2008, and that online communication concerning terrorism is a transboundary phenomenon (this is also clear from the examples below concerning the Noordin Top case as a proxy for Indonesian attacks on Malaysia).

Aside from textual and graphic data, other popular platforms for transmediation are video-sharing websites such as YouTube.com, where online participants can appropriate images and alter them in short video clips. Although there are several older videos about or referring to Noordin Top, the first spike in videos came following the August 8, 2009 raid on suspected terrorists in Temanggung, Central Java, after which police announced that they were "80 percent certain" that they had killed Noordin Top.[13]

In the days following the raid, the supposed death of Noordin Top was a sensation that was quickly deflated by the announcement the following week that DNA and other evidence had shown that the corpse was Ibrohim, who was linked to the 2009 Jakarta bombings, not Noordin Top. The second spike came after a raid that began on the evening of September 16, 2009, in which Noordin Top was actually killed along with three others, and three captured. The third spike came following the press conference and announcement by Mun'im Idris concerning the findings from the autopsy. Although all three are interesting in their own right, the analysis below investigates the third which is the focus of this chapter: rumors of sodomy concerning Noordin Top.

Figure 7.2 A variety of remixed versions of the Noordin Top "wanted" photo

The first YouTube video concerning the accusations appeared the same day as the announcement (September 30), entitled "noordin m top pahlawan malingsia malaysia youtubers" ("Noordin M. Top hero of malingsia [thief + Malaysia] Malaysia youtubers") and posted by a user with the name NusantaraWarrior.[14] This video combines a rebroadcast of Jakarta's MetroTV newscast and NusantaraWarrior's earlier video feminizing Noordin Top, posted on the day of Noordin's demise ("Noordin M Top Tewas Terkencing Kencing 17/09/2009"; "Noordin M Top Killed While Pissing Himself in Fear 17/09/2009").[15] The post-announcement footage features a shot of the police station with police and Mun'im Idris walking toward the camera, and then cuts to a shot of Noordin's corpse. The reporter refers to the condition as "kelainan seks" ("sexual abnormality/anomaly") as a result of "seks menyimpang" ("deviant sex"), and states that a spokesman for Noordin's family denies the allegations. Next, Mun'im is shown in a scrum of reporters, refusing to answer specific questions by explaining that he is on police property, and inviting reporters to talk to him at the Universitas Indonesia campus where he is based. The video ends with images of Noordin's face transposed on to women's bodies; these images, of Noordin Top as a woman, were not created for this video, but rather were used in another video posted by NusantaraWarrior following Noordin Top's death. The video is set to the tune of "Bongkar" by Indonesian pop star Iwan Fals; the term "bongkar" means upside down or out of place and, in the song, it has connotations of a disturbed social order in an era of repression (Iwan Fals was a prominent social critic of Suharto's New Order). Other YouTube videos followed.

The second, fourth, and fifth postings under the search terms "Dubur Noordin Top" are simply rebroadcasts of the news. The third video was created by a user called Gombress, and is the first to incorporate an anti-Malaysian slant; it is entitled "Noordin M. Top liwat pondon sodomi Malaysian hero tewas" ("Noordin M. Top sodomite transvestite sodomy Malaysian hero killed").[16] It begins with a crude joke, then segues to the MetroTV broadcast. Following that is the headline "Club Pondan Noordin M. Top Malaysiana" (Malaysian Transvestite Club Noordin M. Top) and a montage of video clips including a broadcast of a Malaysian news report on a raid on a Malaysian gay club, Mahmoud Ahmadinejad's speech at Columbia University in which he denied that there were homosexuals in Iran, and a flamboyant Malaysian television show host, interspersed with footage of a Western woman laughing hysterically, and with background music of Iwan Fals' song "bongkar." Some of these images were posted by Gombress in earlier digs at Malaysians.

Almost all of Gombress' and NusantaraWarrior's videos feature Indonesian nationalist and anti-Malaysia themes, as do many of their YouTube "friends" in their profile listings. Curiously, both Gombress and NusantaraWarrior state in their profiles that they currently live in Malaysia, the former as a dentist, the latter as a student at Universitas Teknologi Malaysia, the same university that Noordin Top attended. Comments posted for these videos (and others related to Noordin Top) reflect the animosity between some Indonesians and Malaysians, and often spiral downward into cursing and name-calling.

In the days following the announcement, several more YouTube videos appeared regarding the accusations against Noordin. These videos, and the comment threads that follow them, became proxies for the users to lob insults at Malaysia and Malaysians, and for Malaysians to return these insults. They

The case of terrorist Noordin Top 135

refer to recent feuds between Malaysia and Indonesia, such as the dispute over the Ambalat Islands and the Indonesian perception that Malaysia is appropriating its culture to promote tourism, which have much deeper roots (dating to Malaysia's early 1960s decolonization and Indonesia's policy of *Konfrontasi* amid accusations that Malaysia was a post-colonial puppet state).[17]

Over one month later, the news story even spurred a spoof that stayed close to the original, but substituted Noordin Top for the character Jomblo Juhari ("Jomblo" means without a girlfriend or boyfriend), and the author translated the original story into English. Mimicking line for line the original news story in parts, it also injected crude jokes. The goal is clear: Noordin is similar to Jomblo the simpleton, and his activities are reprehensible (*Indonesia Page* 2009).

Netizens ruminated on the posthumous accusations in online forums, blogs, and websites, reflecting the two main tacks associated with the transmediation of the story: criticism of terrorists and Noordin Top himself, and attacks on Malaysia. The criticisms of Noordin and terrorism use words and images to feminize Noordin and terrorists, and the criticisms of Malaysia use Noordin as a symbol or representative of Malaysian identity.

The latent conflict between Malaysia and Indonesia became the predominant theme over time in the transmediation of this rumor. "Noordin Top Appears to be Homosexual (a Reflection of the [religious] Hypocrisy of Malingsia Society)" screamed another *Topix.com* report. The term "Malingsia" combines the word for "thief" with Malaysia, but this rumor has brought to the fore another derogatory term for Indonesians to refer to Malaysians: "Magaysia" (Lundry 2009b).

Because Noordin Top was Malaysian, he has long spurred conspiracy theories that he, and other Malaysians such as Azahari, were sent to Indonesia to perpetrate acts of terror to destabilize Indonesia (Wijaya 2009). Both Malaysian and Indonesian spokespersons have vehemently denied these conspiracies, arguing that the eradication of terrorism is a common goal. There are a few factors that are more likely to be behind terrorists in the region moving to Indonesia to conduct operations. First, Indonesia is poorer than both Singapore and Malaysia, and the state has fewer resources with which to battle terrorism. Second, many of the important members of Jemaah Islamiyah have connections—including family ties—to the Darul Islam movement, a rebellion based in West Java that fought first the Dutch then the Indonesian central government from 1948 to the early 1960s, and there are people who are sympathetic to JI's goals. Third, both Singapore and Malaysia have been fairly successful in cracking down on Islamic militants in the last decade, which is one of the reasons why Abu Bakar Basyir returned to Indonesia from Malaysia in 1999. Finally, with Indonesia's emerging democratic reforms, including freedom of speech, it is more difficult to prosecute those with suspected ties to terrorism without due process and tangible evidence; both Malaysia and Singapore use their Internal Security Acts to hold suspected terrorists for up to two years without charge.

These factors, however, do not seem to matter much to the Indonesian netizens who continue to lob insults at Malaysia. The rumors concerning Noordin Top played perfectly into their pre-existing narrative of Malaysia as a home to deviants who are jealous of Indonesia—especially its varied cultures—and who wish to do it harm. They also allowed the "produsers" to use humor and parody—albeit a sort of primary school humor that targets homosexuality.

The transmediated examples concerning the case of Noordin Top are often done in humorous ways as a means to belittle a terrorist suspected of collusion in the deaths of many Indonesians and foreigners. Robert Hariman (2008: 256) has noted that parody reveals the

> actors behind the masks ... (where) parodic techniques coalesce in the construction of a carnivalesque spectatorship, institutional forms are revealed to be masks, power and status are shown to be acts, and the key to success is not transcendental backing but rather some combination of backstage maneuver and audience gullibility.

Chuck Tryon (2008: 210) notes the decline in importance of traditional media, and argues that online parody can challenge authority and shape political discourse. The humor used by online "produsers" in this case accepts the official government position uncritically (something that the mainstream media in Indonesia did as well, and that a spokesman for gay rights organization GAYa Nusantara refused to refute) but takes it one step further into the realm of ridicule.[18]

J. Michael Waller's (2007) recent work shows the value of ridicule as both a means for terrorists to belittle fellow Muslims who are not willing to join their cause, but also a potential weapon of strategic communication designed to weaken the appeal of extremists' messages among contested populations. As Waller (2007: 97) notes, Osama bin Laden stated that he feared humiliation more than death.

Waller cites both historical and recent examples of ridicule, the latter including the film "Team America: World Police" and its target Kim Jong Il and Muslim terrorists, and a captured unedited version of footage of Abu Musab al-Zarqawi. The "Team America" example is similar to our case as it appeals to adolescent and scatological humor. The raw video of al-Zarqawi portrays someone who wants to promote an image of a capable and fearsome terrorist as one who is somewhat of a bungler; in the video, he is shown to be incapable of fixing a jam in a machine gun he was trying to fire and wearing American-made tennis shoes, and his associate burns his hand after grabbing the searing hot barrel of the recently fired machine gun. These examples and others show the relationship between control of one's image and people's perceptions. Ridicule undermines this control, and shows the weaknesses and vulnerability of the enemy, As Waller (2007: 109) notes:

The case of terrorist Noordin Top   137

Ridicule is a powerful weapon of warfare. It can be a strategic weapon. The United States must take advantage of it against terrorists, proliferators, and other threats. Ridicule is vital because:

- It sticks;
- The target can't refute it;
- It is almost impossible to repress, even if driven underground;
- It spreads on its own and multiplies naturally;
- It can get better with each re-telling;
- It boosts morale at home;
- Our enemy shows far greater intolerance to ridicule than we;
- Ridicule divides the enemy, damages its morale, and makes it less attractive to supporters and prospective recruits; and
- The ridicule-armed warrior need not fix a physical sight on the target. Ridicule will find its own way to the targeted individual.

To the enemy, being ridiculed means losing respect. It means losing influence. It means losing followers and repelling potential new backers. To the enemy, ridicule can be worse than death. Many of our enemies believe death to be a supernatural martyrdom. Ridicule is much worse: defeat without martyrdom, the worst of both worlds. And they have to live with it.

As our results show, it appears as though the ridicule aimed at Noordin Top and his followers (actual or potential) was effective in that his memory became permanently tainted and laudatory communication muted. Although there is little doubt that the memory of Noordin Top will be held in high regard among his fellow extremists and supporters of terror, among those who may have been susceptible to sympathy for him or "contested populations" that have not made a decision to support or reject terrorism in Indonesia, the message certainly had a chilling effect, which was no doubt the goal behind the original announcement.

Conclusion: rumors and implications for counterterrorism performances

In light of growing concerns over the global war on terrorism, the creation and transmediation of rumors regarding terrorists provide a way to analyze extant social anxieties and fears that fuel outcomes associated with counterterrorism and national identities. Rumors have historically been employed in Indonesian politics (Anderson 1990); in this case, they achieve a powerful format by co-conscripting official and unofficial universes of narrative across multiple media platforms. In this way, the study of rumor has multiple implications for counterterrorism strategies and lay tactics of resistance in response to terrorist stories.

138 *C. Lundry and P.H. Cheong*

For counterterrorism concerns, the spread of rumors regarding Top seem to have achieved a chilling effect on his legacy. It is striking to note that, unlike other terrorist leaders who have garnered laudatory acclaim, the discourse surrounding the death of Top (particularly after the release of the rumor) seemed muted. He was notably not gifted with symbols normally associated with martyrdom in the Muslim tradition (i.e., green birds that are posited to hold the souls of martyrs). Recent scholarship on celebrity studies points to the aggregation of fans to mourn for their heroes and idols collectively, and on mediated platforms, which then further inflames their passion and resurrects the fame of deceased celebrities (Sanderson and Cheong 2010). In Top's case, online discourse appeared not to have any such vivifying effects. On the contrary, a significant portion of online content, discussed above, appeared to further diminish his legacy.[19]

It is therefore striking to note the congruence between the rumor and its spread within the cultural crucible of Indonesia and neighboring regions. In many ways, the attempt to posthumously malign Noordin Top by spreading the rumor that he was gay or bisexual—a rumor based on demonstrably false conclusions from mid-nineteenth-century forensic medicine—can be interpreted as an effective multipronged attack on the terrorist. First, it feminizes a cold-blooded killer, and in the minds of some Indonesians makes him mentally ill. Second, it portrays a supposedly pious Muslim as a sinner. Terrorists claim to be acting on behalf of some idealized conceptualization of a "true" Islam, and those who refuse to act or even support them are portrayed as less pious; yet here is someone claiming to be pious, but rather who may have engaged in sodomy. Third, it spreads a rumor that would be difficult, if not impossible, for defenders of Noordin Top to dispel.

In other words, rumor propagation appeared to gain traction on multiple media sites to discredit Top as a terrorist leader martyr as cultural taboos and moral anxieties surrounding homosexuality were evoked. As James Scott (1990: 145) notes:

> As a rumor travels it is altered in a fashion that brings it more closely into line with the hopes, fears and worldview of those who hear it and retell it …The rumor, it appears, is not only an opportunity for anonymous, protected communication, but also serves as a vehicle for anxieties and aspirations that may not be openly acknowledged by its propagators.

On this basis, one must expect rumors to take quite divergent forms depending on the class, strata, region, or occupation in which they circulate and on what counterterrorism purposes they serve. In the context of Islam, it appeared that the accusation against Noordin Top devastated his Muslim "credentials" among followers and those open to his message. Homosexuality is proscribed in Islam, especially so in the puritanical form of Islam espoused by Noordin. Hence, we witnessed how the accusation silenced Noordin's followers, and invited political parodies by others.

The case of terrorist Noordin Top   139

Furthermore, in the contemporary information environment, rumor mash-ups amplify their reach and potential influence. The repetition and reproduction of the colorful visual meme involving Top's body parts, for example his full lips (marked by lipstick) and distorted sexual organs, on various media heightened public awareness of this rumor, beyond the staid mainstream news media representations. It is this extension of rumors into cyber and mediated spaces that requires more in-depth future research into rumor dynamics and how terrorist-related rumors mirror other rumors and stories, and with what effect, as it has been proposed that "the intermodality of the rumor, its ability to piggyback on and intersect with other media, printed and electronic, legitimate and illegitimate, gives it reach and impact" (Bubandt 2008: 796).

Finally, we close with two caveats that are in order. First, it is impossible to know whether Mun'im Idris, Nanan Sukarna, or anyone else was aware that the conclusion of sodomy based on the physical appearance of Noordin Top's corpse was based on discredited science. From the example of Egypt, it is clear that some states continue to base their juridical claims of homosexual behavior on Tardieu's methods. Whether Mun'im or the Indonesian police spread this rumor knowing it was false or not is impossible to ascertain. That being said, the underlying motive behind the accusation seems clear: to discredit Noordin Top among his supporters and would-be supporters in the ways discussed above.

Second, we note the connection between this case and other cases in Southeast Asia in which rumors served key political purposes, as the importance of this case would be easy to overstate. Although the authors have spent a good deal of time conducting research into the topic, especially concerning the viral spread of the story, it was not a widely discussed story. The YouTube videos described in this chapter have comparatively few views, reflecting the low level of internet penetration in Indonesia and suggesting a somewhat insular community of like-minded users, at least among those who profess antipathy toward Malaysia.

There have been similar rumors and deviant sexually related accusations made toward prominent persons in the past. In 1998, accusations of sodomy directed at Malaysian Deputy Prime Minister Anwar Ibrahim led to his dismissal and subsequent imprisonment until 2004. It was also rumored that Anwar was gay and had multiple adulterous relationships. Anwar insisted on his innocence throughout, and there were clear political motives for cutting his political legs out from under him: he was viewed as a symbol of the reform movement, but it was clear that Mahathir Mohammed did not want to give up as Prime Minister. His arrest helped take the wind from the sails of the reform movement in Malaysia, and it produced few long-lasting effects as it did in Indonesia (beginning with the ouster of President Suharto).

Similarly, Habib Rizieq of the Jakarta-based *Front Pembela Islam*, a quasi-legal group of thugs engaged in extortion and protest nominally on behalf of Islam (and native Jakartans, although the movement has spread throughout Indonesia) was rumored to be in possession of pornography following his

140 *C. Lundry and P.H. Cheong*

arrest after an FPI demonstration turned violent at Jakarta's National Monument. Although not charged with a pornography-related offense, he was imprisoned for the violence. The case of Noordin Top, however, is perhaps the first time a *post mortem* rumor of sexual deviance has been spread in order to malign a terrorist. If this strategy is eventually deemed to be a success, perhaps we may see it used again in the future, and perhaps on a terrorist captured alive. We may also see the emergence of a "rumor mosaic" if similar kinds of damning rumors are spread about other extremists and supporters of terror, for example branding them as sexual deviants or hypocritical Muslims (see Bernardi and Ruston, Chapter 3, this volume). In this case, the Noordin Top story appears to have been a successfully employed instance of rumor as an anti-insurgency countermeasure, primarily, perhaps, because of the nature of the source of the rumor as well as its titillating nature, which allowed it to become a meme, gain traction, and spread.

Notes

1 There are variations on the spelling of his name, but the authors will use this spelling for consistency. Subsequent references refer to him by the name Noordin, considered analogous to the last or family name in the West. This applies to references to other individuals in the chapter as well.

2 Nanan stated, "Saya tidak tahu soal itu. Tapi rahasia kedokteran seharusnya itu dirahasiakan. Adak ode etiknya" ("I don't know about that problem. But a medical secret has to be kept secret. There is a code of ethics.") (*Kompas* 2009a).

3 The Indonesia-based jihadist website Prisoner of Joy, for example, posts accounts of the burials of terrorists following their demises, including Bagus Budi Pranato, who was killed with Noordin (Prisoner of Joy 2009a), and Syaifudin Zuhri and Muhammad Syahrir, who played significant roles in the July 17 hotel bombings and who were killed in a raid after Noordin's death (Prisoner of Joy 2009b). Others, such as Air Setiawan and Eko Joko, have been similarly lauded. The posts describe signs that those killed are *shaheed* (martyrs), such as references to the fresh smell of their corpses, blood flowing days after their deaths, and a green bird flying above during their burials, all references to martyrdom in various Hadith.

4 *Ar Rahmah* is a jihadist website based in Indonesia. Its founder, Muhammed Jibriel Abdul Rahman, is currently being tried for links to the July 2009 Ritz-Carlton and J.W. Marriott bombings in Jakarta.

5 George Rousseau (2008) describes Tardieu's debt to sixteenth- to seventeenth-century author on legal medicine, Paolo Zacchia.

6 Prior convictions of sodomy relied on confessions, often obtained through torture, over physical examinations; see Perry (1989).

7 He noted that the habitual sodomite could be identified by his "curled hair, made-up skin, open collar, waist tucked in to highlight the figure; fingers, ears, chest loaded with jewelry; the whole body exuding an odor of the most penetrating perfumes; and in the hand, a handkerchief, flowers, or some needlework; such is the stranger, revolting and rightfully suspect physiognomy that betrays the pederast" (Peniston 2004: 54). These descriptions are laughable today, but his reputation gave them credibility at the time.

8 Rosario (1997: 75–77) notes that the concern over the criminality of sodomites was not a physical concern, but rather due to their "travesties of class and gender"; effeminate affectations were associated with aristocracy, and homosexuals of low

The case of terrorist Noordin Top   141

birth who took these affectations were seen as threatening the social order. Blackmail was another concern. See also Thompson (1996). These claims are repeated in the context of the late-colonial Dutch East Indies. According to Boellstorff (2005: 54), "sex between men seems to have become seen as threatening the racial hierarchy upon which colonial authority rested ...the product of global connection and a threat to social order."

9 *Topix.com* is a popular news aggregator providing localized news.

10 Yuli Esnawati Pengamat, "Jenazah Yang Meninggal Dalam Penggerebekan Di Solo Bukanlah Noordin M Top," Facebook posting, October 1, 2009. Online www.facebook.com/topic.php?uid=34617474664&topic=12213 (accessed 20 November 2009).

11 Al Chaidar is a researcher from Univeritas Malikussaleh in Aceh, in the Faculty of Social Science and Political Science.

12 *Memetic isomorphism* is the process by which a meme or rapidly spreading idea or image on the internet retains its basic elements but is changed in order to fit a different circumstance. In this case, the Mas Selamat wanted poster that originated from the Singaporean site TalkingCock.com became a meme through its viral dissemination, and then Indonesian users adopted the poster's template (including the wording and fonts) but substituted photoshopped images of Noordin Top. The original TalkingCock.com photo can be found online: www.talkingcock.com/html/article.php?sid=2487 (accessed 15 December 2009).

13 The most watched YouTube video under the search "noordin top" is "Detik Detik Penyerbuan Noordin M Top 08/08/09". Originally online at: www.youtube.com/watch?v=rtXp_mo6A3o (accessed 12 August 2009). The video is actually of the August 8 siege in Temanggung, which was not actually Noordin Top. It has over 64,000 views, and it is a rebroadcast of a Televisindo news report, with no sound. Its posting date is August 7, so it must have been posted early in the day on August 8 in Indonesia, and therefore was one, if not the first, of the videos posted, which would help explain its popularity. The video has since been removed, but a copy can be seen at: www.youtube.com/watch?v=7MhHIsnYKBg (accessed 1 July 2012).

14 This video has since been removed from YouTube.

15 *Nusantara* is a term for the Indonesian archipelago based on Sanskrit. It can also refer to Malaysia, or the greater Malay world including Indonesia, Malaysia, Brunei, Singapore, and the Philippines. The video has since been removed from YouTube.

16 The video has since been removed from YouTube

17 Recent spats between Malaysia and Indonesia include the use of a Balinese dance, *Tari Pendent*, the song "Rasa Sayang," and *batik*—all claimed by Indonesians as Indonesian—to promote Malaysian tourism. In the dispute over the Ambalat Islands, the World Court awarded two disputed islands to Malaysia in 2002, rankling Indonesian nationalist sentiment.

18 The mainstream Indonesian media accepted both of the assertions concerning Noordin Top: that he indeed had a funnel-shaped anus, and that a funnel shaped anus was indeed a sign of sodomy. Some argued that it may have been evidence that he had hidden explosives in his anus. With regard to GAYa Nusantara (GN), in a personal communication with spokesman Budi, he acknowledged that he had heard the accusations and the medical evidence to support them, but that GN had no position on the matter. He stated that most Indonesians would not care about the matter, that if Noordin Top was gay it was his business and nobody else's, that Indonesian bloggers were wrong to make generalizations about Malaysians based on one person, and that he had no idea why Noordin's anus would be shaped in such a way (Budi, personal communication, January 11, 2010). That a spokesman for the leading gay rights organization was unwilling to refute claims made on discredited forensic science from the nineteenth century, claims that have been

refuted by gay activists elsewhere, is incredible. The accusation of bisexuality against Noordin continues to this day, where the connection between fundibuliform anus and anal sex appears to be taken as a given, even among gay rights supporters (Bramantyo Prijosusilo 2010).

19 A recent blog post by Indonesian Imbalo (2010) about making pilgrimages to gravesites included a visit to the grave of Noordin Top. In a conversation with Noordin's family, he was apparently told of two green birds appearing during Noordin's burial. Coming from such a source, however, it is clear that the statement reflects his family's interest in providing some kind of positive legacy for Noordin as a martyr.

8 Anxiety and rumor

Exploratory analysis of Twitter posts during the Mumbai terrorist attack

Onook Oh, Manish Agrawal, and H. Raghav Rao

Introduction[1]

Loss of life or damage to property is not the only possible outcomes of a terrorist attack. Other consequences, not always documented or reported, can include psychological harm. Literature in health and psychiatry reports that the experience of terrorism and war can create psychological trauma in individual minds, which may manifest itself as symptoms of anxiety, mental disorder, and stress (Levan 2006). On the other hand, social psychology researchers contend that terrifying collective experiences can lead to group anxiety at the community and/or national levels (Anthony 1973).

In their research on rumor during World War II, Allport and Postman (1947) showed that war and its attendant collective emotional tension (such as anxiety and fear) creates conditions for rumor-mongering. Just as disease is a manifestation of the state of the body, they understood rumor as the disguised expressions of an individual's state of mind. In other words, rumor is a verbal outlet to release emotional tensions such as anxiety, fear, or concern in uncomfortable and unsatisfactory conditions. As for rumor dissemination in a wartime state, they surmised that, unless properly controlled, deleterious or depressing rumors can decrease national morale and plant distrust in government (Allport and Lepkin 1945).

The basic tenets of rumor research in social psychology are that (1) rumor-mongering and the dissemination of rumors are the function of anxiety (Anthony 1973) and (2) "in war time … the conditions for rumor are optimal" (Allport and Postman 1947: 34).

This study applies rumor theory (in the social psychology domain) to analyze the relationship between anxiety and rumor dissemination by analyzing tweets during the Mumbai terrorist attack of November 2008. This was arguably the worst terrorist attack against civilians in the history of India. Through multiple coordinated attacks on a variety of locations throughout Mumbai, the incident killed 165 and injured 304 people in the financial capital of India (Ministry of External Affairs [India] nd). All these scenes were broadcast live through India's mainstream TV media for almost sixty hours without restraint. The scenes were nerve-racking and terrifying enough to create anxiety and ambiguity in the minds of the Indian people (Raman 2010).

144 *O. Oh, M. Agrawal, and H.R. Rao*

Much like the wartime conditions studied by Allport and Postman, we assume that a terrorist situation provides an optimal condition for rumor spread at the community or national level. In addition, we expand the assumption that, in the virtual space of the internet, where the globe is connected through like-minded social network websites and traditional media on a real-time basis, rumor can reach countries half-a-world away synchronously.

One unique feature of the Mumbai terrorist attack of November 2008 was the dynamic participation of networked citizens through social networking websites to report eyewitness accounts of the terrorism situation. On November 26, 2008, as soon as the terrorist attack was mounted, a group of people voluntarily flocked to the Mumbai Twitter pages within minutes (twitter.com/mumbai), and began to transmit eyewitness accounts of the terrorist attack. These tweets were so immediate and spread so rapidly that they drew media attention around the world.

However, despite its contribution, a few concerns were raised regarding the reliability of Twitter as a news source. One concern was that Twitter users repeated headlines they saw or heard from local media instead of posting their own observations. Another concern was that many rumors were circulated without any check. In other words, there was no mechanism to identify and control Twitter reports to minimize fake reports and confirm facts (Gahran 2008; Kievit 2008).

To understand this weakness and to take advantage of Twitter as a participatory open reporting system in the terrorism context, this chapter analyzes the Mumbai tweets from the perspectives of anxiety and rumor. The main focus of this research is to identify the correspondence between the prevalence of anxiety and level of rumor in the context of a terrorist incident. For this analysis, we use rumor theory in the social psychology domain and perform content analysis of Mumbai Twitter posts. This chapter concludes with a few suggested measures to control rumor dissemination over social networking websites in the terrorism context. The contribution of this study is to provide a way to understand rumor-mongering conditions in social media and to control rumor spread via Twitter. The study is expected to enhance the usefulness of Twitter as a participatory emergency reporting system in the terrorism setting.

Theories of rumor

Modern rumor research started with the ground-breaking work of Allport and his colleagues. Their research was based on the analysis of rumors that were widespread during World War II. Expanding on their empirical research, they postulated importance and ambiguity as the key variables in rumor transmission (Allport and Lepkin 1945). Their model of rumor transmission and its description are as follows:

$R \sim i \times a$

Anxiety and rumor 145

[T]his formula means that the amount of rumor circulation will vary with the importance of the subject to the individuals concerned *times* the ambiguity of the evidence pertaining to the topic at issue.

(Allport and Postman 1947: 33)

In this model, the importance (i) represents the affective factor and ambiguity (a), the cognitive factor in rumor transmission (Chorus 1953: 313–34). The affective factor implies that for a rumor to propagate it requires a like-minded group of individuals who find the subject matter important. Consequently, the rumor is more likely to disseminate within a homogeneous circle and less likely to pass across a border of heterogeneous communities. The cognitive factor indicates the need for cognitive interpretation to extract meaning (the rumor content) out of the level of informational ambiguity that is perceived by the community at hand.

According to Allport and Postman (1947: 37), as "our minds protest against chaos," ambiguity and uncertainty cause "intellectual pressure along with the emotional," both of which need to be released. For instance, macabre rumors circulate to release anxiety, scandalous rumor to ooze out sexual desire, and pipe-dream rumors to exemplify feelings of hope or optimism. Simply put, one facet of rumors is to craft a story to "*relieve, justify,* and *explain*" an individual's emotional pressure (Allport and Postman 1947: 36). In contrast, as a positive facet of rumor-mongering, when the uncertain situation or ambiguous information is directed to intellectual pressure, it turns into cognitive endeavors to extract meaning to reduce uncertainty and thereby make the impending event easy to bear.

Anthony (1973) presented a more parsimonious explanation of the rumor transmission phenomenon by subsuming the "importance" and "ambiguity" variables of the rumor formula under the single concept of anxiety. Clarifying the implication of the "importance" variable—which was not well defined by Allport and Postman—she argues that the "importance" variable of rumor can be determined by identifying whether individuals or groups feel anxious about the rumor content. It means that, although rumor recipients may not feel anxious about *un*-important rumor content, if they feel anxious about the rumor content, then it reflects the fact that rumors are important. In this regard, the level of anxiety functions as an indicator of the "importance" variable in rumor transmission.

Unlike Allport and Postman, who explain anxiety as effects of informational and situational "ambiguity," Anthony (1973: 92) separates the anxiety into two dimensions to refine this anxiety concept: "(a) the anxiety level, either chronic or acute, of the group that is to receive the rumor, and (b) the anxiety caused by the rumor content." The first dimension of anxiety exists prior to rumor receipt, and the second one is triggered by ambiguous rumor content. Applying these two dimensions of anxiety to her empirical study, she found that people who had a higher level of chronic anxiety (the first dimension of anxiety) tend to be more active in receiving and relaying rumor to their acquaintances. The conclusion, then, is that the requirement for rumor transmission is that the anxiety caused by ambiguous rumor content (the second dimension of anxiety) and the anxiety level of the group (the first dimension of anxiety) determines the extent of rumor transmission. Using Anthony's anxiety theory, we can refine the explanation of rumor function as follows:

$$R \sim i \times a \times 1 / c^2$$

Critical sensibility (c) follows the notion of Chorus (1953), outlined earlier. This updated formula means that, as the rumor listener's critical sensibility grows, the rumor spread will weaken or stop. In reverse, if the listener's critical sense is low, the rumor is more likely to travel. In this revised formula, c is not a constant, but varies with individual situation, importance, and ambiguity.

The degree of "importance" (i) is a summation of the first and second dimensions of anxiety. Ambiguity (a) indicates the level of ambiguity embedded in the rumor content, and is the source of the second dimension of anxiety.

Although Allport and Postman (1947) did not include anxiety in their rumor formula as a distinct variable, the important role of anxiety in rumor transmission is repeatedly stressed throughout their text. Including Anthony (1973), many later rumor researchers related the anxiety as an indicator of the "importance" variable, and confirmed significant relationships between anxiety and rumor-mongering through empirical studies. As Rosnow's (1991) meta-analysis of the rumor literature shows, anxiety has been the most significant variable in rumor research, followed by the uncertainty and credulity variables.

Accordingly, based on the prior rumor literature, we describe rumor-mongering conditions with three variables of anxiety (as an indicator of the importance of rumor content), ambiguity (or uncertainty), and critical sensibility (or credulity). That is, the most favorable rumor-mongering condition involves high anxiety, high ambiguity, and low critical sensibility. For example, as Rosnow and Fine (1976: 52) exemplified, "disasters and other crises are characterized by high importance, high ambiguity, low critical sensibility, and many rumors." This is consistent with Allport and Postman's (1947: 34) conclusion that "in wartime [...] the conditions for rumor are optimal."

Rumors during the Mumbai terrorist attack

The rumor and anxiety framework provides a useful lens with which to revisit the Mumbai terrorist event of November 2008. We assume that, similar to wartime or disaster conditions, terrorist attacks against civilians in a populous city can cause high anxiety, high ambiguity, and low critical sensibility.

One distinction of the Mumbai terrorist attack from previous ones in India was the dynamic participation of networked citizens through social networking websites. Within minutes of the initial attack on November 26, an eyewitness

Anxiety and rumor 147

of the attacks with the user ID "vinu" uploaded a stream of pictures at the photo-sharing site Flickr.[3] Almost simultaneously, a group of people voluntarily formed a Twitter page (www.twitter.com/mumbai), and began to spread eyewitness accounts of the terrorist attack with photos, links, or texts. The rapid Twitter posts were so up to date and real that worldwide media outlets such as BBC, CBC, CNN, NPR, and Al Jazeera interviewed Twitter users and cited the Twitter posts as their news sources. Literally, "much of the news about the Mumbai attacks reached the world via Twitter" by rapidly spreading to worldwide media Twitter users' eyewitness accounts of the situation in Mumbai (Kievit 2008).

However, despite the rapid propagation of incident reports, a few concerns were raised regarding the reliability of Twitter as a news source (Cellan-Jones 2008; Gahran 2008). One concern was that Twitter users repeated headlines they saw or heard from local media instead of posting their own observations. Another concern was that the mainstream media companies cited Twitter posts as their news sources without checking the reliability of the source message. In some cases, the indicator of source reliability in the mainstream media was merely a link to Twitter pages. Indeed, the supply and distribution chain of Twitter reports was largely composed of (1) Twitter users' citation of mainstream media (especially local live TV), (2) media companies' citation of Twitter posts, and (3) Twitter's link to other sites. In fact, many tweets started with "I heard." For example, some tweets said, "NDTV reports," or had no source identifiers. First-person eyewitness reports that might start with "I saw" were rare.

For example, on the second day of the attacks, *BBC News* (2008) reported that:

Indian government asks for live Twitter updates from Mumbai to cease immediately. "ALL LIVE UPDATES-PLEASE STOP TWEETERING about #Mumbai police and military operations," a tweet says.

The BBC cited this report from a blog,[4] which in turn quoted from a Mumbai Twitter page.[5] After tracking down the source of the message, a motivated blogger calling herself Gahran (2008) found that a junior high school student in Boston posted the original message on the Mumbai Twitter page. According to Gahran's email correspondence with this student, she came to know that the "rumor [*sic*] started via another twitter post that retweeted from another person that was a trusted source IN Mumbai." Also, the student said that he posted another tweet that:

It was confirmed by Mumbai police on video that they don't want live updates. Don't think they mentioned Twitter but it is possible that they did. If not, then that is the rumor that evolved, yet still good practice.[6]

Despite this well-meaning report posted from a country half-a-world away, many tweets were hearsay—rumor—in that they were information received

148   *O. Oh, M. Agrawal, and H.R. Rao*

from ambiguous sources that could not be sufficiently substantiated, or were distorted in transit from mouth to mouth, link to link, link to media, or media to link. It has not been determined whether the message originated from an Indian government source, a local TV interview with a police officer, or was simply misinformation. It still remains a rumor, which may contain a residual particle of truth. However, it is almost impossible to tell what is fact, imaginary elaboration, or distortion. As of now, no authoritative comment on this particular rumor is available.

Related to the above-mentioned tweet, another tweet that has an ambiguous source shows some symptoms of anxiety about collaborative open posts on the military operations of the Indian government against terrorist groups in Mumbai:

> #mumbai RT remember when tweeting details that it is CONFIRMED terrorists have satphone [satellite phone, author corrected] access to net sources + twitter has been noticed @celebcorps, 27 November, 2008, 1:50am.

What we can infer from these two examples of tweets is the fear and anxiety of citizens that terrorist groups equipped with satellite phones may monitor and adversely use live tweets on military and terrorist operations to harm citizens (Oh *et al.* 2011). Using the rumor formula, what we identify is that (1) the Mumbai terrorist situation provided optimal rumor-mongering conditions, and (2) lots of ambiguous information was charged with anxiety.

Analysis of Mumbai Twitter posts

This section describes the correlation patterns between rumor and anxiety found in the Mumbai Twitter page. The main purpose of this section is to verify the significant role of anxiety in rumor dissemination by applying the theory of rumor of Allport and Postman (1947) and Anthony (1973) to a virtual setting during the Mumbai terrorist attack.

For this analysis, we collected all 932 Twitter posts from the Mumbai terror incident page (www.twitter.com/mumbai) during the period of the Mumbai terrorist attack from November 26 to November 29, 2008 and one additional day of November 30. Tweets from November 30 were included in the data sample because many users continued to report situational information after the terrorist attack. This site was formed by a voluntary group of people to report situational information on terrorist attacks in Mumbai. Through this site, online users expressed condolence, encouraged blood donation, posted help-line contact numbers, broadcasted information on their personal safety to family members, reported eyewitness accounts of the situation, and posted links to other news sources about the attack.

The updates on Twitter were so fast they attracted the attention of media outlets such as BBC, CBC, CNN, NPR, and Al Jazeera, playing a significant

Anxiety and rumor 149

role in relaying situational information around the world (Kievit 2008). For this active role of the Mumbai Twitter site, some users added comments such as "twitter rocks – I am getting accurate and better information than MSM like Times Now!" or "CNN has been playing catch up to twitter."[7]

However, despite the rapid updates and widespread dissemination of situational information through Twitter, lots of confusion existed on the site because of the many unidentified sources of information. Many users expressed concerns regarding the reliability of news sources, identified specific users as propagators of unreliable tweets, expressed distrust in media reports in general or Twitter specifically, and requested Twitter users to post only direct observations:

> @Nadia_Sivana that was from earlier. there were massive rumors going around the city that caused panic. news channels had 2 b blacked out
>
> friend in babulnath #mumbai got a house call from the police – to stay indoors, not heed rumors!! MP lives close by;)
>
> @cool_technocrat where did you get that info? its crap. all of this is live on TV. pls stop spreading such stuff without verifying #mumbai
>
> @narayananh sms going around says 5lakhs (500,000 in Hindi [*author added*]). all rumors I think #mumbai
>
> @Kimota please read it carefully – BBC says they got it from a tweet. These rumors have been tweeted all day. BBC is NOT god!!! #mumbai
>
> @innherhike stay calm, @joomp is just instigating a virtual #mumbai riot. everyone should just ignore him. sigh. easier said than done i know mumbai Please tweet only direct observations, RT rumors are just decreasing the signal/noise ratio.

To estimate the level of rumor and anxiety in Twitter, we conducted a content analysis on Twitter posts that could potentially develop into rumors. Following the rumor-mongering condition model of prior research as a baseline for content analysis, we used two classes of lexicon as in Table 8.1: one for rumor and another for emotional tension which represents anxiety (Allport and Postman 1947).

The rumor lexicon chosen implies a subjective connotation that one cannot sufficiently substantiate evidence for their reports. It includes tweets that are not first-person eyewitness observations, or do not provide solid reference sources for their reports. To take into account the contextual implication of reports, we also compared the rumor lexicon that we created against Twitter posts and determined additional words from tweets to be included into the rumor lexicon. The final rumor lexicon that we used for this analysis is presented in Table 8.1.

The anxiety lexicon selection process followed a procedure similar to the rumor words selection process. After defining the anxiety lexicon that represents emotional tension, we closely read through all tweets to check the contextual decorum of the words and to find additional words to be included in

150 *O. Oh, M. Agrawal, and H.R. Rao*

Table 8.1 Rumor word and anxiety word list defined.

Word Class	Rumor Lexicon	Anxiety Lexicon
Verb	expect, might, consider, think, assume, deem, sound, appear, claim, hear/heard, seems/seems to be, believe, doubt, say, said to be, said to have, might, guess, looks like, thought, is helping, confirm, alert, possible,	hate, bitch about,
Adverb	quite, supposedly, perhaps, apparently, maybe, almost, probably, likely	
Adjective	wrong, pretty sure, not sure, unsure, unclear, unreal, surreal, possible,	wild, crashing, pissed, erie, sad, haunting, heartbreaking, sad, scared, painful, stressed, confused, maddening, heartened, terrible, disturbed, overwhelmed, moronic
Noun	belief, someone, story, gossip, anecdote, buzz, tale, rumor, possibility	fatigue, shock, anger, grief, moron, horror, fear, panic, outrage, hatred, retaliation
Unclassifiable	who says?, pls stop spreading such stuff without verifying	F&%@, shit, breaks my heart, heart is beating fast, get the eff out of there, what can we do beyond rhetoric & candles?,

the anxiety lexicon. Most of these words implied emotional tension such as shock, concern, anger, sorrow, blame, or stress that stemmed from the terrorist attack and its attendant uncertain conditions. Example of tweets which contain emotional tension are as follows:

> very sad 2 hear abt the deaths and piling bodies – heart goes out to the 2yr old Israeli girl who lost her parents in Nariman House #mumbai
>
> How will India bounce back? sadly I have no faith in the leadership to take control and stop these heinous acts!
>
> TOTALLY! and unfortunately our police/armed forces are STILL coming off as idiotic! #mumbai

The final emotional tension lexicon which represents anxiety is presented in Table 8.1.

For the coding of Twitter data, two graduate students majoring in management information systems were employed. Before coding, three meetings were held to understand the context of the Mumbai terror attack and the Mumbai Twitter page. It was ensured that the graduate students understood both lexicons of anxiety and rumor. The coding was made in two rounds. The first round was a pilot test with a randomly chosen 100 data sample. In this pilot coding, the kappa value was 0.78. Although acceptable, to improve the mutual agreement, one author moderated discussion with the coders on disagreed data. Through this discussion, the lexicon list was slightly refined. With the final lexicons in Table 8.1, the full 982 data sample was coded. The second coding produced a kappa value of 0.87. The kappa coefficient represents the extent to which the probability of agreed understanding between coders is higher than that which can be obtained by chance (Krippendorff 1980). The remaining disagreed data were discussed and recoded by the first author and two original coders.

Based on the resulting coding, we counted all tweets that implied content for potential rumors and emotional tensions using one-hour time intervals from November 26 to November 30, 2008. The results are shown in Figure 8.1.

Figure 8.1 shows a strong correlational pattern between rumor and emotional tension. The potential rumor content accounts for 23.11 percent (227/982), and emotional tension content 13.14 percent (129/982) of total tweets. That is, following the logic of Anthony's rumor formulation, it can be interpreted that one unit of emotional tension corresponds to 1.76 rumors (23.12/13.14) on the Mumbai Twitter page. However, it should be noted that a more quantitative analysis of the correlational pattern and resulting numbers needs to be carried out.

General implications for rumor control

This section suggests implications for rumor control based on the rumor formula and prior research. As many rumor researchers have pointed out, wartime and natural disaster situations are optimal for rumor dissemination on account of their high levels of anxiety, high levels of situational and

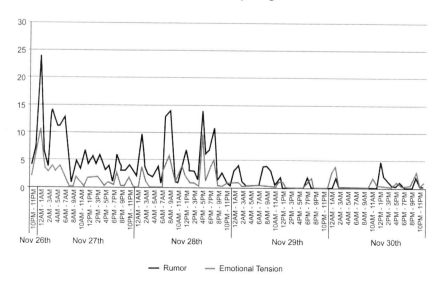

Figure 8.1 Representation of rumor and emotional tension/anxiety

152   O. Oh, M. Agrawal, and H.R. Rao

informational ambiguity, and low critical sense of affected people (Allport and Postman 1947; Rosnow and Fine 1976). They argue that, unless properly managed, negative rumors can lead to a decrease in national morale and distrust in the capacity of government to protect citizens from emergency situations.

An examination of rumors about floods in the city of Port Jervis, New York, in 1955 shows that, when the state government failed to control the momentum of threatening rumors, it caused collective anxiety, which stimulated the exodus of thousands of citizens from their city (Danzig *et al.* 1958). Following Shibutani's (1966) rumor theory, this particular rumor can be seen as mass information-seeking behavior that occurred under conditions of collective informational ambiguity and anxiety. That is, when proper information is not provided to citizens in a timely manner, be it through mass media or loud-speakers, citizens under stress begin to craft stories that are circulated as "improvised news" to fill the hole of collective ambiguity and anxiety (Aguirre and Tierney 2001).

The symptoms of rumor control failure and its deleterious effects were also visible on the Mumbai Twitter pages, when there was no authoritative voice to clarify or correct uncertain information.

> Our Home Minister said "such small incidents happen" http://tr.im/1mqb moronic a*hole #mumbai
>
> How will India bounce back? sadly I have no faith in the leadership to take control and stop these heinous acts!
>
> from karmayog #mumbai We are witnessing a lack of leadership from elected or appointed public representatives, bureaucrats, spiritual leader
>
> I'm super unimpressed with our police force though. Fat, potbellied with tiny revolvers to stand off against AK 47s. #mumbai
>
> amazing ... the shots were definitely coming from AK-47 and our police are there with no life jackets + shit shot rifles! ill-equipped

In the organizational context, Rosnow's (1991) suggestion of rumor control measures is also typically provided in the framework of the rumor formula. Similar to Allport and Postman's suggestion, Rosnow's rumor control measures highlight that reduction in the anxiety level of citizens is the key step to control rumor transmission. As a first rumor control measure, he suggests "[anticipating] events in which anxiety and uncertainty might be optimum for threatening rumors to take hold, and to defuse the situation before damaging consequences develop" (Rosnow 1991: 493). As a next rumor control principle, Rosnow advises paying attention to the types of rumor that can reveal the source of anxiety and uncertainty. In other words, rather than focusing on the rumor itself, he suggests suppressing the source of anxiety that motivates people to spread rumors. Rosnow (1991: 494) insists that the typical police manual style of control measure, "Get the facts promptly and circulate them as widely as possible," is not a good strategy, because it does not consider the main cause of rumor-mongering—anxiety—in its strategy. That is, the focus of his advice is to give priority to the detection and suppression of rumors exhibiting high-anxiety rumor before circulating facts or refuting rumors. Finally, if the aforementioned control measures do not work for operationally sensitive rumors, he suggests that legal action may be appropriate, "If the source can be identified (and presumably the rumor is false), then legal action against the rumor-mongers to enjoin and call attention to their malicious behavior might be considered" (Rosnow 1991: 494).

Such strategies of rumor control provide some insights into developing rumor control measures in a collaborative online setting such as the Mumbai Twitter page. Considering the strength of Web 2.0 technology as an open and collaborative platform, rumor reports generated through voluntary citizens would be beneficial not only in collecting important rumors but in creating a symbiotic relationship between citizens and government in anti-terrorist endeavors. Second, the identification of postings charged with emotional tension, be they through monitoring or automated text-mining, may help prioritize which rumors need to be controlled or addressed first.

However, there still remains a problem with regard to rumor control. Allport and Postman (1947) note that, when people are obsessed with fears, hates, and insidious intentions, the accurate release of information or even the refutation of false stories cannot silence the motivated tongues of rumor spreaders. Although a rumor study by Bordia *et al.* (2005) demonstrates that active rumor denial by reliable sources can control rumor spread, one should be cautious in generalizing these results to the terrorism context. This particular study was conducted in an artificial setting, and the rumors tested were about a computer virus. That is, the level of anxiety associated with a computer virus may not be comparable with that found during a terrorist incident.

The issues of anxiety and uncertainty in the terrorism context raise questions about rumor research which approaches rumor from the perspective of problem-solving or sense-making. For example, rumor research by Bordia and DiFonzo (2004) mainly approaches rumors as a social interaction process to reduce informational uncertainty.

This approach pays more attention to cognitive aspects rather than affective aspects of anxiety. That is, apart from the pressure of emotional tension, they assume that human beings continually try to extract meaning from an uncertain environment. They view sense-making as a collective process of reducing uncertainties to reach an agreement in the community. This notion, we would argue, involves relatively stable environments compared with the setting of a terrorist incident. For instance, to develop a sense-making view of rumor, Bordia *et al.* (2005: 38) investigated rumors such as "Michal Jordan is returning to professional basketball," or "A virus titled 'good times' is being spread by an electronic mail message." In this study, they observed how people in online discussion groups remove uncertain information and arrive at consensual meaning. In this setting, the sense-making or problem-solving view of rumor research assumes a cognitively manageable environment on a

154 O. Oh, M. Agrawal, and H.R. Rao

small scale; at best ten people in a group. However, the rumors found in the Mumbai incident seem to exemplify the affective side of anxiety, which overwhelms our cognitive capacity to extract meaning. In a terrorism setting, the sense-making process involves, at a minimum, diverse entities of government, national security forces, and citizens, which require sophisticated and costly information systems to coordinate them. Therefore, the sense-making view of rumor needs a refinement of the concepts pertaining to uncertainty and anxiety to enable problem-solving and uncertainty removal in the terrorism context. This is an important and challenging task upon which more research is needed.

Conclusion

The Mumbai terrorist attacks of November 2008 raise many questions about Web 2.0, social reporting, and its relationship with rumor dissemination. Given that Twitter's maximum 140-character input interface is best compatible with mobile communication devices such as wireless smart phones, it does have a great potential to be used as an emergency reporting system to relay situational information almost in real time during natural disasters and terrorist attacks (Mills *et al.* 2009).

At the same time, the fact that 140-character short text messages can only deliver sketchy details of a situation without detailed description can cause ambiguity in collaborative social reporting. Especially in the environment of a terrorist attack, which can generate high levels of anxiety and low critical sensibility, social reporting through short text message facilitates rumor-mongering by delivering only sketchy details of situational information in an ambiguous manner.

Two open questions remain with regard to using Twitter as a social reporting system. One, from the citizen's perspective, is about how to enable people to submit accurate information through Twitter during an emergency situation. Another, from the governmental and rumor control perspectives, is about how to reduce uncertainties when ambiguous rumors are circulated. The virtual rumor clinic seems to be a promising strategy to be tested. In other words, while encouraging citizens' collaborative social reporting through Twitter, prompt response systems need to be put in place to (1) refute high-anxiety rumors with professional interpretations of such rumors and (2) distribute such a refutation through multiple communication channels such as retweets, cross-links, RSS, email, text message, or live TV, etc.

Notes

1 Acknowledgment: we thank the editors and referees for their valuable feedback to improve this chapter. We would like to acknowledge NSF for funding this research under grants IIS-0926371 and IIS-0926376. The usual disclaimer applies. The work of the third author has been (partly) supported by Sogang Business School's World Class University Project (R31–20002) funded by Korea Research Foundation.

2 Where: i = 1st dimension of anxiety + 2nd dimension of anxiety; a = ambiguity in the rumor content; c = critical sensibility.
3 See www.flickr.com/photos/vinu/sets/72157610144709049/ (accessed January 3, 2010). The user "vinu" has since removed his photographs from Flickr.
4 See www.lllj.net/blog/?p=555 (accessed January 8, 2010). [Since deleted, although a cached copy can be accessed via the *Wayback Machine*: http://web.archive.org/web/20081201201311/http://www.lllj.net/blog/?p=555 (accessed May 21, 2012).
5 www.twitter.com/Mumbai/status/1026558518 (accessed January 8, 2010).
6 www.twitter.com/mumbaiupdates/status/1026807670 and www.twitter.com/mumbaiupdates/status/1026808444 (accessed January 8, 2010).
7 www.twitter.com/mumbai (accessed April 27, 2010).

9 Rumor—the evil twin of strategic communication

What "white" propaganda can learn from "gray"

Anthony Olcott

Introduction

The Shared Values Initiative (SVI) initiated by the State Department in the wake of 9/11 was a classic example of a sender-controlled messaging effort, designed to provide information that was important to the sender. There was no indication before this initiative was undertaken, however, that the target of this effort—Muslim populations around the world—actually desired this information, nor did the effort itself give them any reason why they should. Not surprisingly, the campaign collapsed. This chapter argues that this campaign, and the institutional assumptions and predispositions that lay behind it, could reasonably be replaced by information campaigns that address issues of genuine concern to the target audience, rather than the issues which the senders think the target *should* want addressed. Because such information—what audiences really worry about—is difficult to obtain, the chapter further argues that the State Department, and other message senders, could profit from techniques developed during World War II for understanding and making use of rumors. Public communicators may hate rumors, but rumors achieve easily what public communicators usually cannot—they generate as if from nowhere and propagate exuberantly, propelling themselves, as one scholar of rumor wrote, "like torpedoes." This chapter argues that rumor should be seen as more than an evil to be battled—rather, it should be employed as a guide for generating and shaping more effective public communications.

The Shared Values Initiative

Within a month of the September 11, 2001 attacks on the World Trade Towers and the Pentagon, the US State Department began a concerted effort to reach out to Arab and Muslim audiences worldwide. Central to that effort was the hiring of Charlotte Beers, who had been a senior executive in both J. Walter Thompson and Ogilvy & Mather, two of the world's largest advertising firms. Brought to Washington, DC as Under Secretary of State and charged with "refurbish[ing] America's image abroad" (*Business Week* 2001),

Rumour and strategic communication   157

Beers aggressively upped the output of messaging to the target audience, overseeing the creation of magazines *Muslim Life in America* and *Hi*, expanding support for the existing radio station *Sawa*, and initiating the process that resulted in the creation of the TV channel *Al-Hurra*.

The intended centerpiece of the campaign, however, was a suite of five "mini-documentaries" that profiled different "ordinary American Muslims," with the goal of illustrating that there is no contradiction between being a Muslim and being an American. Called the "Shared Values Initiative," and dubbed into Arabic, Bahasa, Urdu, and French, the five videos were to be aired during Ramadan 2002 across the Muslim world, partly through free placements, and partly as paid advertisements, for which purpose $15 million was budgeted (US Government Accountability Office [GAO] 2003: 12). Although it is difficult now to be certain where the ads were aired (a surprising amount of the materials related to the campaign, including many of the State Department transcripts of statements by Beers, have disappeared from the web), it appears as though one or more of the five spots ran as paid advertisements in Pakistan, Malaysia, Indonesia, and Kuwait, and as free material in Kazakhstan and Azerbaijan (US Department of State 2003). They also ran as paid content on unspecified "pan-Arab TV satellite stations," permitting the State Department to claim a total viewership of 288 million, with "earned media (press coverage) reaching countless more" (US Department of State 2004b).

What the report quoted above did not mention was that that 'press coverage' was witheringly negative, both in the target regions and in the US. Three key governments—Egypt, Jordan, and Lebanon—publicly refused to air the ads (Tapper 2005), describing them as "propaganda," while elsewhere TV and print journalists heaped scorn on the endeavor (Amos nd). One newspaper likened the effort to a small chamois intended "to polish [the US] image," and another produced a series of cartoon caricatures of the videos (Pratkanis 2009: 115–16). In early December, the campaign was halted, just six weeks after it was begun, when only half the allotted budget had been spent. Charlotte Beers resigned soon afterwards (and appears to have withdrawn from public life), and no further videos were made. Although officially declared to have been a success (Boucher 2003), the Shared Values Initiative was widely regarded as having been a failure—and indeed, was so little regarded that the films themselves disappeared, until 2007, when copies were posted to YouTube.[1]

And what were the messages that these videos sought to convey? According to Ambassador Christopher Ross, the campaign did not "address divisive policy issues directly" but rather tried to "establish broader arenas of mutual interest, common ground, and interaction by talking about such subjects as religious tolerance and family," in order to counteract attitudes in Arab and Muslim countries that the US is "irreligious and hostile to Islam, espousing a culture antithetical to [Muslims'] own culture and values" (Ross 2003).

Both Ross and Ambassador Edward Djerejian, who chaired a study that examined US public diplomacy efforts aimed at the Arab world, described the process by which the decision to make that the focus of the five videos, and

158   *A. Olcott*

the greater campaign, in essentially the same way. Survey data pinpointed a perceived ignorance or misapprehension in the target audience—in the words of the Djerejian report: "The research that led to the campaign ...found that an average of only 12 percent of respondents in nine Muslim and Arab nations surveyed believed Americans respect Arab/Islamic values" (Djerejian 2003). The videos were then shaped (apparently by a fairly large committee, given Djerejian's complaint that it took five months to get approval for the project and another eight or nine months to complete the videos) to supply the target audiences with images and words intended to demonstrate that that belief was in error.

Public diplomacy, polling, and people's interests

The opinion survey results, which so dismayed the Djerejian committee and led to the hiring of Ms. Beers, were both facets of an approach to communication that had grown up in the era after World War I, and then come to full fruition after World War II. The notion that an abstract entity such as a "public"—an anonymous but somehow coherent mass of individuals—could share opinions, and that, moreover, those opinions were of interest and value, was one that had sprung up in the first part of the twentieth century. As one survey of that development notes, this process had an iterative quality, developing tools and techniques that could measure this new phenomenon, while also helping to create the notion that there exist things about which people can and should have opinions (see Osborne and Rose 1999).

Early practitioners of polling were divided, though, about what to do with the information that their new science generated. To some, the point of discovering what opinions held sway was to shape policy, but to a much larger group, the use of opinion polling was the reverse, to find ways in which opinion could be shifted to fall more into line with existing or proposed policies (see Habermas 1971, especially Chapter 5). This inclination was paralleled by the growth of the advertising industry, which also relied upon the creation of desires and demands in large masses of people for goods and services that they had not previously known they wanted.[2]

A recent paper points out an important confluence between these two uses of public opinion, that both were suffused with a general disposition toward positivism in how their practitioners assumed that humans process information (Heath and Feldwick 2007). "Opinion" was widely regarded as being in error, whereas the job of opinion-makers—and thus, by extension, advertisers—was to correct that error with better factual information. As the authors of that paper point out, those assumptions themselves were deeply nested in rational actor theories of social behavior, which posited that people process information in order to make choices that will lead logically to their greatest personal advantage. Thus communication is viewed as an entirely one-way transaction, with information being transferred from those in possession of "the facts" to those who are in error.

Rumour and strategic communication   159

One of the persistent circularities of public opinion research, however, is that it is the poser of the question—the would-be purveyor of the information—who defines the subjects about which the target audience is found to be ignorant. It is the poll-taker, after all, who both shapes and poses the question, thus making it possible that the poll is defining ignorance about a topic in which the respondent has no particular desire to be enlightened (Sussman 2010). In the case of the Shared Values Initiative, although poll-takers were able to secure a numeric distribution of how their target audiences answered the question "Do Americans respect Arab/Islamic values?," there is no evidence offered that, absent a poll-taker, people in the target audience would have asked themselves that question.

Put another way, it seems quite likely that $7.5 million and a considerable amount of energy, time, and imagination were devoted to providing "corrective" information on a topic about which no one in the target audience cared whether they were uninformed—in effect, putting out an answer to a question that no one had asked.

As Corman *et al.* (2007) argue, the continued insistence of US public communicators to "shape the message" ignores both that other senders are also "shaping messages" and, more importantly, that the messages that are received, and the *way* in which they are received, are determined not by the senders but by the receivers. The "message influence" models of communication have long been contested by another group of theories, which focus not on the information senders, but rather on the audience. Called "uses and gratification theory," this general approach argues that, if messaging is to have any opportunity to be successful, it must either have utility for a would-be receiver, or provide some kind of pleasure, comfort, or satisfaction (Rubin and Windahl 1986). Although the "uses and gratification" approach fell into disfavor for a time, the recent explosion in media among which audiences may make choices has led to renewed interest in the theory, precisely because it has at its heart what scholar Thomas Ruggiero (2000) called "the basic questions"—"Why do people become involved in one particular type of mediated communication … and what gratifications do they receive from it?"

"Our opponents use propaganda—we use truth"

The uses and gratifications theories of communication intersect with public diplomacy efforts in an interesting way because, at least until relatively recently, it was an unspoken assumption of most public diplomacy efforts that the "American story" was one that audiences would naturally want to hear, and would respond to. Telling that story was sharply differentiated from "propaganda"—something about which most Americans were deeply suspicious (indeed, so much so that the Smith–Mundt Act was drafted to outlaw the "propagandizing" of domestic audiences).[3] There is an abiding faith that the US "story" is so compelling that it needs only be articulated, not sold. Indeed, one of the ambassadors who later held a post similar to that of Beers

160 *A. Olcott*

is reported to have had a briefing slide which read: "Our opponents use propaganda—we use truth."[4]

There had been a time, though, when the US was very actively involved in dissecting, understanding, and making use of precisely what we might today call "propaganda." First the British, and then the US, saw the Nazis' stunning military success as the product of a well-established propaganda process for creating doubt, fear, and confusion among target populations in advance of their attacks. The Underground Propaganda Committee (UPC) in Britain and, slightly later, the Office of Special Services (OSS) in the US used their study of Nazi techniques to fight back, battling for the minds of European populations as assiduously as others fought for European soil.[5]

Importantly, virtually the only medium that those would-be "communicators" had at their command was rumors. Newspapers and radios in the captured countries were closed or their content changed to meet the occupiers' ends, and there were few other means of implanting or reinforcing counter-messages into the territories they wished to reach. One of the great advantages of rumors was that, as one of the practitioners from the period, Robert Knapp (1944: 28), put it, successful rumors are "self-propelling," meaning that the target audience itself embraces and disseminates the information, without further effort required on the part of the originator of the rumor.

For many official communicators, it is precisely that ability to appear as if from nowhere, and to prove almost impossible to kill, that makes rumors so feared, and so loathed. Kapferer (1990) has documented several of these persistent, self-propagating and self-sustaining rumors, which even huge corporate communicators have battled strenuously but with mixed success at best. The Procter & Gamble Company, for example, waged a seven-year battle against rumors which asserted that their corporate seal included secret Satanic symbols and, in the end, only quashed the rumors by removing their logo from products entirely, even though they had been using it for almost a century (Kapferer 1990: 21–22).

For other paid communicators, however, that capacity for self-propulsion that helped message-senders in a medium-poor environment is also the most highly coveted attribute of messaging in the media-saturated environment of today. To have a message become self-propelling, or as it is now called, to "go viral"[6]—to be picked up and transmitted to a desired audience by members of that audience themselves, without further intervention (or, importantly, expenditure) by the message originator—is the dream of everyone now competing for audience attention.

It is striking, therefore, that one of the texts singled out by a blogger, on a website devoted to the sales of luxury goods, as a guide for how to make messaging go viral was a secret memo that researcher Robert Knapp had written for the OSS in 1943, "Criteria of a Successful Rumor."[7] As the blogger marveled, although "a military document written during World War Two is going to have different objectives and a different tone" than would a marketing memo today, "it is striking how much the [Knapp] briefing reads like a best practice checklist of how brands can create compelling and viral brand narratives."[8] In Knapp's formulation, a successful rumor is:

1. easy to remember, because it is brief, simple, uses familiar and concrete details and persons, offers a memorable slogan or phrase and, if possible, has humor;
2. follows a familiar plot, recapitulating precedents and traditions from the history and folklore of the target audience, and so is "the oldest story in the newest clothes";
3. is a function of the momentary interests and circumstances of the target group, fills a knowledge gap, and contains verifiable or accepted details;
4. and exploits the emotions and sentiments of the target group, using the "emotional disposition" shared by the group.[9]

Knapp also argued that rumors will find fertile ground particularly among two groups of people: those who are most eager for information about events that affect them; and those with fears, hopes, and hostilities.

If Robert Knapp had been in charge of the Shared Values Initiative ...

There are important differences, of course, between the Shared Values Initiative and the rumors that Knapp and his British counterparts were trying to create in World War II. The Shared Values Initiative, just like all public diplomacy and strategic communications campaigns, was intended as an exercise in what Knapp would have called "white propaganda,"[10] or a message that is ascribed to its true source. As the marketing bloggers who have embraced the declassified Knapp memo understand, however, there are important principles in the creation of rumors that could have increased, if not the impact of the films, then at least the likelihood that they might at least have been looked at.

Examined through this lens, the Shared Values Initiative almost certainly made a good choice of target audiences—as defined by Knapp. In the months following the September 11 attacks on New York and Washington, potential viewers in the Middle East would have been eager for information about events that had already or would soon affect them, and they would have possessed "hopes, fears, and hostilities" in abundance. However, in all other ways, the five films failed to meet most or all of Knapp's recommendations:

- Although the five videos all use real people, they lack any memorable slogans or "bumper sticker lines," they certainly lack humor, and—most important—there is no indication at all of what the video expects the audience to *do* after viewing them. The films have no clear point or purpose—and thus there is nothing memorable about them.

162   *A. Olcott*

- The films may have used "accepted details"—as one Indonesian viewer said, "We know that there's religious freedom in America" (Rampton 2007)—but they failed to address the "interests and circumstances of the target group" (Knapp 1943).
- To the extent that the videos have any plot line, it is an American one, of "rags to riches" through personal effort. The "American-ness" of the films is reinforced by such details as baseball in the "teacher" segment or a state fair in the "baker" segment. Most American of all is the "doctor" film, which ends with its protagonist meeting President Bush. Nothing in the films suggests familiarity with or interest in the narratives of the target audience.

It is perhaps anachronistic to criticize those responsible for the Shared Values Initiative for having ignored another of Knapp's injunctions, that message creation should take into account the form in which the message is planned for delivery. Even so, making the campaigns' segments as TV spots left delivery decisions entirely in the hands of intermediaries—most of whom declined to participate. Although delivery options that would have made it easier for the videos to become "self-propelling"—such as online video (YouTube and others)—were still about two years away from realization at the time of Beers' campaign, even in 2002, there were already online delivery options such as Flash or PowerPoint that could at least have provided a potential for the films to "self-propel," rather than leaving the State Department reliant upon Egyptian state broadcasting as a platform for dissemination.

In addition to being "locked down" in the ways in which they could have been distributed, the films were also what might be called "locked down" in an artistic sense. Although filmed in a seemingly informal, almost amateur style, the videos all had a deep professionalism that attempted strenuously to control and shape audience reaction. A close study of the lighting, editing, and other structural elements of the films shows how tightly managed all the segments were. In the "teacher" segment, for example, the subject's son swings his baseball bat, after which the camera cuts immediately to a shot of people in the stands turning their heads, as if to follow a ball he had hit.[11]

Ample research exists to show that people are surprisingly adept at perceiving such subtleties and, even if unable to call them out specifically, will sense them as attempts at manipulation and "false notes"—in short, as "advertising." Unfortunately, this "covert falseness" of the five films, the manipulation that derives from the skill of the film makers, was also confirmed by an "overt falseness"—all five TV spots ended with a banner claiming them to have been a presentation not of the State Department or the US Government, but rather of "The Council of American Muslims for Understanding ...and the American people." As the internet was quick to make clear, this Council did not exist, but rather was a front organization established by the State Department (Rampton 2007)—thus making the Shared Values Initiative an exercise not in "white propaganda," but in "gray."

One more thing rumor might do

The use of a false-front sponsor suggests that Beers and her team were sufficiently aware of their target audiences to understand how ineffective "official information" was likely to have been, given the long and dismal history of state broadcasting in the target region. Had they studied Knapp, they might have built upon that understanding to also profit from his recommendation that successful messaging required "intelligence" (his word) about the target audience's "fears, hopes, and hostilities" in relation to the message sender, as well as their "customary and traditional ways of expressing their anxieties, hopes, and aggressions, especially in conditions of national crisis" (Knapp 1943).

How might such "intelligence" have been obtained, given the known weaknesses of polling, and the general difficulties of doing survey research in the area?

Captain Stephanie Kelley, a student at the Naval Postgraduate School, made the ingenious suggestion in 2004 that it is precisely the study of the rumors that exist in a given area that might prove the best guide for knowing what "white rumors," or desired information, should be about. Issued first as a Master's thesis (Kelley 2004), and then—in a shortened and revised form— as a journal article (Kelley 2005), Kelley's proposal to aggregate, categorize, and—most importantly—*listen* to rumors was based on her close study of nearly 1,000 rumors that had been circulating in Iraq in the aftermath of the US invasion, between October 2003 and August 2004. Kelley's reasoning, as laid out at some length in her dissertation, was based on the rich literature that has emerged about how rumors are generated and transmitted.

Kelley based her argument on the classic rumor studies of Allport and Postman (1946, 1947) and Knapp (1944), who argued that rumor is the product of two elements, a topic's importance and its ambiguity, and also Tamotsu Shibutani (1966), who argued further that rumors are a kind of *improvised news*: spontaneously generated and modified popular "explanations" for phenomena of concern, about which there is either insufficient information or where the audience has insufficient trust in the formal purveyors of news. To this, however, Kelley also added the work of Ralph Rosnow, who had stipulated that, in addition to the factors posited by Allport and Postman, Knapp, and Shibutani, should be added what Rosnow (1991: 486) called "outcome-relevant involvement" or, more simply, the obvious but important notion that people only create rumors about things that they care about and are interested in.

This suggests that, of necessity, the rumors that survive and thrive are not only going to be good indicators of the issues that concern people, but also will capture what people understand to be the main actors in a given situation, the motivations and purposes of those actors, and what those people understand to be causal in a given society. This is shown clearly in Kelley's study, which was based on the rumors regularly reported by *The Baghdad Mosquito*, a weekly compilation of media stories and other information that

164   A. Olcott

was circulating in Iraq following the US invasion. The *Mosquito*'s purpose was to alert those conducting information operations in the country to what "the street" was saying. The rumors were solicited from native informants, who were able to provide further context about how viable the rumors were.

There are some obvious methodological difficulties, not least of which would be how to account for the biases of native informants willing to work for the coalition forces in recording and interpreting the rumors of their countrymen in that fractured and fractious nation. Even in a more benign setting, however, we should account for the differences between strategic communication efforts undertaken—such as the work of *The Baghdad Mosquito*—and the public diplomacy efforts of teams such as that of Charlotte Beers. Although the boundaries between the two kinds of public communication can be blurry—sometimes the easiest way to distinguish the two is to define strategic communication as what the Pentagon does, whereas public diplomacy is what the State Department does—in general, strategic communication tends to have a more immediate goal than does public diplomacy, preparing a population for a military action to come or explaining one that has just taken place. Public diplomacy, in contrast, tends to be more about trying to create attitudes and opinions in target audiences, and has sometimes been quite narrowly defined as the administration of exchanges and international information programs (Paul 2009).[12]

Because *The Baghdad Mosquito* rumors that form the basis of Kelley's thesis derive from a more military purpose, it is possible that they omit rumors that did not bear so directly on issues of immediate safety and security. Still, the data Kelley presents suggest how systematic collection and categorization of rumors could serve to better inform official efforts to manage public perceptions in places of interest. Using approximately 1,000 rumors collected between October 2003 and August 2004, Kelley argued that they could be grouped into eight "overarching concerns." These concerns were: (1) government and politics [26.6 percent of all rumors]; (2) quality of life [18.1 percent]; (3) insurgency [17 percent]; (4) security [16.7 percent]; (5) terrorism [9.3 percent]; (6) US military [7.2 percent]; (7) communication [3.5 percent]; and (8) detainees [1.7 percent].

Although her data were collected after the Shared Values Initiative videos were aired (and Iraqis were not at the time one of the target audiences), Captain Kelley's taxonomy still suggests ways in which information campaigns might be better focused. The systematic collection and categorization of rumors would at the very least tell would-be communicators the issues that most concern the audiences they wish to reach. It is worth noting, for example, that the subject which the Shared Values Initiative saw as the top priority to address—US respect for Muslims—appears in Kelley's tabulation only under the "communication" rubric, which was the general theme of only about 3 percent of the rumors collected.

The same point emerges from a different treatment of the rumors that Kelley collected, when she tries to group the rumors not by topic, but rather

Rumour and strategic communication 165

by what she posits is the motivation behind the rumor (or, the human need that rumor is attempting to fill). Again, the topic of the Shared Values Initiative campaign might be said potentially to address the motivation of "curiosity," or trying to make sense of the world through "pseudo-news." The fact that more than one in five rumors collected seemed to be motivated by this need suggests how fertile an area it might have been for public diplomacy to address, whether as 'white' or as 'gray' information. As Kelley's cross-categorization suggests, however, what people were curious about was not what life might be like in America, but rather about what was happening *in their own country.*

Where Kelley's data suggest that Knapp's approach might have proven particularly fruitful, however, is in the category of rumors that Kelley calls "wish motivated." Intuitively, it is here that a perception management team might find the topics, and their desired outcomes, that the target audience most favors. That does not necessarily mean that such communicators would try to make those wishes "come true," but knowing that—in Kelley's examples— rumors were circulating that the American forces were going to provide housing for poor Iraqis or hire large numbers of local laborers for construction work would at least have provided indicators of possible areas of attention.

Conclusion

Clearly, Captain Kelley's suggestions for the collection and categorization of rumors in regions of interest would need considerable refinement before they could be fully operational. Consideration would also have to be given to the various ways in which official communicators might respond to them, whether by transforming "wish rumors" into reality, providing reliable information on topics that rumors suggest lack it, or by attempting to debunk them (although all research suggests that this last is extremely difficult to do with even partial success). What her research does suggest, however, is that learning to pay attention to rumors is one way in which public communicators might be able to move away from the "message influence" model of public diplomacy that proved so ineffective in the Shared Values Initiative, and begin to move more toward a "uses and gratification model." Rumors, in other words, are one means through which outsiders might learn what those with whom they would like to engage in conversation are already talking about. Unlike the case with the Shared Values Initiative, such an approach might at least allow officials to offer answers to questions that people are already asking, and thus offer information on topics about which they would truly like to be enlightened.

Notes

1 The SVI videos are: "Shared Values: Teacher" at: www.youtube.com/watch? v=Iu3dR7F0Cz8; "Shared Values: Firefighter" at: www.youtube.com/watch?

166   *A. Olcott*

v=d7KkzF-9_X4; "Shared Values: Journalist" at: www.youtube.com/watch?v=errfBCc-NXE; "Shared Values: Doctor" at: www.youtube.com/watch?v=Cpxco8qn_V8; "Shared Values: Baker" at: www.youtube.com/watch?v=PlEALpiFBW0 (all accessed May 21, 2012).

2 J. Walter Thompson, the agency where Beers began her career, was a pioneer of "scientific advertising." See Kreshel (1990). The international dimensions of this effort are captured in Merron (1999).

3 Two interesting books on this subject are Cull (2008) and Gary (1999).

4 I am unable to find written confirmation of this assertion, but I have been told by several who would be in a position to have seen this person's briefings that this is true.

5 An online repository of archival material related to this can be found at *PsyWar. org*: www.psywar.org/sibs.php

6 There are literally thousands of examples of "things that have gone viral"—for quick reference, this website offers 47 examples: www.ignitesocialmedia.com/viral-marketing-examples/ (accessed 11 March 2013).

7 The memo is available online at: upload.wikimedia.org/wikipedia/commons/2/27/Doctrine_Regarding_Rumors.pdf (accessed 10 March 2013).

8 "What can luxury brands learn from secret military documents?," *Agenda Inc.* blog, agendainc.com/blog/?p=664 (accessed 12 December 2009). The website is unfortunately no longer active but it was reblogged at: wearchive.tumblr.com/post/346312129/we-what-can-luxury-brands-learn-from-secret (accessed 12 March 2013).

9 *Ibid.* See also Robert Knapp, "The Criteria of a Successful Rumor," *Office of Strategic Services Planning Group* Memo P.G. 28, June 2, 1943. Online at: www.agendainc.com/media/rumor.pdf

10 Traditionally, "black" propaganda is deliberately misattributed information, whereas "gray" is unattributed, but usually designed to mislead. "White" propaganda identifies the source of the information.

11 Why the target audience would care about baseball, or even know what the boy was doing, is another question.

12 This survey by Paul (2009) points out that the Department of Defense Dictionary of Military and Associated Terms gives an official—albeit very broad—definition for "strategic communication," whereas no definitive counterpart for "public diplomacy" seems to exist.

Conclusion

Greg Dalziel

Two broad questions motivated this project. First, what relationship did rumors have to the political and social fields of society? This question found itself broadly situated within Asia for a variety of reasons. Second, what implications did rumor have for state strategic communication strategies and practices? The works featured in this volume address these questions to varying degrees and, in doing so, raised a number of questions that we were not necessarily cognizant of at the beginning of the project; they point the way towards future research into rumor and related forms of social communication.

We first attempt to summarize the authors' combined insights and findings with regard to the two main orienting questions: the political and social impact of rumor and the implications of rumor for state strategic communication strategies and practices. In a sense, looking at rumor through the framework of strategic communication tells us less about the problem that rumor poses for such work and more about problems that may be inherent in the logic that underpins strategic communication. We then move on to the variety of hunches, insights, and potential research paths for the future that emerged out of the hard labor of the authors in this volume. These are our own insights, however, and do not expect that all the authors would necessarily concur with our findings. We argue that rumor research needs to better take into account variations in meanings and context in addition to being more reflexive. Second, rumor research should focus less on rumor content and more on the work done by people categorizing and classifying information and knowledge as rumor. This can focus particularly on who is doing the categorizing, in what context, and to what effect. Finally, the role of the internet and social media is explored in terms of both rumor diffusion but also the impact of these phenomena on rumor research itself.

The political and social impact of rumors

As we noted in the Introduction, rumors are often perceived in the literature to have a negative effect on society. Rumors are seen to have some kind of causal effect on: starting episodes of collective violence; impeding participation

168   *G. Dalziel*

in useful state-run social programs; fomenting and sustaining mistrust between social groups; deceiving and leading people astray. As we look deeper into the exact effects that rumor is supposed to exert—that is, in what manner they are a problem—we find that the problem of rumor is one asymmetrically distributed. That is, rumors are not equally a problem for every social group one might find distributed across a society. Historically, rumor is constructed as a problem for those within the state or other large organizations (there is an element of power, then, in the perception of rumor). Rumors are a thing to be dealt with. Research, then, is often designed around figuring out underlying dynamics so that rumors may be properly ameliorated. It is why so much of the literature revolves around offering specific prescriptions for refuting rumor or repairing rumor's assumed damage.

Yet the cases in this book present a rather mixed view of rumor. Certainly, in Woodward's case, for example, rumors are seen to have a negative social impact. But this appears less a product of any properties inherent in rumor and more the combination of the production of knowledge married to a hegemonic, coercive power. In this particular case, the state has some ability to shape the contours of knowledge about the events of the 1965 coup and the role that groups of Indonesians did or did not play. The variety of ways in which the state can utilize power is directed, as Woodward demonstrates, in the enactment of symbolic boundaries that are propped up and maintained through state-propagated rumors. These rumors are used to divide good from bad, right from wrong, and the way that particular events are remembered. These symbolic boundaries and the discursive practices associated with them are used to "enforce, maintain, normalize, or rationalize social boundaries" that still exert an impact on Indonesian society today (Lamont and Molnár 2002: 186).

At the same time, rumors were used to resist, reshape, and reinterpret Suharto and his political regime. We see similar processes at work in the Iranian election and Noordin Top cases, where attempts by state organizations to propagate particular understandings were resisted. Focusing on the interactive process of communication means that seeing rumor as a "problem" may be limiting. In the case of Iran, this was through networks of opposition both inside Iran and outside via the connectivity offered by the internet. For the Noordin Top case, technologies were used to reshape and repurpose images and video in combination with official and unofficial narratives to create rumor mash-ups.

In all these cases, then, the process of the generation of meaning is dynamic, interactive, and ongoing, which can throw out novel results in a process of emergence. It can also be highly contentious. The problem for the state is that the generation of meaning for political purposes, what the sociologist Andreas Glaeser (2012) calls *political epistemics*, is one that requires a certain amount of consensus and conformity. Propaganda is often created in order "to prevent subjectivist interpretation" (quoted in Glaeser 2012: 129). Rumors represent differences in collective definitions of the situation; they underscore the relative instability of meanings which constitute the very institutions underpinning social and political life. Such failures in influencing understandings are, for elites, often "profoundly disturbing" (Moscovici 1976: 68). It is why one typically finds communication that resists state-imposed narratives categorized as rumor and why a typical response by the state to rumor is attempting to engage in the "social control of communicative behavior" via regulation and monitoring of communication channels (Shibutani 1961: 128). The most prominent example of this is the rumor control clinics that started in the US during World War II and continued through the 1970s (Knopf 1975; Ponting 1973), and the recent attempts by the Japanese government to monitor internet communications for *fuhyo higai* ("harmful rumors") about the Fukushima nuclear disaster (Matsuda 2011; Schafer 2012).

Although a lack of consensus arising out of communication interactions may be unsettling for state elites, both Gelfert and Dentith argue that it is better to come to terms with this process rather than trying to engage in restricting communicative behavior. As a matter of course, Gelfert argues, it is unfeasible to expect that everyone fastidiously checks the reliability and verifiability of their sources of information. Indeed, as Dentith writes, confusing rumor with conspiracy theory or intentional deception (rumor-mongering) elides the fact that rumors are generally reliable forms of testimony.

A solution, then, to the "problem" of rumor is to bolster trust in one's fellow citizens and the various institutions that make up society. Not only is the free flow of communication important, but the ability to participate in communication interactions without the state constantly inserting itself is recommended. This does not mean, as Gelfert writes, that everyone will at all times agree with one another. Lack of consensus is not inherently a problem and may be the sign of a "healthy" society. If the state is disappointed in the outcomes of these communication interactions, then the fault may not be inherent in the assumed properties of one genre of communication or the other, but in more exogenous factors. Shibutani (1978: 427), for example, wrote that "definitions that may be constructed are limited by the availability of relevant information from trusted communication channels." Secrecy and repression, for example, often generate the type of communication categorized as rumor. Communal violence rarely occurs, one might assume, in places where people get along. The negative focus on rumor-as-problem, then, may draw attention away from more consequential structural conditions or environmental factors and make it more likely that proposed solutions will be along the lines of censorship, regulation, and monitoring, which will do little to alleviate such underlying problems and may only increase the likelihood they will generate further rumors.

Rumor and strategic state communication

The second aspect of the research on rumor presented in this book was framing it within the context of strategic state communication strategies and

170   *G. Dalziel*

practices. For those professionals whose main work is defined by communication, what impact did rumors and rumor dynamics have? A key element of the institutional logic of strategic state communication is the goal of persuading particular publics to support (or not actively oppose) state policy or action, or to change behaviors in support of a particular goal. Another core part of strategic state communication are practices centered around the reflexive management of organizational reputations; by "institutional logic" we mean the "central logic ...which constitutes its organizing principles and which is available to organizations and individuals to elaborate" (Friedland and Alford 1991: 248; see also Thornton *et al.* 2012: 2).

Research into a variety of differing professions has documented the way in which people engage in practices of defining, enacting, and maintaining boundaries towards a variety of ends, such as professionalization, institutionalization, or legitimacy (Abbott 1988, 1995; Lamont and Molnár 2002; Lamont and Thevenot 2000; Sarfatti-Larson 1977). Rumor appears to be quite problematic for communication professionals. Its problematization—indeed, the kinds of information that gets defined as rumor by members of such professions—may be a by-product of boundary work occurring within the professional field. White (2000: 210), discussing differences between social groups in the categorization of information, writes, "rumor is the officials' term for information they have not engendered, shaped, or controlled." Communication may be more likely to be negatively categorized as rumor if it represents an encroachment on to the professional field of those whose work is defined by defining reality for others.

Bernardi and Ruston, for example, found rumors to be problematic for those engaged in communication work within the US military in Iraq. The problem for these professionals was trying to persuade local Iraqis to participate in agricultural projects sponsored by the US military. However, gaining participation was problematic and rumors of American's poisoning of cows reportedly not only seemed believable to locals but also worked to dissuade (at least in the eyes of the Americans) locals from participating in the program.

The believability of these rumors and the apparent impact they had on behavior were problematic for these communication professionals. Bernardi and Ruston argue that these rumors filled a "knowledge gap" and "capitalized on a lack of official information." Yet for the locals, it is not clear what counts as 'official information'; in this context, it seems as though the US military lacked the authority to ascribe truth or falsity to a particular set of truth claims. This would be a frustrating situation for those tasked with, from their perspective, communicating the truth and trying to engage with local Iraqis to better their living standards through improving agricultural practices. What is "official information" to these professionals is most likely self-evident. Official information is information that comes from approved, designated representatives of the US or Iraqi governments. It has gone through the necessary steps to be official: via the proper organizational channels, it has been approved by the relevant committees who ensure the

Conclusion 171

message fits the overall "policy" or "strategy," received the proper approval, with the proper signatures in the correct locations on the right forms and the relevant information entered in the databases and spreadsheets. It has been released and publicized in the prescribed fashion to the proper people and distributed by assigned personnel via relevant channels. At some point, a PowerPoint is made.

This is official information. It can be trusted precisely because it has gone through these rational steps. More importantly, it can be trusted because it is *true*, they would argue. *Of course* Americans are not poisoning cows! they say. That would be *absurd*.

Such conflicts might usefully be seen as examples of "incommensurable institutional logics" (Friedland 2009: 2) where competing rationalities are at work. Viewing rumor in this perspective highlights some of the work that occurs in such conflicts (see Friedland 2009; Mohr 2000; Thornton *et al.* 2012). Friedland (2009: 2) writes that "institutional logics join subjects, practices, and objects into bundled sets which have an inner referentiality [and] performative order." As such, the institutional logic of strategic state communication, geared as it is around maneuvering representations in the services of a larger organization in order to persuade others, is violated by the persistence of communication that is called rumor. Those with a stake in defining situations, or communicating organizationally approved definitions of the situation, dislike alternative attempts at constructing such definitions. Indeed, for those with roles in state organizations or professions associated with communication work, the often messy business of figuring out what is going on or (and even more difficult) defining what is going on for others can be disconcerting. The neat ordering of reality that bureaucracy aims for is often upended in such situations, and the persistence of alternative explanations represents troubling failures for communication professionals in the chosen and sanctified techniques of their field.

In addition, it is not clear whether rumors themselves have the sort of impact that is often attributed to them; in the Iraq case, for example, in influencing (or persuading) Iraqis not to participate in the agricultural program; this is not to argue whether they did or did not believe the views they were expressing, just whether such rumors were in and of themselves a causal influence in the decision not to participate in the agricultural program. Some research suggests that "individuals are *remarkably bad* at giving consistent reasons for their behavior" (Vaisey 2009: 1678; emphasis in the original).[1] It may simply be that cooperating with the American occupiers was not seen as acceptable conduct for local Iraqis at that time; such actions may not have seemed conceivable or meaningful. Bernardi and Ruston argue that the rumors were seen by the strategic communication professionals to be "degrading the efficacy of the bovine inoculation campaign," but it is also possible that the mere fact it was an *American* bovine inoculation campaign served to dissuade participation. It is easier to explain organizational failure in strategic communication if it is because of external factors such as troublesome rumors or a recalcitrant target audience; failure can also be explained by the message

172   *G. Dalziel*

simply being not expressed using the right language, or the right format, or at the right time. But explaining failure as embedded in the organization itself is a tad more troublesome.

A recent "lessons learned" meta-study by a division of the US Department of Defense (2012) about the organizational experiences in Iraq and Afghanistan identified a number of problems for US military strategic communication professionals. The report states that insurgents—unlike the US military—were "unconstrained by the truth" (US Department of Defense 2012: 11)[2] and used a narrative to illustrate the problems facing the US military. In this particular case, an explosion caused by the premature denotation of an improvised explosive device planted by insurgents killed a number of civilians; however it was "quickly (and falsely) reported to be a Predator [drone] strike. Though not true, years later, locals still believed the casualties came from a coalition airstrike [sic]" (US Department of Defense 2012: 11–12). False narratives impede true narratives, and people end up holding false beliefs that impinge on the reputation of the US military and make it more difficult to garner cooperation by civilians. Remedies proffered in this report include, for example, changing organizational structures or speeding up organizational decision-making in order to release information faster. The assumptions, however, and what they say about the viability of the institutional logic of strategic communication, are striking. What this organizational narrative of failure cannot take into account is precisely the role that plausibility and reputation play in the endurance and persistence of narratives, regardless of their epistemic validity. Why did such civilians believe it plausible that a US Predator drone could—accidentally or otherwise—kill a group of civilians?

There is a tension in the institutional logic of strategic state communication that views communication as a form of power by which "the perspectives of men are shaped" (Shibutani and Kwan 1965: 228). Rumors represent not only a failure of this power but also a failure of consensus and a diversion from definitions of the situation. Shibutani, in his study on ethnic stratification, theorized that "the extent to which different individuals are able to develop consensus depends upon their participation in common communication channels" (Shibutani and Kwan 1965: 573), and that participation is a function of social distance between different groups. In an earlier piece, Shibutani (1961: 128) writes that "except under unusual circumstances men who are within one another's range do not enter readily into communicative transactions. In all groups there is differential contact and associations." Communication itself is stratified. It is therefore unclear precisely how effective communication in situations such as Iraq can be given that (1) strategic communication practitioners may not, it is presumed, be participating in the same communication channels as the people they are trying to communicate with and (2) the greater the social distance between strategic communication practitioners and audience, the more difficult consensus will be.

As we noted earlier, the cow poisoning rumor in Iraq appeared to practitioners to be absurd; absurdity is an oft-overlooked quality of rumor.

Conclusion 173

Absurdity is a property of novelty and surprise. Differences in communication channels resulting from social distance would seem to increase the likelihood of surprise occurring and, hence, the generation of communication experienced as absurdity and categorized as rumor. Shibutani (1986: 274) writes that

> When such definitions [of the situation] are subsequently discovered to have been mistaken, they are dismissed as rumors. When adaptive efforts turn out to be successful, however, consensus constructed in this manner is not so condemned.

Communication is an interactive process, and understandings or collective meanings reached are liable to change. When they do so, Shibutani argues, we discard previous understandings as "rumor." People are fallible and can end up mistaken. Events can change and new information be acquired. Knowledge changes. That is an unfortunate fact of life, but the dynamics of social distance, Shibutani argues, increases the chances of failures to reach consensus (Shibutani and Kwan 1965: 572–78).

Commonly, problems in strategic communication efforts are often seen as failures in *communication*. Either the message was not the right one at the right time, or there was perhaps a mismatch between words and deeds that, although troubling, was unavoidable. However, failures may be embedded in the organization itself (as discussed earlier), or they may be shaped by broader structural dynamics such as the structure of communication channels. Shibutani has been widely cited in this volume (and elsewhere) for his work on rumor, but his other work on stratification and communication interactions holds lessons for strategic communication practices.

It is also not clear how useful—or necessary—the involvement of the state is in the process of a public coming up with meaningful understandings or consensual definitions of the situation. Certainly the necessity of state involvement has been rationalized. Dalziel's chapter argues that strategic state communication efforts can, in fact, influence collective sense-making outcomes but, in this sense, they do not alleviate the production of rumors, but merely serve as additional fodder in the production of collective definitions of the situation (i.e., the output of collective sense-making efforts). As such, although Olcott (among others) argues that understanding rumors can lead to "smarter" strategic state communication practices, this does not necessarily mean it will also lead to no rumors.

Oh *et al.*'s case focuses on a number of problems that rumors combined with Twitter and other social media platforms have for state communication practices during a crisis. In the Mumbai case, they find that the volume and immediacy of information via social media platforms was a problem for authorities. Information appeared that was counter to what authorities were releasing to the public, was information that authorities had no knowledge of, or was information that could have benefited the terrorists operationally. In addition, the volume and immediacy of information was seen as diffusing not just knowledge but also negative emotional states—the classic anxiety factor.

174 *G. Dalziel*

Finally, space constraints on Twitter and other social media platforms are seen as problematic because it means important information may be stripped away, increasing the chances of ambiguity or misunderstanding.[3]

One novel suggestion by Oh *et al.* was the employment in such situations of "virtual rumor clinics." This is worth exploring in greater detail in future research. One may find analogous practices and similar types of organizations among those that deal with "brand management," "reputation management," or the various kinds of social media "monitoring." Given the failure, however, of non-virtual rumor clinics in the past and current research on information diffusion, we are uncertain how effective virtual rumor clinics will be (see Graham 2009; Knopf 1975, 2006[1975]; Ponting 1973). Their appeal to state organizations, however, is undeniable. Beyond the sense of control they offer, rumor clinics represent the sort of busy work that bureaucracy and bureaucrats thrive upon.

Some research suggests that people are able to function quite well in situations involving ambiguous meanings (Swidler 2001). Additionally, recent research on communication interactions on Twitter after the 2010 Chile earthquake finds that, as people engage in collective sense-making efforts, information that is true ends up diffusing for a longer period of time and to more people, as opposed to information that is subsequently deemed false (Mendoza *et al.* 2010). People acting in concert can often come to a meaningful understanding or consensual definition of the situation without the interjection of state authorities.

Oh *et al.* argue that previous (social psychology) research into the sense-making functions of rumor is suspect because "it involves relatively stable environments compared to the setting of a terrorist incident" such as the Mumbai attacks in which they situate their study. This is true for social psychology research that is conducted in a laboratory setting. But, as discussed later, historically, rumor research is found in situations that are not particularly stable. The influence of the relative stability of the environment on sense-making outcomes is worth investigating further. In sociology, for example, Swidler (2001: 131) argues that, during unsettled periods, people "must construct new lines of action." In order to do so, Swidler writes in an earlier piece, "people formulate, flesh out, and put into practice new habits of action" (1986: 279), which also "makes possible new strategies of action" (1986: 280). For Ball-Rokeach (1973), situations of what she terms "pervasive ambiguity" are typified by people not having a definition of the situation as a prerequisite to action: "cut off from external sources of information, the construction and the validation of a definition of the situation had to take place entirely within the collective" (Ball-Rokeach 1973: 387). Both Swidler and Ball-Rokeach point to the idea that collective sense-making outcomes are dynamic and capable of producing novel and surprising interpretations, and these novel interpretation are more likely to persist during unsettled times than in settled times (see also Tilly 1993, 2002). We explore in further detail the role of context in rumor research in the next section.

Future directions for rumor research

Although some researchers acknowledge that "rumor has multiple meanings" (Fine and Turner 2001: 18), in practice the assumption often is that it has a fixed meaning both within and between cases. Abbott (1992: 433) argues that this "univocal meaning assumption" is prevalent across the social sciences. This assumption, however, increases the chances that there is a disjunct between the concept deployed by the researcher and that of the subjects under study (although more often than not the focus is on rumor content, and those actually engaged in the diffusion of rumor are removed from the picture).

Kapferer (1990:1) wrote that "the concept [of rumor] in fact slips away just when one believes one has pinned it down." Yet the instability of the rumor concept, the disjunct between research and subject's concepts needs to be taken into account (see Bourdieu and Wacquant 1992; Flyvbjerg 2001; Giddens 1982; Martin 2011). Discrepancies in the meaning of rumor between researcher and subject ensure that, rather than measuring the structure of plausibility within a subject (or community of subjects), it is more likely that what is being measured is the structure of plausibility of the researcher. Rather than trying to polish their rumor concepts into nice, shiny, and predictable billiard balls, it may be more useful to view rumor as a form of categorization and classification (see Dalziel, forthcoming).

Such a turn opens new avenues of rumor research that incorporate a growing body of literature broadly situated within sociology, particularly in the related subfields of culture and organizations, that may offer useful insights and methods (for example, see Cerulo 2000; DiMaggio 1997; Goldberg 2011; Lamont and Molnár 2002; László 1990; Zerubavel 1991).

These sets of literature are often quite comfortable dealing with not only a multivocality of meanings within a case, but also taking into account context; in policy studies, one also finds a wide-ranging literature in this vein (Chock 1995; Lasswell 1970; Swaffield 1998; Torgerson 1985).

The question of meaning as it relates to culture and action can be found addressed in work broadly situated within relational approaches to sociology that sees meanings as "[embedded] within a broader system of relationships" (Mohr 2000: 27).[4] As Emirbayer (1997: 300) writes, "the meaning of one concept can be deciphered only in terms of its 'place' in relation to the other concepts in its web." Rumors only come into being through people noticing and attending to information and categorizing such information as *rumor* or otherwise. Such categorization varies and is only done in relation to other items of information, to previously held frames or schemas, to the context and situation at hand, and in relation to other actors. Similarly, the meaning of *rumor* itself is not fixed and is variable within and between cases.

With regard to context, we mean simply "the phenomenon surrounding a case" (Abbott 1995: 94); we suspect that institutional setting has an important impact on rumor meaning and categorization efforts. Historically, the context of rumor is usually post-crisis or -disaster situations. Similarly, rumors are

176 *G. Dalziel*

fairly well studied in the context of financial markets (Kosfeld 2005; Rose 1951; Schindler 2007) or in organizational contexts whether it is on employee performance (Caplow 1947; Michelson and Mouly 2000, 2004) or corporate reputation (Blackshaw and Iyer 2008; DiFonzo 2008; DiFonzo and Bordia 2000, 2002; McConnell 1989; Saffery 2004). Missing from these analyses, however, are comparative studies of variation between organizational and institutional contexts.

In many settings, rumors are not only viewed negatively, but the data chosen by the analyst are invariably false (and should have been seen as obviously false by those spreading it). However, when one looks at examples of rumor data in the financial sector, one finds a high likelihood of "true" rumor being spread (Dalziel, forthcoming). Rumors in the financial sectors may be "true," but they also pose a problem; it is just that the nature of this problem is different from other settings. They are suspicious because rumors may convey an unfair advantage over others if one has information before others. In strategic communication, however, rumors are suspicious because the underlying institutional logic of that field is persuasion using the "truth". Rumors in political settings (especially during wartime) are a problem because they identify a lack of consensus and unity in the polity. At the same time, rumors circulating in someone else's political field are useful because they may tell one something that is true or about the emotions of that populace.

Such an analysis of multiple meanings and context dependence might seem a matter of empirics, yet in some academic fields (we are looking in the direction of political science and international relations at this point) doing so would seem to rely on interpretivist or hermeneutic qualitative methods that are often *verboten*. However, Mohr and Duequenne (1997), for example, use quite formal quantitative structuralist techniques to model the structure of categories and their relation to organizational practices (see also Mohr 1998 on methods). In their study on the provision of social services in New York City, Mohr and Duequenne (1997: 343) demonstrate how "the meaning of various poverty classifications can be deduced through an examination of the ways in which those categories were used." In doing so, the authors reveal "the logic of social relief by understanding how cultural distinctions and forms of actions were meaningfully differentiated." In a more recent study, Krinsky (2010) takes a formal approach to examine the relation of power to such meaning variations. A similar use of such techniques may be of use in understanding the changing logic of state communication practices in general and organizational practices as they relate to rumor meanings. Revisiting work on state practices related to rumor, then, such as rumor control clinics, may be worth exploring in such a framework.

Rumors and the internet

Finally, work on rumors and related genres of communication will inevitably include more analysis using data garnered from the internet (whether from

Conclusion 177

"social media" or otherwise), given the ability to collect, organize, and analyze previously unobtainable amounts of data on communication interactions. The sheer size of such data is impressive—a recent article utilized five million 'tweets' [Twitter postings] (Mendoza *et al.* 2010). One is able to obtain data on communication interactions and expressed sentiments over a wide geographical area or narrowed to fairly specific publics (Donovan 2004; Jansen *et al.* 2009). This can allow the researcher to track how particular narratives develop and evolve over time (Yardi and Boyd 2010).

Future research might include analysis of the variety of narratives that develop (in both online and "offline" settings), which ones persist, and in what ways (if any) they influence future narratives. In the same way that some of the narratives of the Hua Nang murder were used to frame the MSK escape in Singapore, for example, the collective definitions (narratives) of the MSK escape were then subsequently reused and integrated into narrative understandings of unrelated events in the future.[5]

Tracking the development of these narratives and how they are reused in different situations may give insight into the dynamics of what one might call *narrative sedimentation*. Much like how particular kinds of regular and repeated social interactions can "concatenate" into durable social structures (Martin 2009; see also Godart and White 2010), some types of communication interactions may concatenate into narrative structures. This can aid in providing a framework for understanding why particular narratives are reused and refashioned in collective sense-making activities whereas others seem to be discarded and forgotten.

Online media also provide an opportunity for researchers to understand rumors in formats beyond the spoken and written word. As Lundry and Cheong showed, the effects of *transmediation* and "produsers" expand rumors from simply written or oral discourse to online videos and photoshopped pictures. What one finds, then, are *rumor mash-ups*. Lundry and Cheong's case, in fact, suggests that there are types of communication interactions that differ significantly from past forms, increasing the roles that people can take within such interactions and complicating research that is traditionally oriented around rhetoric and discourse.

Indeed, the internet means that social communication is often very *public* as opposed to in the past. During the 1940s, rumor researchers had to employ volunteers in barbershops, bars, and diners to pass along overheard tidbits (much like the Stasi in East Germany; Glaeser 2012), or relied upon readers of weekly magazines to respond to advertisements soliciting rumors. Communication, then, was in many respects more private or limited within particular networks. The internet allows for a much wider diffusion of social communication—which is admittedly a very facile observation—but it also allows for a more public communication. This increases the roles that participants and audiences can take in the diffusion of information, and the creation of meanings.[6]

In addition, Jenkins' (2006) concepts of *convergence culture*, with narratives diffusing across different media formats and platforms, along with that of

178   G. Dalziel

participatory culture, where people are actively engaged in the production, diffusion, and consumption of culture (equivalent to Bruns' "produsers" concept), changes the way in which we can look at rumor diffusion. A passive audience is often assumed in communication practices and is indicative of early communication theories (e.g., Berlo 1960; Shannon and Weaver 1964). Contemporary strategic communication practices often implicitly support this view with a persistent focus around *the message*. This is often mirrored in rumor research with the focus on content (Bordia 1996; Bordia and Rosnow 1998; Bordia *et al.* 1999). That is, "meaning is treated as something audiences construct in response to a specific message" (Cerulo 2000: 24) rather than in response to specific *social situations*. These new concepts along with the broader changes that the internet has brought about in the traditional divide between "mass media" and public, between the producers of "news" and those that spread "unofficial" information that in the past characterized rumor meanings highlights how previous rumor concepts utilized by researchers may quickly become inadequate if they have not done so already.

One issue, however, with using internet data for rumor research is understanding and putting into context broader media consumption patterns. For example, in an "aging society" such as Japan, studies consistently find that older generations still get their information via "traditional" media communication channels such as the radio, television, and newspapers (Hirata *et al.* 2011; Saito 2010). Rumor, then, may remain a profoundly oral and localized activity among such groups.

Age is an unexplored framework through which to study rumor. One finds a strong bias towards youth in reviewing previous rumor research. Experiments are conducted using undergraduates; surveys circulated among university students; or, in more recent years, data are gathered from communication channels dominated by youth (Allport and Postman 1946, 1947; Bordia *et al.* 2005; DiFonzo and Bordia 2007; Fragale and Heath 2004; Higham 1951; Schall *et al.* 1950; Smith 1947). There are some exceptions, of course. Research in anthropology has tended to avoid this problem, while Morin's (1971) classic work on rumors in the French town of Orleans and Renard's (1991) article on the diffusion of LSD rumors between North America and France both largely focused on women (specifically mothers) and middle-class professionals. If rumors are indeed a way to identify distinct cognitive subcultures, or variances in structures of plausibility, then understanding precisely who is a member of such a community (and whether these patterns affect plausibility, for example) is equally as important as the content of rumors themselves (Ito *et al.* 2010).

Conclusion

This project started many years ago with a workshop centered around the political and social impact of rumors and the relation of this phenomenon to state strategic communication practices. In the course of this project, the

Conclusion 179

research presented in this volume has extended our knowledge of rumor while opening up new avenues for future research.

The more one studies rumor, the more difficult a phenomenon it appears, as Kapferer noted. One thing is clear, however, and that is rumor is not going away no matter states' and organizations' attempts to either provide more information or, conversely, prevent less communication as a salve. Understanding the world around us involves communication and interaction. The production of knowledge is never as clean nor as ordered as bureaucratic rationality would presuppose. And the behavior that produces meaning and generates knowledge not only can produce the sort of repetitive interaction characterized as institutions or structure but is also capable of producing emergent behavior that can appear novel or unsettling. Rumors are not objects waiting to be discovered, but the product of people's attempts to understand the world around them.

Work on rumor often ends up focusing on falsehoods. As we noted, this appears to be at some level a product of institutional context. Unfortunately, refereeing the epistemic validity of information does not offer many insights into communicative behavior. Nor does this improve or align differing definitions of the situation. For the social scientist, regulating truth can offer a self-satisfied feeling of certainty; after all, a PhD must be good for something. For the bureaucrat, maintaining clear epistemic boundaries separates lines of responsibility and provides a rational basis for decision-making (Swaffield 1998). A better focus, however, is on "who has the authority to describe a particular set of truth claims as unsecured, unverified, and suspect?" (Fine 1995: 125). To this, we would add that a focus on power and organization should be included. In all the cases in this book, we see competition over this question of authority, attempts to impose authority, and resistance to such attempts.

State organizations should learn to tolerate communication categorized as rumor. The social ills often associated with rumor are the products of much deeper forces, and the presence of rumor is either a manifestation of these problems or a function of social distancing between elites and subject communities in which problematic discourse is dismissed as rumor. More importantly, the lack of any information called rumor in a society does not indicate perfect trust in "official" information nor the sort of perfectly functioning order and harmony that state organizations often strive for. Such an environment, in fact, could only be the product of a complete lack of communication and interaction that is generally only achievable through *rigor mortis.*

A possible solution—and one instituted to varying degrees by many states—might be to engage in more, or more finely tuned, censorship practices. This is technically a "solution" in that it can give the appearance of solving the problem and everyone can be home in time for tea. It might reduce "rumors" (however defined) on a particular communication channel. But the result is much like sticking your fingers in your ears and humming a pleasant tune when you do not want to hear what someone has to say: you can't hear them, but that doesn't mean they're not talking.

Notes

1 Swidler (1986, 2001) is the most well-known (and cited) author in this line of work on culture, but see also Lizardo and Strand (2010).
2 This, of course, is a common trope—or hoary chestnut, whichever one prefers—in the problems facing states communicating in a conflict where "we" only engage in truth-telling while "they" deal in propaganda or falsehood.
3 This is less of a problem for languages relying on logographic alphabets such as Chinese or Japanese.
4 See also Emirbayer (1997); Fine and Kleinman (1983); Godart and White (2010); Mohr (1998).
5 For example, when the Singapore government went over budget for the 2010 Youth Olympics, the MSK incident was repeatedly used as a similar example of government "failure."
6 The role of technology and social communication has been studied in the past in topics such as "xeroxlore" (or "photocopylore") and "faxlore" in relation to the diffusion of urban legends (see Brunvand 2001; Hatch and Jones 1997; Preston 1974, 1994).

Bibliography

Abbott, Andrew. 1988. *The System of Professions: An Essay on the Division of Expert Labor.* Chicago, IL: University of Chicago Press.

———. 1992. From Causes to Events: Notes on Narrative Positivism. *Sociological Methods & Research* 20(4): 428–455.

———. 1995. Things of Boundaries. *Social Research* 62(4): 857–882.

———. 2004. *Methods of Discovery: Heuristics for the Social Sciences.* New York: 2004.

Adams, Abigail E. 1999. Gringas, Ghouls and Guatemala: The 1994 Attacks on North American Women Accused of Body Organ Trafficking. *Journal of Latin American Anthropology* 4(1): 112–133.

Adkins, Karen C. 1996. *Knowledge Underground: Gossipy Epistemology.* Unpublished PhD Dissertation: University of Massachusetts-Amherst.

Aguirre, B.E. and Kathleen J. Tierney. 2001. *Testing Shibutani's Prediction of Information Seeking Behavior in Rumor.* Working Paper #307. University of Delaware: Disaster Research Center.

al-Husni, Khairil Ghazali. 1999. *15 Dalil Mengapa Suharto Masuk Neraka.* Jakarta: Pustaka Muthmainnah.

Allport, Floyd. H. and Milton Lepkin. 1945. Wartime Rumors of Waste and Special Privilege: Why Some People Believe Them. *Journal of Abnormal and Social Psychology* 40(1): 3–36.

Allport, Gordon W. and Leo Postman. 1946. An Analysis of Rumor. *The Public Opinion Quarterly* 10(4): 501–517.

———. 1947. *The Psychology of Rumor.* New York: Russel & Russel.

Althaf. 2009. Noordin M Top Rajai Yahoo Selama 2009. *Ar-Rahmah* [Blog]. 12 December. Online at: www.arrahmah.com/index.php/news/read/6243/noordin-m-top- (accessed 15 December 2009).

Amos, Sandy. nd. Selling Brand America. *Globalization and Media* [Blog]. Online at: homepage.newschool.edu/~chakravs/sandy.html (accessed 4 December 2009).

Anderson, Benedict. 1990. *Language and Power: Exploring Political Cultures in Indonesia.* Ithaca, NY: Cornell University Press.

Anthony, Susan. 1973. Anxiety and Rumor. *Journal of Social Psychology* 89(1): 91–98.

Arjomad, Said A. 1989. *The Turban for the Crown: The Islamic Revolution in Iran.* Oxford: Oxford University Press.

Artha, Arwan. 2007a. *Dunia Spiritual Soeharto. Menelusiri Laku Ritual, Tempat-Tempat dan Guru Spiritualnya.* Yogyakarta: Galang Press.

———. 2007b. *Bu Tien, Wangsit Keprabon Soeharto.* Yogyakarta: Galang Press.

182 *Bibliography*

Assmann, Aleida and Corinna Assmann. 2010. Neda – The Career of a Global Icon, pp. 225–242 in *Memory in a Global Age: Discourse, Practices, and Trajectories*, edited by Aleida Assmann and Sebastian Conrad. New York: Palgrave.

Ayim, Maryann. 1994. Knowledge through the Grapevine: Gossip as Inquiry, pp. 85–99 in *Good Gossip*, edited by Robert F. Goodman and Aharon Ben-Ze'ev. Lawrence: University Press of Kansas.

Azra, Azyumardi. 2003. Death of Religious Tolerance? *Jakarta Post*, 3 January.

Bahrampour, Tara. 2009. Rumors and Theories Swirl around Protests. *The Washington Post*, 27 June.

Bakhash, Shaul. 1998. Iran's Remarkable Election. *Journal of Democracy* 9(1): 80–94.

Bakhtin, Mikhail. 1981. *The Dialogic Imagination: Four Essays by M.M. Bakhtin*. Austin: University of Texas Press.

Baldwin, Daniel A. 1997. The Concept of Security. *Review of International Studies* 23 (1): 5–26.

Ball-Rokeach, Sandra J. 1973. From Pervasive Ambiguity to a Definition of the Situation. *Sociometry* 36(3): 378–389.

Bangerter, Adrian and Chip Heath. 2004. The Mozart Effect: Tracking the Evolution of a Scientific Legend. *British Journal of Social Psychology* 43(4): 605–623.

Bartlett, F.C. 1932. *Remembering: A Study in Experimental and Social Psychology*. Cambridge: Cambridge University Press.

Basham, Lee. 2003. Malevolent Global Conspiracy. *Journal of Social Philosophy* 34 (1): 91–103.

Bauer, Raymond A. and David B. Gleicher. 1953. Word-of-Mouth-Communication in the Soviet Union. *Public Opinion Quarterly* 17(3): 297–310.

Baumgartner, Jody C. 2007. Humor on the Next Frontier: Youth, Online Political Humor, and the JibJab Effect. *Social Science Computer Review* 25(3): 319–338.

BBC News. 2008. As It Happened: Mumbai Attacks 27 Nov. 27 November. Online at: news.bbc.co.uk/2/hi/south_asia/7752003.stm (accessed 16 December 2009).

——. 2010. US Denies Killing Iran Scientist Massoud AliMohammadi. 12 January. Online at: news.bbc.co.uk/2/hi/middle_east/8455593.stm (accessed 12 March 2013)

Benedict, Ruth. 1946. *The Chrysanthemum and the Sword: Patterns of Japanese Culture*. Boston, MA: Houghton Mifflin.

Benford, Robert D. and David A. Snow. 2000. Framing Processes and Social Movements: An Overview and Assessment. *Annual Review of Sociology* 26: 611–639.

Berger, Peter L. and Thomas Luckman. 1967. *The Social Construction of Reality: A Treatise in the Sociology of Knowledge*. Garden City, NY: Doubleday.

Bergmann, Jorg R. 1993. *Discreet Indiscretions: The Social Organization of Gossip*. New York: Aldine de Gruyter.

Berlo, David K. 1960. *The Process of Communication: An Introduction to Theory and Practice*. New York: Holt, Rinehart and Winston.

Bernard, Viola, Perry Ottenberg and Fritz Redl. 2002 [1965]. Dehumanization: A Composite Psychological Defense in Relation to Modern War, pp. 64–82 in *Behavior Science and Human Survival*, edited by Milton Schwebel. Lincoln, NE: iUniverse.

Bernardi, Daniel *et al*. 2012. *Narrative Landmines: Rumors, Islamist Extremism, and the Struggle for Strategic Influence*. Rutgers, NY: Rutgers University Press.

Birch, David. 1992. Talking Politics: Radio in Singapore. *Continuum: The Australian Journal of Media & Culture* 6(1): 75–101.

Bird, Donald, Stephen C. Holder and Diane Sears. 1976. Walrus is Greek for Corpse: Rumor and the Death of Paul McCartney. *Journal of Popular Culture* 10(1): 110–121.

Bibliography   183

Blackmore, Susan. 2000. *The Meme Machine.* New York: Oxford University Press.

Blackshaw, Pete and Karthik Iyer. 2008. *Rumors and Issues on the Internet: Using the Web to Manage Reputations and Crises ... Before it's Too Late.* Corporate Report: Intelliseek.

Boellstorff, Tom. 2005. *The Gay Archipelago: Sexuality and Nation in Indonesia.* Princeton, NJ: Princeton University Press.

Boey, David. 2008. Every Moment He's Out 'a Significant Danger'. *The Straits Times,* 28 February.

Bolter, Jay D. and Richard Grusin. 2000. *Remediation: Understanding New Media.* Cambridge: MIT Press.

Bordia, Prashant. 1996. Studying Verbal Interaction on the Internet: The Case of Rumor Transmission Research. *Behavior Research Methods* 28(2): 149–151.

——, and Nicholas DiFonzo. 2002. When Social Psychology Became Less Social: Prasad and the History of Rumor Research. *Asian Journal of Social Psychology* 5 (1): 49–61.

——, and Nicholas DiFonzo. 2004. Problem Solving in Social Interactions on the Internet: Rumor as Social Cognition. *Social Psychology Quarterly* 67(1): 33–49.

——, and Ralph Rosnow. 1998. Rumor Rest Stops on the Information Highways: Transmission Patterns in a Computer-Mediated Rumor Chain. *Human Communication Research* 25(2): 163–179.

——, Nicholas DiFonzo and Artemis Chang. 1999. Rumor as Group Problem Solving: Development Patterns in Informal Computer-Mediated Groups. *Small Group Research* 30(1): 8–28.

—— et al. 2005. Rumors Denials as Persuasive Messages: Effects of Personal Relevance, Source, and Message Characteristics. *Journal of Applied Social Psychology* 35 (6):1301–1311.

Bormann, Ernest G. 1972. Fantasy and Rhetorical Vision: The Rhetorical Criticism of Social Reality. *The Quarterly Journal of Speech* 58(4): 396–407.

Boucher, Richard. 2003. US Spokesman Says Media Publicity Campaign in Muslim World 'Successful'. Excerpt from US State Department Daily Press Briefing, 16 January. Online at: www.worldofradio.com/dxld3011.txt (accessed 23 November 2009).

Bourdieu, Pierre. 1977. The Economics of Linguistic Exchanges. *Social Science Information* 16(6): 645–668.

——. 1979. Public Opinion Does Not Exist, pp. 124–130 in *Communication and Class Struggle,* edited by A. Matterlat and S. Siegelaub. New York: International General.

——. 1993. *The Field of Cultural Production.* Cambridge: Polity Press.

——. 1998. *Practical Reason.* Stanford, CA: Stanford University Press.

——. 2003 [1991]. *Language and Symbolic Power.* Cambridge, MA: Harvard University Press.

——. and Loïc J.D. Wacquant. 1992. *An Invitation to Reflexive Sociology.* Chicago, IL: University of Chicago Press.

Bramantyo Prijosusilo. 2010. Hostility, Not Homosexuality, Flies in The Face of True Koranic Teachings. *Jakarta Globe,* March 29. Online at: www.thejakartaglobe.com/opinion/hostility-not-homosexuality-flies-in-the-face-of-true-koranic-teachings/366516 [accessed 1 May 2010].

Brekhus, Wayne. 1998. A Sociology of the Unmarked: Redirecting our Focus. *Sociological Theory* 16(1): 34–51.

Bridger, Jeffrey C. and David R. Maines. 1998. Narrative Structures and the Catholic Church Closings in Detroit. *Qualitative Sociology* 21(3): 319–340.

184 *Bibliography*

Brison, Karen J. 1992. *Just Talk: Gossip, Meetings, and Power in a Papua New Guinea Village*. Berkeley, CA: University of California Press.

Brownlee, Jason. 2007. *Authoritarianism in an Age of Democratization*. Cambridge: Cambridge University Press.

Brumberg, Daniel. 2001. *Reinventing Khomeini: The Struggle for Reform in Iran*. Chicago, IL: Chicago University Press.

Bruns, Axel. 2008. *Blogs, Wikipedia, Second Life, and Beyond: From Production to Produsage*. New York: Peter Lang.

Brunvand, Jan H. 2001. *The Truth Never Stands in the Way of a Good Story*. Champaign: University of Illinois Press.

Bubandt, Nils. 2000. Conspiracy Theories, Apocalyptic Narratives and the Discursive Construction of 'the Violence' in Maluku. *Antropologi Indonesia* 63(24): 15–28.

——. 2008. Rumors, Pamphlets, and the Politics of Paranoia in Indonesia. *Journal of Asian Studies* 67(3): 789–817.

Buckner, H. Taylor. 1965. A Theory of Rumor Transmission. *The Public Opinion Quarterly* 29(1): 54–70.

Burgess, Adam. 2007. Mobile Phones and Service Stations: Rumour, Risk and Precaution. *Diogenes* 54(1): 125–139.

Burke, Timothy. 1998. Cannibal Margarine and Reactionary Snapple: A Comparative Examination of Rumors about Commodities. *International Journal of Cultural Studies* 1(2): 253–270.

Business Week. 2001. Charlotte Beers' Toughest Sell: Can She Market America to Hostile Muslims Abroad? *Business Week*, 17 December.

Butt, Leslie. 2005. 'Lipstick Girls' and 'Fallen Women': AIDS and Conspiratorial Thinking in Papua, Indonesia. *Cultural Anthropology* 20(3): 412–442.

Campion-Vincent, Veronique. 1992. Disassembled Babies: A New Latin-American 'Legend'. *Cahiers Internationaux de Sociologie* 39(93): 299–319.

——. 2007. Rumors and Urban Legends. *Diogenes* 54(1): 162–199.

Caplow, Theodore. 1947. Rumors in War. *Social Forces* 25(3): 298–302.

Carpini, Michael X.D. 1994. The Making of a Consensual Majority: Political Discourse and Electoral Politics in the 1980s, pp. 232–273 in *An American Half Century: Postwar Culture and Politics in the USA*, edited by Michael Klein. London: Pluto Press.

Cellan-Jones, Rory. 2008. Twitter – the Mumbai Myths. *BBC News*, 1 December. Online at: www.bbc.co.uk/blogs/technology/2008/12/twitter_the_mumbai_myths.html (accessed 12 May 2012).

Cerulo, Karen A. 2000. The Rest of the Story: Sociocultural Patterns of Story Elaboration. *Poetics* 28(1): 21–45.

——. 2010. Mining the Intersections of Cognitive Sociology and Neuroscience. *Poetics* 38(2): 115–132.

Chadwick, Thomas. 1932. *The Influence of Rumour on Human Thought and Action*. Manchester: Sherrat & Hughes.

Chandrasekaran, Rajiv. 2006. *Imperial Life in the Emerald City: Inside Iraq's Green Zone*. New York: Knopf.

Chatman, Seymour. 1978. *Story and Discourse: Narrative Structure in Fiction and Film*. Ithaca, NY: Cornell University Press.

Chia, Sue-Ann. 2004. Govt Worries about Soft Terror Targets: SM Goh. *The Straits Times*, 20 September.

Chicago Commission on Race Relations. 1922. *The Negro in Chicago: A Study of Race Relations and a Race Riot*. Chicago, IL: University of Chicago Press.

Chin, Yolanda. 2010. Community Confidence and Security, pp. 443–461 in *Management of Success: Singapore Revisited*, edited by Terrence Chong. Singapore: ISEAS.

Chock, Phyllis P. 1995. Ambiguity in Policy Discourse: Congressional Talk about Immigration. *Policy Sciences* 29(2): 165–184.

Chorus, A. 1953. The Basic Law of Rumor. *Journal of Abnormal and Social Psychology* 48(2): 313–314.

Chua, Beng Huat. 1995. *Communitarian Ideology and Democracy in Singapore.* London: Routledge.

Clarke, Steve. 2002. Conspiracy Theories and Conspiracy Theorizing. *Philosophy of the Social Sciences* 32(2): 131–150.

——. 2006. Appealing to the Fundamental Attribution Error: Was it All a Big Mistake? pp. 129–132 in *Conspiracy Theories: The Philosophical Debate*, edited by David Coady. Aldershot: Ashgate

Coady, C.A.J. 1992. *Testimony: A Philosophical Study.* Oxford: Oxford University Press.

——. 2006. Pathologies of Testimony, pp. 253–271 in *The Epistemology of Testimony*, edited by Jennifer Lackey and Edgar Sosa. Oxford: Oxford University Press.

Coady, David. 2003. Conspiracy Theories and Official Stories. *International Journal of Applied Philosophy* 17(2): 197–209.

——. 2006a. Rumour Has It. *International Journal of Applied Philosophy* 20(1): 41–53.

——. 2006b. An Introduction to the Philosophical Debate about Conspiracy Theories, pp. 1–13 in *Conspiracy Theories: The Philosophical Debate*, edited by David Coady. Aldershot: Ashgate.

——. 2007. Are Conspiracy Theorists Irrational? *Episteme: A Journal of Social Epistemology* 4(2): 193–204.

Code, Lorraine. 1994. Gossip, or In Praise of Chaos, pp. 100–105 in *Good Gossip*, edited by Robert F. Goodman and Aaron Ben-Ze'ev. Lawrence: University Press of Kansas.

Collins, Louise. 1994. Gossip: A Feminist Defense, pp. 106–116 in *Good Gossip*, edited by Robert F. Goodman and Aharon Ben-Ze'ev. Lawrence: University Press of Kansas.

Collins, Randall. 1981. On the Microfoundations of Macrosociology. *American Journal of Sociology* 86(5): 984–1014.

Committee of Inquiry (Singapore). 2008. *Report of the Committee of Inquiry on the Escape of Jemaah Islamiyah Detainee, Mas Selamat bin Kastari, from the Whitley Road Detention Centre.*

Cook, M.A. 2003. *Forbidding Wrong in Islam.* Cambridge: Cambridge University Press.

Corman, Steven R. and Kevin J. Dooley. 2008. *Strategic Communication on a Rugged Landscape: Principles for Finding the Right Message.* Working Paper #0801. Arizona State University: Consortium for Strategic Communication.

——., Angela Tretheway and H.L. Goodall, Jr. 2007. *A 21st Century Model for Communication in the Global War of Ideas: From Simplistic Influence to Pragmatic Complexity.* Working Paper #0701. Arizona State University: Consortium for Strategic Communication.

Cottee, Simon. 2010. Mind Slaughter: The Neutralizations of Jihadi Salafism. *Studies in Conflict & Terrorism* 33(4): 330–352.

Council of Europe. 2007. *Secret Detentions and Illegal Transfers of Detainees Involving Council of Europe Member States.* Report by Committee on Legal Affairs and

186 Bibliography

Human Rights. Online at: assembly.coe.int/ Documents/WorkingDocs/Doc07/edoc1 1302.pdf (accessed 1 March 2010).

Cull, Nicholas J. 2008. *The Cold War and the United States Information Agency: American Propaganda and Public Diplomacy, 1945–1989.* Cambridge: Cambridge University Press.

Cuonzo, Margaret A. 2008. Gossip: An Intention-based Account. *Journal of Social Philosophy* 39(1): 131–140.

Craig, Edward. 1990. *Knowledge and the State of Nature: An Essay in Conceptual Synthesis.* Oxford: Oxford University Press.

Cribb, Robert. 1990. *The Indonesian Killings, 1965–1966.* Clayton: Centre of Southeast Asian Studies, Monash University.

Dabashi, Hamid. 2010. *Iran, The Green Movement and the USA: The Fox and the Paradox.* London: Zed Books.

Dalziel, G.R. 2011. Assessing the Terrorist Threat to the Food Supply: Food Defence, Threat Assessments, and the Problem of Vulnerability. *International Journal of Food Safety, Nutrition and Public Health* 4(1): 12–28.

———. Forthcoming. Making Distinctions: A New Approach to the Study of Rumor, in *Genre-Text-Interpretation: Multidisciplinary Perspectives on Folklore and Beyond,* edited by Kaarina Koski. Helsinki: Finnish Literature Society/Studia Fennica.

D'Andrade, Roy. 1995. *The Development of Cognitive Anthropology.* Cambridge: Cambridge University Press.

Danzig, Elliot R., Paul W. Thayer and Lila R. Galanter. 1958. *The Effects of a Threatening Rumor on a Disaster-Stricken Community.* Washington, DC: National Academy of Sciences – National Research Council.

Das, Veena. 2005. *Life and Words: Violence and the Descent into the Ordinary.* Berkeley: University of California Press.

De Bellaigue, Christopher. 2007. *The Struggle for Iran.* New York: New York Review Books.

DeClerque, Julia *et al.* 1986. Rumor, Misinformation and Oral Contraceptive Use in Egypt. *Social Science Medicine* 23(1): 83–92.

Defense Science Board (US). 2007. *Report of the Defense Science Board Task Force on Strategic Communication in the 21st Century.*

de Ipola, Emilio. 2007. Bembas: The Life and Death of Rumors in a Political Prison (Argentina 1976–83). *Diogenes* 54(1): 140–161.

De Sousa, Ronald. 1994. In Praise of Gossip: Indiscretion as a Saintly Virtue, pp. 25–33 in *Good Gossip,* edited by Robert F. Goodman and Aharon Ben-Ze'ev. Lawrence: University Press of Kansas.

DiFonzo, Nicholas. 2008. *The Watercooler Effect: A Psychologist Explores the Extraordinary Power of Rumors.* Avery: New York.

———. and Prashant Bordia. 2000. How Top PR Professionals Handle Hearsay: Corporate Rumors, their Effects, and Strategies to Manage Them. *Public Relations Review* 26(2): 173–190.

———. and Prashant Bordia. 2002. Corporate Rumor Activity, Belief and Accuracy. *Public Relations Review* 28(1): 1–19.

———. and Prashant Bordia. 2007. *Rumor Psychology: Social and Organizational Approaches.* Washington, DC: American Psychology Association.

DiMaggio, Paul. 1997. Culture and Cognition. *Annual Review of Sociology* 23: 263–287.

Dinnie, Keith. 2007. *Nation Branding: Concepts, Issues, Practice.* Burlington, MA: Elsevier.

Bibliography 187

Djerejian, Edward P. 2003. *Changing Minds Winning Peace: A New Strategic Direction for US Public Diplomacy in the Arab & Muslim World.* Report of the Advisory Group on Public Diplomacy for the Arab and Muslim World. Online at: www.state. gov/documents/organization/24882.pdf (accessed 1 April 2012).

Dodoo, Alexander *et al.* 2007. When Rumors Derail a Mass Deworming Exercise. *The Lancet* 370[9586]: 465–466, 11 August.

Donovan, Pamela. 2004. *No Way of Knowing: Crime, Urban Legends, and the Internet.* New York: Routledge.

Drake, Richard A. 1989. Construction Sacrifice and Kidnapping Rumor Panics in Borneo. *Oceania* 59(7): 269–279.

Dunbar, Robin I.M. 1996. *Grooming, Gossip, and the Evolution of Language.* London: Faber.

Dundes, Alan. 1965. *The Study of Folklore.* Englewood Cliffs, IL: Prentice-Hall.

Ehteshami, Anoushiravan and Mahjoob Zweiri. 2007. *Iran and the Rise of its Neo-conservatives: The Politics of Tehran's Silent Revolution.* London: I.B. Tauris.

Eliade, Mircea. 1954. *The Myth of Eternal Return or Cosmos and History.* Princeton, NJ: Princeton University Press.

Emirbayer, Mustafa. 1997. Manifesto for a Relational Sociology. *American Journal of Sociology* 103(2): 281–317.

Emler, N. 1994. Gossip, Reputation, and Social Adaptation, pp. 117–138 in *Good Gossip*, edited by Robert F. Goodman and Aaron Ben-Ze'ev. Lawrence: University Press of Kansas.

Engineer, Asghar A. 1995. Bhagalpur Riot Enquiry Commission Report. *Economic and Political Weekly* 30(28): 1729–1731, 15 July.

Esfandiari, Golnaz. 2010a. Iran State TV Suggests Neda's Iconic Death was 'Faked'. *Radio Free Europe*, 7 January. Online at: www.rferl.org/content/Iran_State_TV_Suggests_ Iconic_Protest_Death_Faked/1923414.html [accessed 20 January 2010].

——. 2010b. Twitter Devolution. *Foreign Policy*, 7 June. Online at: www.foreignpolicy. com/articles/2010/06/07/the_twitter_revolution_that_wasnt (accessed 20 June 2010).

Espeland, Wendy N. and Michael L. Stevens. 1998. Commensuration as a Social Process. *Annual Review of Sociology* 24: 313–343.

Esposito, James L. and Ralph Rosnow. 1984. Cognitive Set and Message Processing: Implications of Prose Memory Research for Rumor Theory. *Language and Communication* 4(4): 301–315.

Evans, Dominic and Frederik Dahl. 2009. Mousavi Camp Waging Velvet Revolution: Iran Guards. *Reuters*, 10 June. Online at: www.reuters.com/assets/print?aid=USTRE 55920M20090610 (accessed 12 April 2010).

Fadly. 2009. Noordin M Top, Selamat Jalan Wahai Mujahid. *Ar-Rahmah* [Blog]. 19 September. Online at: www.arrahmah.com/index.php/news/read/5703/noordin-m-top -selamat-jalan-wahai-mujahid/P200/ (accessed 20 October 2010).

Farge, Arlette, Jacques Revel and Claudia Mieville. 1991. *The Vanishing Children of Paris: Rumor and Politics before the French Revolution.* London: Polity Press.

Faye, Cathy. 2007. Governing the Grapevine: The Study of Rumor during World War II. *History of Psychology* 10(1): 1–21.

Feldman, Allen. 1997. Violence and Vision: the Prosthetics and Aesthetics of Terror. *Public Culture* 10(1): 24–60.

Feldman-Savelsberg, Pamela, Flavien T. Ndonko and Bergis Schmidt-Ehry. 2000. Sterilizing Vaccines or the Politics of the Womb: Retrospective Study of a Rumor in Cameroon. *Medical Anthropology Quarterly* [new series] 14(2): 159–179.

188   *Bibliography*

Fenster, Mark. 1999. *Conspiracy Theories: Secrecy and Power in American Culture.* Minneapolis: University of Minnesota Press.

Festinger, Leon. 1962. *A Theory of Cognitive Dissonance.* Stanford, CA: Stanford University Press.

Fine, Gary A. 1992. *Manufacturing Tales: Sex and Money in Contemporary Legends,* Knoxville, TN: University of Tennessee Press.

——. 1993. The Sad Demise, Mysterious Disappearance, and Glorious Triumph of Symbolic Interactionism. *Annual Review of Sociology* 19: 61–87.

——. 1995. Accounting for Rumor: The Creation of Credibility in Folk Knowledge, pp. 123–136 in *Folklore Interpreted: Essays in Honor of Alan Dundes,* edited by Regina Bendix and Rosemary L. Zumwalt. New York: Garland Publishing.

——. 2001. *Difficult Reputations: Collective Memories of the Evil, Inept, and Controversial.* Chicago, IL: University of Chicago Press.

——. 2007. Rumor, Trust and Civil Society: Collective Memory and Cultures of Judgment. *Diogenes* 54(5): 5–18.

——. and Bill Ellis. 2010. *The Global Grapevine: Why Rumors of Terrorism, Immigration, and Trade Matter.* New York: Oxford University Press.

——. and Irfan Khawaja. 2005. Celebrating Arabs and Grateful Terrorists: Rumor and the Politics of Plausibility, pp. 189–206 in *Rumor Mills: The Social Impact of Rumor and Legend,* edited by Gary A. Fine, Veronique Campion-Vincent and Chip Heath. New Brunswick, NJ: Transaction Publishers.

——. and Sherry Kleinman. 1983. Network and Meaning: An Interactionist Approach to Structure. *Symbolic Interaction* 6(1): 97–110.

——. and Patricia A. Turner. 2001. *Whispers on the Color Line: Rumor and Race in America.* Berkeley, CA: University of California Press.

——., Veronique Campion-Vincent and Chip Heath (eds) 2005. *Rumor Mills: The Social Impact of Rumor and Legend.* New Brunswick, NJ: Transaction Publishers.

Firth, Raymond. 1956. Rumor in a Primitive Society. *The Journal of Abnormal and Social Psychology* 53(1): 122–132.

Fisher, Walter. 1984. Narration as a Human Communication Paradigm: The Case of Public Moral Argument. *Communication Monographs* 51: 1–22.

——. 1987. *Human Communication as Narration: Toward a Philosophy of Reason, Value, and Action.* Columbia, SC: University of South Carolina Press.

Flyvbjerg, Bent. 1998. *Rationality and Power: Democracy in Practice.* Chicago: Chicago University Press.

——. 2001. *Making Social Science Matter: Why Social Inquiry Fails and How it Can Succeed Again.* Cambridge: Cambridge University Press.

——. 2004. Phronetic Planning Research: Theoretical and Methodological Reflections. *Planning Theory & Practice* 5(4): 283–306.

Fong, Tanya. 2005. Took Strolled Across Causeway. *The Straits Times,* 14 July.

Fragale, Alison and Chip Heath. 2004. Evolving Informational Credentials: The (Mis)Attribution of Believable Facts to Credible Sources. *Personality and Social Psychology Bulletin* 30(2): 226–236.

Fraser, Nancy. 1990. Rethinking the Public Sphere: A Contribution to the Critique of Actually Existing Democracy. *Social Text* 25(26): 56–80.

Friedland, Roger. 2009. The Endless Fields of Pierre Bourdieu. *Organization* 16(6): 887–917.

——. and Robert R. Alford. 1991. Bringing Society Back in: Symbols, Practices, and Institutional Contradictions, pp. 232–266 in *The New Institutionalism in*

Organizational Analysis, edited by Walter W. Powell and Paul DiMaggio. Chicago, IL: University of Chicago Press.

Fukuyama, Francis. 1992. *The End of History and the Last Man*. New York: Harper.

Gahran, Amy. 2008. Tracking a Rumor: Indian Government, Twitter, and Common Sense. *Contentious.com* [Blog]. Online at: www.contentious.com/2008/11/27/tracking-a-rumor-indian-government-twitter-and-common-sens/ (accessed 2 December 2010).

Gant, Samuel G. 1906. *Diseases of the Rectum and Anus*. Philadelphia, PA: F.A. Davis Company.

Garrett, R. Kelly. 2011. Troubling Consequences of Online Political Rumoring. *Human Communication Research* 37(2): 255–274.

——, and James N. Danziger. 2011. Internet Electorate. *Communication of the ACM* 54(3): 117–123.

Gary, Brett. 1999. *The Nervous Liberals: Propaganda Anxieties from World War I to the Cold War*. New York: Columbia University Press.

Geertz, Clifford. 1991. Deep Play: Notes on the Balinese Cockfight, pp. 239–277 in *Rethinking Popular Culture: Contemporary Perspectives in Cultural Studies*, edited by Chandra Mukerji and Michael Schudson. Berkeley, CA: University of California Press.

Gelfert, Axel. 2006. Kant on Testimony. *British Journal for the History of Philosophy* 14(4): 627–652.

——. 2008. Learning from Testimony: Cognitive Cultures and the Epistemic Status of Testimony-Based Beliefs, pp. 34–56 in *Culture, Nature, Memes*, edited by Thorsten Botz-Bornstein. Newcastle: Cambridge Scholars Publishing.

——. Forthcoming. Communicability and the Public Misuse of Communication: Kant on the Pathologies of Testimony, in *Proceedings of the Eleventh International Kant Congress* held in Pisa, Italy, 22–26 May 2010. Berlin: de Gruyter.

Genette, Gerard. 1980. *Narrative Discourse*. Ithaca, NY: Cornell University Press.

Gheissari, Ali and Vali Nasr. 2006. *Democracy in Iran: History and the Quest for Liberty*. Oxford: Oxford University Press.

——, and Kaveh-Cyrus Sanandaji. 2009. New Conservative Politics and Electoral Behavior in Iran, pp. 275–298 in *Contemporary Iran: Economy, Society, Politics*, edited by Ali Gheissari. Oxford: Oxford University Press.

Gheytanchi, Elham and Babak Rahimi. 2009. The Politics of Facebook in Iran. *Open Democracy*, 1 June. Online at: www.opendemocracy.net/article/email/the-politics-of-facebook-in-iran (accessed 30 June 2012).

Giddens, Anthony. 1982. *Profiles and Critiques in Social Theory*. Berkeley, CA: University of California Press.

Gilbert, Daniel T. 1991. How Mental Systems Believe. *American Psychologist* 46(2): 107–119.

——, Douglas S. Krull and Patrick S. Malone. 1990. Unbelieving the Unbelievable: Some Problems in the Rejection of False Information. *Journal of Personality and Social Psychology* 59(4): 601–613.

——, Romin W. Tafarodi and Patrick S. Malone. 1993. You Can't Not Believe Everything You Read. *Journal of Personality and Social Psychology* 65(2): 221–233.

Gladwell, Malcolm. 2000. *The Tipping Point: How Little Things Can Make a Big Difference*. Boston, MA: Little, Brown.

Glaeser, Andreas. 2012. *Political Epistemics: The Secret Police, the Opposition, and the End of East German Socialism*. Chicago, IL: University of Chicago Press.

Gluckman, Max. 1963. Gossip and Scandal. *Current Anthropology* 4(3): 307–316.

190 *Bibliography*

Godart, Frederic C., and Harrison C. White. 2010. Switchings under Uncertainty: The Coming and Becoming of Meanings. *Poetics* 38(6): 567–586.

Goffman, Erving. 1959. *The Presentation of Self in Everyday Life*. New York: Doubleday.

Goldberg, Amir. 2011. Mapping Shared Understandings Using Relational Class Analysis: The Case of the Cultural Omnivore Reexamined. *American Journal of Sociology* 116(5): 1397–1436.

Goldman, Alvin I. 1999. *Knowledge in a Social World*. New York: Oxford University Press.

Goodman, Robert F. and Aaron Ben-Ze'ev (eds). 1994. *Good Gossip*. Lawrence: University Press of Kansas.

Gorka, Sebastian and David Kilcullen. 2009. Who's Winning the Battle for Narrative? Al-Qaida Versus the United States and its Allies, pp. 229–240 in *Influence Warfare: How Terrorists and Governments Fight to Shape Perceptions in a War of Ideas*, edited by James J.F. Forest. Westport, CT: Praeger Security International.

Gosseries, Axel. 2008. Publicity. *The Stanford Encyclopedia of Philosophy* (Fall 2008 edition), edited by Edward N. Zalta. Online at: plato.stanford.edu/archives/fall2008/entries/publicity/ (accessed 1 February 2010).

Graham, Jeffrey. 2009. *'Loose Lips Sink Ships': A History of Rumor Control in the United States*. Unpublished PhD Dissertation: City University of New York.

Gramsci, Antonio. 1971. *Selections from the Prison Notebooks of Antonio Gramsci*. London: Lawrence and Wishart.

Gray, Colin S. 1999. Strategic Culture as Context: The First Generation of Theory Strikes Back. *Review of International Studies* 25(1): 46–69.

Gray, Matthew. 2010. *Conspiracy Theories in the Arab World: Sources and Politics*. New York: Routledge.

Grossman, Lev. 2009. Iran Protests: Twitter, the Medium of the Movement. *Time*, 17 June. Online at: www.time.com/time/printout/0,8816,1905125,00.html (accessed 20 September 2010).

Guha Ranajit. 1983. *Elementary Aspects of Peasant Insurgency in Colonial India*. Delhi, India: Oxford University Press.

Gus Rachmat. 2009. Kerusakan Dubur Noordin M Top Akibat Penetrasi Benda Tumpul. *Ar-Rahman Solution* [Blog]. Online at: http://gusrachmat.wordpress.com/2009/10/01/kerusakan-dubur-noordin-m-top-akibat-penetrasi-benda-tumpul/ (accessed 30 June 2012).

Gwee, Ah Leng. 1963. Koro: A Cultural Disease. *Singapore Medical Journal* 4(3): 119–122.

———. 1968. Koro: Its Origin and Nature as a Disease Entity. *Singapore Medical Journal* 9(1): 3–6.

Habermas, Jurgen. 1971. *Toward a Rational Society: Student Protest, Science, and Politics*. Boston, MA: Beacon Press.

Hahn, Steven. 1997. 'Extravagant Expectations' of Freedom: Rumour, Political Struggle, and the Christmas Insurrection Scare of 1865 in the American South. *Past and Present* 157(2): 122–158.

Halverson, Jeffry R., H.L. Goodall, Jr. and Steven R. Corman. 2011. *Master Narratives of Islamist Extremism*. New York: Palgrave.

Hardin, Russell. 2002. The Crippled Epistemology of Extremism, pp. 3–22 in *Political Extremism and Rationality*, edited by Albert Breton *et al*. Cambridge: Cambridge University Press.

Hariman, Robert. 2008. Political Parody and Public Culture. *Quarterly Journal of Speech* 94(3): 247–272.

Harsin, Jayson. 2006. The Rumour Bomb: Theorising the Convergence of New and Old Trends in Mediated US Politics. *Southern Review: Communication, Politics & Culture* 39(1): 84–110.

Hart, Bernard. 1916. The Psychology of Rumor. *Proceedings of the Royal Society of Medicine (Section of Psychiatry)* 9(1): 1–26.

Hashemi, Nader and Danny Postel (eds). 2010. *The People Reloaded: The Green Movement and the Struggle for Iran's Future*. Brooklyn, NY: Melville House.

Hatch, Mary J. and Michael O. Jones. 1997. Photocopylore at Work: Aesthetics, Collective Creativity and the Social Construction of Organizations. *Studies in Cultures, Organizations and Societies* 3(2): 263–287.

Heath, Robert and Paul Feldwick. 2007. Fifty Years of Using the Wrong Model of Advertising. *International Journal of Market Research* 50(1): 29–59.

Heine-Geldern, Robert. 1942. Conceptions of State and Kingship in Southeast Asia. *Far Eastern Quarterly* 2(1): 15–30.

Hempel, Carl G. 1983. Valuation and Objectivity in Science, pp. 73–100 in *Physics, Philosophy and Psychoanalysis: Essays in Honor of Adolf Grünbaum*, edited by Robert S. Cohen. Dordrecht: Reidel.

Herbst, Susan. 1993. The Meaning of Public Opinion: Citizens' Construction of Political Reality. *Media, Culture & Society* 15(3): 437–454.

Herriman, Nicholas. 2010. The Great Rumor Mill: Gossip, Mass Media, and the Ninja Fear. *Journal of Asian Studies* 69(3): 732–748.

Herman, Judith. 1997. *Trauma and Recovery: The Aftermath of Violence from Domestic Abuse to Political Terror*. New York: Basic Books.

Hermawan, B. 2009. Polri: Dubur Noordin Tak Diutak-Utik. *Inilah* [Blog], 1 October. Online at: www.inilah.com/berita/2009/09/30/161702/polri-dubur-noordin-tak-diutak-atik/ (accessed 12 November 2009).

Hersh, Seymour M. 2004. *Chain of Command*. New York: HarperCollins Publishers.

Higham, T.M. 1951. The Experimental Study of the Transmission of Rumour. *British Journal of Psychology* 42(1/2): 42–55.

Hirata, Akiro, Emi Morofuji and Hiroshi Arakami. 2011. Television Viewing and Media Use Today: From 'The Japanese and Television 2010' Survey. *NHK Broadcasting Studies* 9: 1–46.

Hiratsuka, Chihiro. 1996. Disaster Information in the Multimedia Age. *Studies of Broadcasting* 32: 77–114. Broadcasting Culture Research Institute (NHK).

Hiroi, Osamu. 1996. The Development of Disaster Broadcasting in Japan. *Studies of Broadcasting* 32: 7–32. Broadcasting Culture Research Institute (NHK).

Hopf, Ted. 2002. *Social Construction of International Politics: Identities and Foreign Policies, Moscow, 1955 and 1999*. New York: Cornell University Press.

Human Rights Watch. 2004. *In a Time of Torture: Egypt's Crackdown on Homosexual Conduct*. New York: Human Rights Watch.

Hussain, Zakir. 2008. 'Ruthless' JI Chief Planned Attacks Here. *The Straits Times*, 28 February.

Ibrahim, Yaacob. 2003. Speech by Dr Yaacob Ibrahim, Acting Minister for Community Devt and Sports and Minister-in-Charge of Muslim Affairs, at the Debate in Parliament on the White Paper on JI Arrests and the Threat of Terrorism, 21 January 2003. *Singapore Government Press Release*. Online at: stars.nhb.gov.sg/stars/public/viewHTML.jsp?pdfno=2003012109 (accessed 30 June 2012).

Ikutaro, Shimizu. 2011 [1937]. *Ryugen Higo*. Tokyo: Chikuma Shobo.

192 Bibliography

Imbalo. 2010. Kuburan dan Wisata. *Imbalo Namaku* [Blog], 21 April. Online at: imbalo.wordpress.com/2010/04/21/kuburan-dan-wisata/ (accessed 30 June 2012).

Indonesia Page: All About Indonesia. 2009. Jomblo Juhari [Blog]. Online at: indonesiapage.-blogspot.com/2009/11/jomblo-juhari.html (accessed 12 November 2009).

International Crisis Group. 2006. Terrorism in Indonesia: Noordin's Networks. *International Crisis Group Asia Briefing*, May 5. Online at: www.crisisgroup.org/en/regions/asia/south-east-asia/indonesia/114-terrorism-in-indonesia-noordins-networks.aspx (accessed 30 June 2012).

Isikoff, Michael and David Corn. 2007. *Hubris*. New York: Three Rivers Press.

Ito, Masami. 2011. Edano Denies Flying Family Abroad. *The Japan Times*, April 12.

Ito, Mizuko *et al*. 2010. *Hanging Out, Messing Around, and Geeking Out: Kids Living and Learning with New Media*. Cambridge, MA: MIT Press.

Jacobsen, David J. 1948. *The Affair of Dame Rumor*. New York: Rinehart & Co.

Jansen, Bernard J. *et al*. 2009. Twitter Power: Tweets as Electronic Word of Mouth. *Journal of the American Society for Information Science & Technology* 60(11): 2169–2188.

Jenkins, Henry. 2006. *Convergence Culture: Where Old and New Media Collide*. New York: New York University Press.

Johnston, Alastair I. 1995. *Cultural Realism: Strategic Culture and Grand Strategy in Chinese History*. Princeton, NJ: Princeton University Press.

Jose, Lydia N.Y. 2012. The Koreans in Second World War Philippines: Rumour and History. *Journal of Southeast Asian Studies* 43(2): 324–339.

Jung, Carl G. 1964. Flying Saucers: A Modern Myth of Things Seen in the Skies, pp. 307–418 in *Civilization in Transition*. New York: Bollingen Foundation.

Kaler, Amy. 2009. Health Interventions and the Persistence of Rumor: The Circulation of Sterility Stories in African Public Health Campaigns. *Social Science & Medicine* 68(9): 1711–1719.

Kalmre, Eda. 1996. Legends of the Afghanistan War: The Boy Saved by the Snake. *Folklore: Electronic Journal of Folklore* 1(1): 51–61. Online at: www.folklore.ee/folklore/nr1/afga.htm [accessed 30 June 2012].

Kant, Immanuel. 1900. *Kant's Gesammelte Schriften* (Academy Edition = AA). Berlin: Verlag von Georg Reimer, Walter de Gruyter

——. 1991 [1795]. *Kant: Political Writings*. Edited by Hans S. Reiss. Cambridge: Cambridge University Press.

——. 1996. *The Metaphysics of Morals*. Translated and edited by Mary J. Gregor. Cambridge: Cambridge University Press.

——. 1997. *Lectures on Ethics*. Edited by Peter Heath and J.B. Schneewind. Translated by Peter Heath. Cambridge: Cambridge University Press.

——. 1998a [1781]. *Critique of Pure Reason*. Translated and edited by Paul Guyer and Allen W. Wood. Cambridge: Cambridge University Press.

——. 1998b. *Unveröffentlichte Nachschriften I. Logik Bauch*. Edited by Tillmann Pinder. Hamburg: Felix Meiner.

——. 2006 [1798]. *Anthropology from a Pragmatic Point of View*. Translated and edited by Robert Louden. Cambridge: Cambridge University Press.

Kapferer, Jean-Noel. 1990. *Rumors: Uses, Interpretations, and Images*. New Brunswick, NJ: Transaction Publishers.

Keeley, Brian. 1999. Of Conspiracy Theories. *Journal of Philosophy* 96(3): 109–126.

Kelley, Stephanie R. 2004. *Rumors in Iraq: A Guide to Winning Hearts and Minds*. Unpublished MSc Thesis, Naval Postgraduate School.

Bibliography 193

———. 2005. Rumors in Iraq: A Guide to Winning Hearts and Minds. *Strategic Insights* 4(2). Online at: ics-www.leeds.ac.uk/papers/pmt/exhibits/2667/kelleyfeb05.pdf (accessed 30 June 2012).

Kelsey, Charles B. 1893. *Diseases of the Rectum and Anus, Their Pathology, Diagnosis and Treatment*. New York: William Wood and Company.

Kievit, Rob. 2008. Twitter Messages Feed Major News Channels. *Radio Netherlands*. Online at: www.expatica.com/es/news/news_focus/Twitter-messages-feed-major-news -channels_13314.html (accessed 21 May 2012).

Kirsch, Stuart. 2002. Rumor and Other Narratives of Political Violence in West Papua. *Critique of Anthropology* 22(1): 53–79.

Klapp, Orrin E. 1972. *Currents of Unrest: An Introduction to Collective Behavior*. New York: Holt, Rinehart and Wilson.

Klintberg, Bengt A. 1986. *Råttan i pizzan: Folksägner i vår tid* [The Rat in the Pizza: Folk Legends of our Time]. Stockholm: Nordstedts.

———. 1994. *Den stulna njuren: sägner och rykten i vår tid* [The Stolen Kidney: Legends and Rumors of our Time]. Stockholm: Nordstedts.

Knapp, Robert H. 1943. The Criteria of a Successful Rumor. *Office of Strategic Services Planning Group Memo P.G. 28*, 2 June 1943. Online at: www.icdc.com/~paul-wolf/oss/rumormanual2june1943.htm (accessed 30 June 2012).

———. 1944. A Psychology of Rumor. *Public Opinion Quarterly* 8(1): 22–37.

Knopf, Terry A. 1975. Rumor Controls: A Reappraisal. *Phylon* 36(1): 23–31.

———. 2006 [1975]. *Rumors, Race and Riots*. New Brunswick, NJ: Transaction Publishers.

Koenig, Frederick W. 1985. *Rumors in the Market Place: The Social Psychology of Commercial Hearsay*. Dover, MA: Auburn House Publishing.

———. 1992. Comment. *Public Opinion Quarterly* 56(2): 254.

Kompas. 2009a. Nanan: Soal Dubur Noordin Seharusnya Dirahasiakan, 30 September. Online at: nasional.kompas.com/read/2009/09/30/17405148%20/nanan (accessed 30 June 2012).

———. 2009b. Forensik Temukan Kelainan di Tubuh Jenazah Noordin, 30 September. Online at: http://nasional.kompas.com/read/2009/09/30/1628014/Forensik.Temukan. Kelainan.di.Tubuh.Jenazah.Noordin (accessed 1 July 2012).

Koro Study Team. 1969. The Koro 'Epidemic' in Singapore. *Singapore Medical Journal* 10(4): 234–242.

Kosfeld, Michael. 2005. Rumors and Markets. *Journal of Mathematical Economics* 41 (6): 646–664.

Kreshel, Peggy J. 1990. John B. Watson at J. Walter Thompson: The Legitimation of 'Science' in Advertising. *Journal of Advertising* 19(2): 49–59.

Krinsky, John. 2010. Dynamics of Hegemony: Mapping Mechanisms of Cultural and Political Power in the Debates over Workfare in New York City, 1993–1999. *Poetics* 38(6): 625–648.

Krippendorff, Klaus H. 1980. *Content Analysis: An Introduction to its Methodology* [1st edn]. Beverly Hill, CA: Sage Publications.

Kroeger, Karen A. 2003. AIDS Rumors, Imaginary Enemies, and the Body Politic in Indonesia. *American Ethnologist* 30(2): 243–257.

Kuran, Timur. 1997. *Private Truth, Public Lies: The Social Consequences of Preference Falsification*. Cambridge, MA: Harvard University Press.

Lackey, Jennifer. 2006. Introduction, pp. 1–21 in *The Epistemology of Testimony*, edited by Jennifer Lackey and Edgar Sosa. Oxford: Oxford University Press.

194 *Bibliography*

Lai, Gina and Odalia Wong. 2002. The Tie Effect on Information Dissemination: The Spread of a Commercial Rumor in Hong Kong. *Social Networks* 24(1): 49–75.

Lamont, Michele and Virag Molnár. 2002. The Study of Boundaries in the Social Sciences. *Annual Review of Sociology* 28: 167–195.

——. and Laurent Thevenot (eds). 2000. *Rethinking Comparative Cultural Sociology: Repertoires of Evaluation in France and the United States.* Cambridge: Cambridge University Press.

Land, Isaac. 2006. 'Sinful Propensities:' Piracy, Sodomy, and Empire in the Rhetoric of Naval Reform, 1770–1870, pp. 90–114 in *Discipline and the Other Body: Correction, Corporeality, Colonialism*, edited by Anupama Rao and Steven Pierce. Durham, NC: Duke University Press.

Langlois, Janet L. 2005. 'Celebrating Arabs': Tracing Legend and Rumor Labyrinths in Post-9/11 Detroit. *Journal of American Folklore* 118(468): 219–236.

Lasswell, Harold. 1970. The Emerging Concept of Policy Sciences. *Policy Sciences* 1 (1): 3–14.

László, Janos. 1990. Images of Social Categories vs Images of Literary and Non-Literary Objects. *Poetics* 19(3): 277–291.

Lebarre,Weston. 1972. *The Ghost Dance: The Origins of Religion.* New York: Delta.

Leifer, Michael. 2000. *Singapore's Foreign Policy: Coping with Vulnerability.* London: Routledge.

Levan, Itzhak. 2006. Terrorism and Its Effects on Mental Health. *World Psychiatry* 5 (1): 35–36.

Levi-Strauss, Claude. 1966. *The Savage Mind.* Chicago, IL: University of Chicago Press.

Levy, Neil. 2007. Radically Socialized Knowledge and Conspiracy Theories. *Episteme* 4(2): 181–192.

Life Magazine. 1942. Rumor Clinic. *Life Magazine* 12(15): 12 October.

Liow, Joseph S. 2006. *Muslim Resistance in Southern Thailand and Southern Philippines: Religion, Ideology, and Politics.* Washington, DC: East–West Center.

Lizardo, Omar and Michael Strand. 2010. Skills, Toolkits, Contexts and Institutions: Clarifying the Relationship between Different Approaches to Cognition in Cultural Sociology. *Poetics* 38(2): 204–227.

Long, Scott. 2004. When Doctors Torture: The Anus and the State in Egypt and Beyond. *Health and Human Rights* 7(2): 114–140.

Long, S.R. Joey. 2008. Winning Hearts and Minds: US Psychological Operations in Singapore, 1955–1961. *Diplomatic History* 32(5): 899–930.

——. 2011. *Safe for Decolonization: The Eisenhower Administration, Britain, and Singapore.* Kent, OH: Kent State University Press.

Lotan, Gilad *et al.* 2011. The Revolutions were Tweeted: Information Flows During the 2011 Tunisian and Egyptian Revolutions. *International Journal of Communication* 5: 1375–1405. Online at: ijoc.org/ojs/index.php/ijoc/article/view/1246 (accessed 30 June 2012).

Lundry, Chris. 2009a. Possible New JI/AQ Offshoot Claims Jakarta Bombings. *COMOPS Journal*, 30 July. Online at: comops.org/journal/-2009/07/29/possible-new-jiaq-offshoot-claims-jakarta-bombings/ (accessed 30 June 2012).

——. 2009b. Getting to the Bottom of Explosive Rumors Concerning Noordin Top. *COMOPS Journal*, 1 October. Online at: comops.org/journal/2009/10/01/getti ng-to-the-bottom-of-explosive-rumors-concerning-noordin-top/ (accessed 30 June 2012).

Luo, Serene. 2008. Shock over Court Escape Bids. *The Straits Times*, 13 June.

MacDougall, John A. 1976. Birth of a Nation: National Identification in Singapore. *Asian Survey* 16(6): 510–524.

MacIntyre, Alasdair. 1984. *After Virtue: A Study in Moral Theory.* Notre Dame, IL: University of Notre Dame Press.

Mackey, Charles. 1996 [1841]. *Extraordinary Popular Delusions and the Madness of Crowds.* London: J. Wiley & Sons.

Mackey, Robert. 2010. Iranian TV Sees Conspiracy in Neda Video. *The New York Times (Lede Blog)*, 7 January. Online at: thelede.blogs.nytimes.com/2010/01/07/iranian-tv-sees-conspiracy-in-neda-video/?partner=rss&emc=rss (accessed 30 June 2012).

Maines, David R. 1999. Information Pools and Racialized Narrative Structures. *The Sociological Quarterly* 40(2): 317–326.

———. 2000. The Social Construction of Meaning. *Contemporary Sociology* 29(4): 577–584.

Mains, Daniel. 2004. Drinking, Rumor, and Ethnicity in Jimma, Ethiopia. *Africa: Journal of the International African Institute* 74(3): 341–360.

Malinowksi, Bronislaw. 1926. *Crime and Custom in Savage Society.* London: Kegan Paul.

Manoukian, Setrag. 2010. Where is this Place? Crowds, Audio Vision, and Poetry in Postelection Iran. *Public Culture* 22(2): 237–263.

Martin, John L. 2009. *Social Structures.* Princeton, NJ: Princeton University Press.

———. 2011. *The Explanation of Social Action.* Oxford: Oxford University Press.

Matsuda, Misa. 2011. Rumors and 'fuhyo higai (harmful rumors)' During the Ongoing Disaster. *Chuo Online* [Blog]. Online at: www.yomiuri.co.jp/adv/chuo/dy/research/20110602.htm (accessed June 20 2012).

McAdams, Mindy. 2008. Twitter, Mumbai, and 10 Facts about Journalism Now. *Teaching Online Journalism* [Blog]. Online at: mindymcadams.com/tojou/2008/twitter-mumbai-and-10-facts-about-journalism-now/ (accessed 3 January 2010).

McConnell, Brian. 1989. The Corporate Folk-Legend: Marketing Invention or Consumer Response?, pp. 231–249 in *The Questing Beast: Perspectives on Contemporary Legend Volume IV*, edited by Gillian Bennett and Paul Smith. Sheffield: Sheffield Academic Press.

McSweeney, Bill. 1999. *Security, Identity and Interests: A Sociology of International Relations.* Cambridge: Cambridge University Press.

Meikle, Graham. 2008. Whacking Bush: Tactical Media as Play, pp. 367–382 in *Digital Media and Democracy: Tactics in Hard Times*, edited by Megan Boler. Cambridge, MA: MIT Press.

Mendoza, Marcelo, Barbara Poblete and Carlos Castillo. 2010. Twitter Under Crisis: Can We Trust What We RT? *1st Workshop on Social Media Analytics (SOMA '10), July 25, Washington, DC.*

Merron, Jeff. 1999. Putting Foreign Consumers on the Map: J. Walter Thompson's Struggle with General Motors. *Business History Review* 73(3): 465–504.

Merten, Klaus. 2009. Zur Theorie des Gerüchts. *Publizistik* 54(1): 15–42.

Michelson, Grant and Suchitra Mouly. 2000. Rumour and Gossip in Organisations: A Conceptual Study. *Management Decision* 38(5): 339–346.

———. 2004. Do Loose Lips Sink Ships?: The Meaning, Antecedents and Consequences of Rumour and Gossip in Organisations. *Corporate Communications: An International Journal* 9(3): 189–201.

Miller, Dan E. 1992. 'Snakes in the Greens' and Rumor in the Innercity. *Social Science Journal* 29(4): 381–393.

———. 2006. Rumor: An Examination of Some Stereotypes. *Symbolic Interaction* 28(4): 505–519.

196 *Bibliography*

Mills, Alexander *et al.* 2009. Web 2.0 Emergency Applications: How Useful Can Twitter Be for Emergency Response. *Journal of Information Privacy and Security* 5 (3): 3–26.

Ministry of External Affairs (India). nd. Mumbai Terror Attacks: Dossier of Evidence. Online at: www.hindu.com/nic/dossier.htm (accessed 3 January 2010).

Ministry of Home Affairs (MHA) (Singapore). 2002. *A Singapore Safe for All.* Online at: www.mha.gov.sg/get_blob.aspx?file_id=645_1008_312_ISA_Booklet-English.pdf (accessed 30 June 2012).

——. 2003. *White Paper: The Jemaah Islamiyah Arrests and the Threat of Terrorism.*

——. 2008. Ministry of Home Affairs News Release on Mas Selamat bin Kastari (press release), 27 February. Online at: www.mha.gov.sg/news_details.aspx?nid=MT E2NQ%3D%3D-%2BZANEx6LKCM%3D (accessed 30 June 2012).

Misztal, Barbara. 1996. *Trust in Modern Societies: The Search for the Bases of Social Order.* London: Polity Press.

Mitzen, Jennifer. 2006. Ontological Security in World Politics: State Identity and the Security Dilemma. *European Journal of International Relations* 12(3): 341–370.

Mohr, John W. 1998. Measuring Meaning Structures. *Annual Review of Sociology* 24: 345–370.

——. 2000. Introduction: Structures, Institutions, and Cultural Analysis. *Poetics* 27(2/3): 57–68.

——. and V. Duquenne. 1997. The Duality of Culture and Practice: Poverty Relief in New York City, 1888–1917. *Theory and Society* 26(2/3): 305–356.

Morin, Edgar. 1971. *Rumor in Orleans.* London: Blond.

Morozov, Evgeny. 2009. Texting Towards Utopia: Does the Internet Spread Democracy? *Boston Review,* March/April. Online at: bostonreview.net/BR34.2/morozov.php (accessed 30 June 2012).

——. 2011. *The Net Delusion: The Dark Side of Internet Freedom.* New York: Public Affairs.

Moscovici, Serge. 1976. *Social Influence and Social Change.* London: Academic Press.

Moulin, Carolina. 2010. Border Languages: Rumors and (Dis)Placements of (Inter) National Politics. *Alternatives* 35(4): 347–371.

Mubarok, Mufti M. and Affan Rasyidin. 2008. *Soeharto Tak Pernah Mati: Jejak Besar Sang Jenderal Besar.* Surabaya: Institute for Development Economic.

Mullen, Patrick B. 1972. Modern Legend and Rumor Theory. *Journal of the Folklore Institute* 9(2/3): 95–109.

Musambachime, Mwelwa C. 1988. The Impact of Rumor: The Case of the Banyama (Vampire Men) Scare in Northern Rhodesia, 1930–1964. *The International Journal of African Historical Studies* 21(2): 201–215.

Nadarajan, Ben. 2004. Body of Missing China Girl Found; Malaysian Arrested. *The Straits Times,* 1 November.

——. and Teh Joo Lin. 2008. Have You Seen These Clothes Discarded Anywhere? *The Straits Times,* 5 March.

Naji, Kasra. 2009. *Ahmadinejad: The Secret History of Iran's Radical Leader.* London: I.B. Tauris.

National Security Coordination Secretariat (NSCS) (Singapore). 2006. *1826 Days: A Diary of Resolve. Securing Singapore since 9/11.* Singapore: SNP-Reference.

——. 2008. *Fight Terrorism? Don't Joke!* Singapore: National Security Coordination Secretariat.

Bibliography 197

———. 2009. *Teacher's Guide to 'Fight Terrorism? Don't Joke!* Singapore: National Security Coordination Secretariat.

Navaro-Yashin, Yael. 2002. *Faces of the State: Secularism and Public Life in Turkey*. Princeton, NJ: Princeton University Press.

Neubauer, Hans-Joachim. 1999. *The Rumor: A Cultural History*. London: Free Association Books.

Nigam, Adita. 2002. Theatre of the Urban: The Strange Case of the Monkeyman in *Sarai Reader 2002: The Cities of Everyday Life*, edited by Ravi Vasudevan *et al*. Delhi: Sarai & CSDS+ The Society for Old and New Media. Online at: www.sarai.net/publications/readers/02-the-cities-of-everyday-life/05theatre_urban.pdf (accessed 30 June 2012).

Nye, Joseph. 2004. *Soft Power: The Means to Success in World Politics*. New York: Public Affairs.

Odum, Howard W. 1997 [1943]. *Race and Rumors of Race: The American South in the Early Forties*. Baltimore, MD: The Johns Hopkins University Press.

Oh, Onook, Manish Agrawal and H.R. Rao. 2011. Information Control and Terrorism: Tracking the Mumbai Terrorist Attack through Twitter. *Information Systems Frontiers* 13(1): 33–43.

Olcott, Anthony. 2012. *Open Source Intelligence in a Networked World*. London: Continuum Books.

Oman, Charles W.C. 1922. *The Unfortunate Colonel Despard and Other Studies*. London: E. Arnold & Co.

O'Neill, Onora. 2009a. Making Reason Public: Necessary Conditions for Dialogue and Discourse. *Annual Oslo Lecture on Mind in Nature* (unpublished lecture). University of Oslo, 2 September.

———. 2009b. Ethics for Communication? *European Journal of Philosophy* 17(2): 167–180.

Ono, Shinji. 1994. A Deliberate Rumor: National Anxiety in China on the Eve of the Xinhai Revolution, pp. 25–40 in *China's Republican Revolution*, edited by Shinkichi Eto and Harold Z. Schiffrin. Tokyo: University of Tokyo Press.

Open Source Center. 2007. *Thinking Ahead: How New-Media Tools are Shifting Political Dynamics*. Washington, DC: Office of the Director of National Intelligence.

Osborne, Thomas and Nikolas Rose. 1999. Do the Social Sciences Create Phenomena?: The Example of Public Opinion Research. *British Journal of Sociology* 50(3): 367–396.

Owens, Geoffrey R. 2005. The Secret History of TANU: Rumor, Historiography and Muslim Unrest in Contemporary Dar Es Salaam. *History and Anthropology* 16(4): 441–463.

Pamungkas, K. 2007. *Rahasia Supranatural Soeharto*. Yogyakarta: Penerbit Narasi.

Paul, Christopher. 2009. *Whither Strategic Communication? A Survey of Current Proposals and Recommendation*. Working Paper/Occasional Papers OP-250-RC. RAND Corporation. Online at: www.rand.org/pubs/occasional_papers/2009/RAND_OP250.pdf (accessed 30 June 2012).

———. *et al*. 2009. Challenges to Shaping Civilian Attitudes and Behaviors in a Theater of Operations, pp. 173–194 in *Influence Warfare: How Terrorists and Governments Fight to Shape Perceptions in a War of Ideas*, edited by James J.F. Forest. Westport, CT: Praeger Security International.

Pels, Peter. 1992. Mumiani: The White Vampire – A Neo-Diffusionist Analysis of Rumor. *Etnofoor* 5(1–2): 165–187.

Pendleton, Susan C. 1998. Rumor Research Revisited and Expanded. *Language & Communication* 18(1): 69–86.

198 *Bibliography*

Peniston, William A. 2004. *Pederasts and Others: Urban Culture and Sexual Identity in Nineteenth Century Paris.* New York: Harrington Park Press.

Perry, Mary E. 1989. The 'Nefarious Sin' in Early Modern Seville. *Journal of Homosexuality* 16(1/2): 67–90.

Peterson, Warren and Noel P. Gist. 1951. Rumor and Public Opinion. *American Journal of Sociology* 57(2): 159–167.

Phillips, Susan E. 2007. *Transforming Talk: The Problem with Gossip in Late Medieval England.* University Park: The Pennsylvania State University Press.

Pigden, Charles. 1995. Popper Revisited, or What is Wrong with Conspiracy theories? *Philosophy of the Social Sciences* 25(1): 3–34.

——. 2006. Complots of Mischief, pp. 139–166 in *Conspiracy Theories: The Philosophical Debate*, edited by David Coady. Aldershot: Ashgate.

Pliskin, Karen L. 1980. Camouflage, Conspiracy, and Collaborators: Rumors of the Revolution. *Iranian Studies* 13(1): 55–81.

Ponting, J.R. 1973. Rumor Control Centers as Intermittent Organizations. A Study of a Neglected Organizational Type. Unpublished PhD dissertation: The Ohio State University.

Popper, Karl. 1945. *The Open Society and Its Enemies.* London: Routledge and Kegan Paul.

——. 1974. *The Open Society and Its Enemies Volume 2: The High Tide of Prophecy: Hegel, Marx, and the Aftermath* [4th edn]. London: Routledge and Kegan Paul.

Prasad, Jumana. 1935. The Psychology of Rumor: A Study Relating to the Great Indian Earthquake of 1934. *British Journal of Psychology* 26(1): 1–15.

——. 1950. A Comparative Study of Rumours and Reports in Earthquakes. *British Journal of Psychology* 41(3/4): 129–144.

Pratkanis, Anthony. 2009. Public Diplomacy in International Conflicts: A Social Influence Analysis, pp. 111–153 in *Routledge Handbook of Public Diplomacy*, edited by N. Snow and P. Taylor. New York: Routledge.

——. *et al.* 1988. In Search of Reliable Persuasion Effects: III. The Sleeper Effect is Dead. Long Live the Sleeper Effect. *Journal of Personality and Social Psychology* 54 (2): 203–218.

Press TV. 2009a. US, Israel behind Iran Vote-Rigging Rumors: Ejei, 28 June. Online at: edition.presstv.ir/detail/99291.html (accessed 30 June 2012).

——. 2009b. BBC Provoked Post-Vote Unrest: Iran Police Chief, 5 July. Online at: edition.presstv.ir/detail/99861.html (accessed 30 June 2012).

Preston, Michael J. 1974. Xerox-Lore. *Keystone Folklore* 19(1): 11–26.

——. 1994. Traditional Humor from the Fax Machine: 'All of a Kind'. *Western Folklore* 53(2): 147–169.

Prisoner of Joy. 2009a. Chronology of Ash-Shaheed Urwah's Janaza Reception [Blog]. Online at: prisonerofjoy.blogspot.com/2009/10/chronology-of-ash-shaheed-urwahs-janaza.html (accessed 30 June 2012).

——. 2009b. Accused as Terrorists, Their Janazas are Smiling. Online at: prisonerofjoy. blogspot.com/2009/10/accused-as-terrorists-their-janazas-are.html (accessed 30 June 2012).

Quek, Christine. 2008. Massive Manhunt Continues. *The Straits Times*, 29 February.

Rahimi, Babak. 2011. The Agonistic Social Media: Cyberspace in the Formation of Dissent and Consolidation of State Power in Postelection in Iran. *The Communication Review* 14(3): 158–178.

Rainie, Lee and Barry Wellman. 2012. *Networked: The New Social Operating System.* Cambridge, MA: MIT Press.

Bibliography 199

Ramakrishna, Kumar. 2002. *Emergency Propaganda: The Winning of Malayan Hearts and Minds, 1948–1958*. Richmond: Curzon.

——. 2009a. *Radical Pathways: Understanding Muslim Radicalization in Indonesia*. Westport, CT: Praeger Security International.

——. 2009b. A Holistic Critique of Singapore's Counter-Ideological Program. *CTC Sentinel* 2(1): 8–11.

Raman, B. 2010. Mumbai Terrorist Attack – Dossier of Evidence. *The Hindu*. Online at: www.hindu.com/nic/dossier.htm [accessed 3 January 2010].

Rampton, Sheldon. 2007. Shared Values Revisited. *Counterpunch* Weekend Edition, 19–21 October. Online at: www.counterpunch.org/2007/10/19/shared-values-revisited/ (accessed 30 June 2012).

Rancière, Jacques. 1999. *Disagreement: Politics and Philosophy*. Minneapolis: University of Minnesota Press.

Reals, Tucker. 2009. Does Letter Prove Iran Election Fraud? *CBS News.com*, 18 June. Online at: www.cbsnews.com/8301-503543_162-5095195-503543.html (accessed 30 June 2012).

Rekhi, Shefali. 2008. Fugitive May Link up with JI Comrades. *The Straits Times*, 29 February.

Renard, Jean-Bruno. 1991. LSD Tattoo Transfers: Rumor from North America to France. *Folklore Forum* 24(2): 3–26.

Renne, Elisha P. 1993. *The Stolen Pregnancy and Other Rumors of Reproduction*. Unpublished Conference Paper presented at the African Studies Association Annual Meeting, Boston.

Ricks, Thomas E. 2007. *Fiasco*. New York: Penguin.

Rosario, Vernon A. 1997. *The Erotic Imagination: French Histories of Perversion (Ideologies of Desire)*. New York: Oxford University Press.

——. 1999. The Rise and Fall of the Medical Model: The Pathologization of Homosexuality from 1881 to 1973. *The Harvard Gay & Lesbian Review* 6(4): 31–34.

Rose, Arnold M. 1951. Rumor in the Stock Market. *Public Opinion Quarterly* 15(3): 461–486.

Rosnow, Ralph L. 1988. Rumor as Communication: A Contextualist Approach. *Journal of Communication* 38(1): 12–28.

——. 1991. Inside Rumor: A Personal Journey. *American Psychologist* 46(5): 484–296.

——. and Gary A. Fine. 1976. *Rumor and Gossip: The Social Psychology of Hearsay*. New York: Elsevier Inc.

——, John Yost and James L. Esposito. 1986. Belief in Rumor and Likelihood of Rumor Transmission. *Language and Communication* 6(3): 189–194.

Ross, Christopher. 2003. Pillars of Public Diplomacy. *Harvard International Review* 25 (2): 22–28.

Ross, Norbert. 2004. *Culture & Cognition: Implications for Theory and Method*. London: Sage Publications.

Rousseau, George. 2008. Policing the Anus: Stuprum and Sodomy according to Paolo Zacchia's Forensic Medicine, pp. 75–91 in *The Sciences of Homosexuality in Early Modern Europe*, edited by Kenneth Borris and George Rousseau. New York: Routledge.

Rubin, Alan M. and Sven Windahl. 1986. The Uses and Dependency Model of Mass Communication. *Critical Studies in Mass Communication* 3(2): 184–199.

Ruggiero, Thomas E. 2000. Uses and Gratification Theory in the 21st Century. *Mass Communications and Society* 3(1): 3–37.

200 Bibliography

Saffery, Marion. 2004. *Corporate Rumors: Causes, Formation, and Refutation*. Unpublished MA Thesis, University of Southern California.

Saito, Kensaku. 2010. Older People and Television Viewing in Japan. *NHK Broadcasting Studies* 8: 63–95.

Sanderson, Jimmy and Pauline H. Cheong. 2010. Tweeting Prayers and Communicating Grief over Michael Jackson Online. *Bulletin of Science, Technology and Society* 30(5): 328–340.

Sarfatti-Larson, Magali. 1977. *The Rise of Professionalism*. Berkeley, CA: University of California Press.

Sasaki, Tomomi. 2011. Japan: Toxic Rain, Earthquake Weapons and other False Rumors. *Global Voices Online* website. Online at: globalvoicesonline.org/2011/03/13/japan-toxic-rain-earthquake-weapons-and-other-false-rumors/ (accessed 30 March 2011).

Sato, Kenji. 1995. *Ryugen Higo: Uwasa-banashi o yomite oku saho*. Tokyo: Takafumi, Inc.

Schacter, Stanley and Harvey Burdick. 1955. A Field Experiment on Rumor Transmission and Distortion. *Journal of Abnormal Psychology* 50(3): 363–371.

Schafer, Fabian. 2012. Fukushima: Rumours, Emotions and Rousseau's General Will in the Digital Age. *Open Democracy*, 17 May. Online at: www.opendemocracy.net/fabian-sch%C3%A4fer/fukushima-rumours-emotions-and-rousseau%E2%80%99s-general-will-in-digital-age (accessed 28 June 2012).

Schall, Herbert M., Bernard Levy and M.E. Tresselt. 1950. A Sociometric Approach to Rumor. *Journal of Social Psychology* 31(1): 121–129.

Schindler, Mark. 2007. *Rumors in Financial Markets: Insights into Behavioral Finance*. Chichester: Wiley.

Schmeidler, Gertrude R. and Gordon W. Allport. 1944. Social Psychology and the War Effort: May 1943–May 1944. *Journal of Social Psychology* 20(1): 145–180.

Scott, James C. 1985. *Weapons of the Weak: Everyday Forms of Peasant Resistance*. New Haven: Yale University Press.

——. 1990. *Domination and the Arts of Resistance: Hidden Transcripts*. New Haven, CT: Yale University Press.

Sedikides, Constantine and Craig A. Anderson. 1992. Causal Explanations of Defection: A Knowledge Structure Approach. *Personality & Soc Psych Bulletin* 18(4): 420–429.

Seko, Sipri. 2009. Ahli Forensik: Dubur Noordin Rusak. *Kupang Pos*, 30 September. Online at: properti.kompas.com/read/2009/09/30/17134388/Ahli.Forensik.Dubur.Noordin.Rusak (accessed 30 June 2012).

Shahrokni, Nazanin. 2012. The Politics of Polling: Polling and the Constitution of Counter-publics during 'Reform' in Iran. *Current Sociology* 60(2): 202–221.

Shannon, Claude E. 1948. A Mathematical Theory of Communication. *The Bell Systems Technical Journal* 27: 379–423, 623–656.

——. and Warren Weaver. 1964. *The Mathematical Theory of Communication*. Urbana, IL: University of Illinois Press.

Shibutani, Tamotsu. 1944. *Rumors in a Crisis Situation*. Unpublished MSc Dissertation, University of Chicago.

——. 1948. *The Circulation of Rumors as a Form of Collective Behavior*. Unpublished PhD Dissertation, University of Chicago.

——. 1955. Reference Groups as Perspectives. *American Journal of Sociology* 60(6): 562–569.

——. 1961. *Society & Personality: An Interactionist Approach to Social Psychology*. New Brunswick, NJ: Transaction Publishers.

——. 1966. *Improvised News: A Sociological Study of Rumor.* Indianapolis: The Bobbs-Merrill Company.

——. (ed.). 1970. *Human Nature and Collective Behavior: Papers in Honor of Herbert Blumer.* Englewood Cliffs, NJ: Prentice Hall.

——. 1978. *The Derelicts of Company K: A Sociological Study of Demoralization.* Berkeley, CA: University of California Press.

——. 1986. *Social Processes: An Introduction to Sociology.* Berkeley, CA: University of California Press.

——. and K. Kwan. 1965. *Ethnic Stratification: A Comparative Approach.* New York: Macmillan.

Shoelhi, Mohammad. 2008. *Rahasia Pak Harto.* Jakarta: Grafindo.

Singh, M. 2002. Revealed: This was their Revenge Target because. *The New Paper,* 26 September.

Singleton, Stephanie L. 2008. *According to Rumor, it's a Conspiracy: Conspiracy Theory as a Paradigmatic Construct.* Unpublished MA Thesis, Indiana University.

Sinha, Duganand. 1952. Behaviour in a Catastrophic Situation: A Psychological Study of Reports and Rumours. *British Journal of Psychology* 43(3): 200–209.

——. 1954. Rumors as Factors in Public Opinion during Election. *The Eastern Anthropologist* 8(2): 63–72.

Skadian, Carl. 2008a. Massive Manhunt: Thousands of Officers Fan Out After Dangerous JI Terrorist Leader Flees Detention Centre. *The Straits Times,* 28 February.

——. 2008b. '72 Hours into the Search'. *The Straits Times,* 2 March 2008.

Smith, George H. 1947. Beliefs in Statements Labeled Fact and Rumor. *Journal of Abnormal Psychology* 42(1): 80–90.

Smith, Steven A. 2006. Talking Toads and Chinless Ghosts: The Politics of 'Superstitious' Rumors in the People's Republic of China, 1961–1965. *The American Historical Review* 111(2): 405–427.

Snow, Nancy and Phil Taylor (eds). 2009. *Routledge Handbook of Public Diplomacy.* New York: Routledge.

Soempeno, Femi A. 2008. *Prabowo Titisan Soeharto? Mencari Pemimpin Baru di Mada Paceklik.* Yogyakarta: Galang Press.

Sofsky, Wolfgang. 2008. *Privacy: A Manifesto.* Princeton, NJ: Princeton University Press.

Sokefield, Martin. 2002. Rumours and Politics on the Northern Frontier: The British, Pakhtun Wali and Yaghestan. *Modern Asian Studies* 36(2): 299–340.

Somers, Margaret and Gloria D. Gibson. 1994. Reclaiming the Epistemological 'Other': Narrative and the Social Constitution of Identity, pp. 37–99 in *Social Theory and the Politics of Identity,* edited by Craig Calhoun. Oxford: Blackwell Publishers.

Soumalainen, A. *et al.* 2007. Congenital Funnel Anus in Children: Associated Anomalies, Surgical Management and Outcome. *Pediatric Surgery International* 23 (12): 1167–1170.

Sperber, Dan. 1975. *Rethinking Symbolism.* Cambridge: Cambridge University Press.

——. 1985. *On Anthropological Knowledge.* Cambridge: Cambridge University Press.

Sreberny, Annabelle and Gholan Khiabany. 2010. *Blogistan: The Internet and Politics in Iran.* New York: I.B. Tauris.

Stadler, Jonathan. 2003. Rumor, Gossip and Blame: Implications for HIV/AIDS Prevention in the South African Lowveld. *AIDS Education and Prevention* 15(4): 357–368.

Stanley. 1999. Penggambaran Gerwani Sebagai Kumpulan Pembunnuh dan Setan. (Fitnah dan Fakta Penghancuran Organisasi Perempuan Terkemuka). Paper

202 *Bibliography*

presented at Seminar, 'Tragedi Nasional 1965', Masyarakat Sejarawan Indonesia, Serpong, 8 September.

The Star Online (Malaysia). 2009. Noordin may have Hidden Explosives in his Anus, Experts say, 2 October. Online at: www.thestar.com.my/news/story.asp?file=/2009/10/2/nation/4826681&sec=nation (accessed 30 June 2012).

Stelter, Brian. 2011. How the Bin Laden Announcement Leaked Out. *The New York Times*, 1 May. Online at: mediadecoder.blogs.nytimes.com/2011/05/01/how-the-osama-announcement-leaked-out/ (accessed 1 July 2012).

Stern, William L. 1902. Zur Psychologie der Aussage: Experimentelle Untersuchungen über Erinnerungstreue. *Zeitschrift für die gesamte Strafechtswissenschaft* 22(2/3): 315–370.

Stewart, Pamela J. and Andrew Strathern. 2003. *Witchcraft, Sorcery, Rumors and Gossip*. Cambridge: Cambridge University Press.

The Straits Times. 2003. Terror Suspect Arrested in Indonesia not to be Extradited to Singapore, 4 February.

——. 2008a. The Escape Raises Posers, 1 March.

——. 2008b. Unlikely He's Left Country, say Security Experts, 1 March.

Suczek, Barbara. 1972. The Curious Case of the 'Death' of Paul McCartney. *Journal of Contemporary Ethnography* 1(1): 61–76.

Sunstein, Cass R. 2002. On a Danger of Deliberative Democracy. *Daedalus* 131(4): 120–124.

——. 2008. 'She Said What?' 'He Did That?': Believing False Rumors. *Harvard Public Law Working Paper*, No. 08-56. Online at: http://ssrn.com/abstract=1304268 (accessed 15 January 2010).

——. 2009. *On Rumors: How Falsehoods Spread, Why We Believe Them, What Can Be Done*. New York: Farrar, Strauss and Giroux.

——. and Adrian Vermeule. 2009. Conspiracy Theories: Causes and Cures. *Journal of Political Philosophy* 17(2): 202–227.

Sussman, Dalia. 2010. Opinion Polling: A Question of What to Ask. *The New York Times*, 26 February.

Swaffield, Simon. 1998. Contextual Meanings in Policy Discourse: A Case Study of Language Use Concerning Resource Policy in the New Zealand High Country. *Policy Sciences* 31(3): 199–224.

Swidler, Ann. 1986. Culture in Action: Symbols and Strategies. *American Sociological Review* 51(2): 273–286.

——. 2001. *Talk of Love: How Culture Matters*. Chicago, IL: University of Chicago Press.

Tai, Zixue and Tao Sun. 2011. The Rumouring of SARS During the 2003 Epidemic in China. *Sociology of Health & Illness* 33(5): 677–693.

Tambiah, Stanley J. 1996. *Leveling Crowds: Ethnonationalist Conflicts and Collective Violence in South Asia*. Berkeley, CA: University of California Press.

Tan, Andrew. 2003. The Indigenous Roots of Conflict in Southeast Asia: The Case of Mindanao, pp. 97–115 in *After Bali: The Threat of Terrorism in Southeast Asia*, edited by Kumar Ramakrishna and Tan See Seing. Singapore: World Scientific Publishing.

Tan, Tania *et al.* 2008. Schools Beef Up Security at All Levels. *The Straits Times*, February 29.

Tanner, Ralph E.S. 1978. Rumor and the Buganda Emergency, 1966. *The Journal of Modern African Studies* 16(2): 329–338.

Tapper, Jake. 2005. Would You Buy a US Foreign Policy From This Man? *Salon.com*, 25 April. Online at: www.salon.com/2003/04/25/propaganda_10/ (accessed 1 July 2012).

Taussig, Michael. 1986. *Shamanism, Colonialism, and the Wild Man: A Study in Terror and Healing*. Chicago, IL: University of Chicago Press.

Taylor, Gabriel. 1994. Gossip as Moral Talk, pp. 34–36 in *Good Gossip*, edited by Robert F. Goodman and Aaron Ben-Ze'ev. Lawrence: University Press of Kansas.

Taylor, Phil. 2005. Towards a New Magic Bullet? *Defence Management Journal* 30: 64–65. Online at: www.defencemanagement.com/article.asp?id=192&content_name=Communications&article=4753 (accessed 1 July 2012).

——. and Nancy Snow. 2006. The Revival of the Propaganda State: US Propaganda at Home and Abroad since 9/11. *The International Communication Gazette* 68(5&6): 389–408.

Thompson, Victoria E. 1996. Creating Boundaries: Homosexuality and the Changing Social Order in France, 1830–1870, pp. 102–127 in *Homosexuality in Modern France*, edited by Jeffrey Merrick and Bryant T. Ragan Jr. New York: Oxford University Press.

Thornton, Patricia H., William Ocasio and Michael Lounsbury. 2012. *The Institutional Logics Perspective: A New Approach to Culture, Structure, and Process*. Oxford: Oxford University Press.

Tilly, Charles. 1993. Contentious Repertoires in Great Britain, 1758–1834. *Social Science History* 17(2): 253–280.

——. 2002. *Stories, Identities, and Political Change*. Oxford: Rowman & Littlefield Publishers.

Topix.com. 2009. Fakta! Noordin Sering Disodomi, 1 October. Online at: www.topix.com/forum/world/indonesia/TQQPE0QUKS4KL0DDH (accessed 1 July 2012).

Torgerson, Douglas. 1985. Contextual Orientation in Policy Analysis. *Policy Sciences* 18(3): 241–261.

Tryon, Chuck. 2008. Pop Politics: Online Parody Videos, Intertextuality, and Political Participation. *Popular Communication* 6(4): 209–213.

Tsuganesawa, Toshihiro. 1996. Media Reporting and Rumor Following the Great Hanshin Earthquake. *Studies of Broadcasting* 32: 115–140. Broadcasting Culture Research Institute (NHK).

Turner, Patricia A. 1987. Church's Fried Chicken and The Klan: A Rhetorical Analysis of Rumor in the Black Community. *Western Folklore* 46(4): 294–306.

Ueussner, Ki M. 2008. Social Media a Lifeline, Also a Threat? *ABC News*. Online at: http://abcnews.go.com/Technology/International/story?id=6350014&page=1 [accessed 8 January 2010].

US Army and Marine Corps. 2007. *The US Army/Marine Corps Counterinsurgency Field Manual*. Chicago, IL: University of Chicago Press.

US Department of Defense. 2012. *Decade of War, Volume 1: Enduring Lessons from the Past Decade of Operations*. Online at: blogs.defensenews.com/saxotech-access/pdfs/decade-of-war-lessons-learned.pdf (accessed 29 June 2012).

US Department of State. 2003. *Daily Press Briefing. January 16*. Online at: http://2001-2009.state.gov/r/pa/prs/dpb/2003/16717.htm (accessed 27 January 2013).

——.2004a. *Patterns of Global Terrorism 2003*. Online at: www.state.gov/documents/organization/31912.pdf [accessed 1 July 2012].

——. 2004b. *Strategic Goal 11: Public Diplomacy and Public Affairs*. Online at: www.state.gov/s/d/rm/rls/perfplan/2004/20495.htm (accessed 1 July 2012).

——. 2007. *Country Reports on Terrorism 2006*. Online at: www.state.gov/documents/organization/83383.pdf (accessed 1 July 2012).

204 *Bibliography*

US Government Accountability Office [GAO]. 2003. *US Public Diplomacy: State Department Expands Efforts but Faces Significant Challenges.* GAO Report GAO-03-951. September 2003. Online at: www.gao.gov/new.items/d03951.pdf (accessed 1 July 2012).

Vaisey, Stephen. 2009. Motivation and Justification: A Dual-Process Model of Culture in Action. *American Journal of Sociology* 114(6): 1675–1715.

Van der Kroef, Justus M. 1959. Javanese Messianic Expectations: Their Origins and Cultural Context. *Comparative Studies in Society and History* 1(4): 299–323.

Vasu, Norman. 2008. (En)Countering Terrorism: Multiculturalism and Singapore. *Asian Ethnicity* 9(1): 17–32.

——. and Yolanda Chin. 2007. *The Ties that Bind and Blind: A Report on Inter-racial and Inter-religious Relations in Singapore.* Singapore: Centre of Excellence for National Security (CENS), S. Rajaratnam School of International Studies (RSIS), Nanyang Technical University (NTU). Online at: www.rsis.edu.sg/publications/reports/RSIS%20Social%20resilience%20report.pdf (accessed 1 July 2012).

——. and Yolanda Chin. 2012. *The Ties that Bind and Blind: A Report on Inter-racial and Inter-religious Relations in Singapore 2012.* Singapore: CENS, RSIS, NTU. Online at: www.rsis.edu.sg/cens/PDF/RSIS_TiesthatBind.pdf (accessed 1 July 2012).

——. and Bernard Loo. 2010. National Security and Singapore: An Assessment, pp. 462–488 in *Management of Success: Singapore Revisited*, edited by T. Chong. Singapore: Institute of Southeast Asian Studies (ISEAS).

——. and Kumar Ramakrishna. 2006. Countering Terrorism: Multiculturalism in Singapore. *Connections: The Quarterly Journal* 5(4): 143–155.

Velayutham, Selvaraj. 2007. *Responding to Globalization: Nation, Culture and Identity in Singapore.* Singapore: ISEAS.

Vijayan, K.C. 2004. Huang Na Touches Nation's Heart. *The Straits Times*, 22 October.

Virtanen, Leea. 1987. *Varastettu isoäiti. Kaupungin kansantarinoita* [Stolen grandmother. Folk legends of the city]. Helsinki: Tammi.

——. 1996. *Apua! Maksa ryömii. Nykyajan tarinoita ja huhuja* [Help! The liver crawls. Contemporary legends and rumors]. Helsinki: Tammi.

Wallace, Anthony F.C. 1956. Revitalization Movements. *American Anthropologist* 58 (2): 264–281.

Waller, J. Michael. 2007. *Fighting the War of Ideas like a Real War: Messages to Defeat the Terrorists.* Washington, DC: The Institute of World Politics Press.

Warner, Michael. 2005. *Publics and Counterpublics.* New York: Zone Books.

The Washington Times. 2009. Iran's Twitter Revolution (Editorial), 16 June. Online at: www.washingtontimes.com/news/2009/jun/16/irans-twitter-revolution/ (accessed 30 June 2012).

Weick, Karl. 1995. *Sensemaking in Organizations.* Thousand Oaks, CA: Sage.

Weiner, Michael A. 1989. *The Origins of the Korean Community in Japan, 1910–1923.* Manchester: Manchester University Press.

White, Luise. 1994. Between Gluckman and Foucault: Historicizing Rumour and Gossip. *Social Dynamics* 20(1): 75–92.

——. 2000. *Speaking with Vampires: Rumor and History in Colonial Africa.* Berkeley, CA: University of California Press.

Wieringa, Saskia E. 2003. The Birth of the New Order State in Indonesia: Sexual Politics and Nationalism. *Journal of Women's History* 15(1): 70–91.

Wijaya, Taufik. 2009. 'Fakta' Bukan Jaringan Islamiyah (JI) Pimpinan Noordin M Top. *Detik News*, 25 July. Online at: news.detik.com/read/2009/07/25/162611/

1171439/10/fakta-bukan-jaringan-islamiyah–ji–pimpinan-noordin-m-top (accessed 23 September 2009).

Wong, Kan Seng. 2003. ISD Intelligence Service Promotion Ceremony on Thursday, 3 April at Copthorne Waterfront Hotel, Grand Ballroom – Speech by Mr Wong Kan Seng, Minister for Home Affairs. Online at: www.mha.gov.sg/news_details.aspx?nid=OTA5-AJbbOx6zQXU%3D (accessed 1 July 2012).

——. 2004. Launch of the International Centre for Political Violence and Terrorism Research, Institute of Defence and Strategic Studies at Nanyang Technological University – Speech by Mr Wong Kan Seng, Minister for Home Affairs, 20 February 2004. Online at: www.mha.gov.sg/news_details.aspx?nid=Nzk5-5px2Iw6F2z0%3D (accessed 1 July 2012).

——. 2008a. Escape of JI Detainee Mas Selamat From Detention – Comments by Deputy Prime Minister and Minister for Home Affairs Wong Kan Seng in Parliament, 28 February 2008. Online at: www.mha.gov.sg/news_details.aspx?nid=MTE2Ng%3D%3D-7jdNkWa0yXk%3D (accessed 1 July 2012).

——. 2008b. Ministerial Statement by the Minister for Home Affairs Made in Parliament on Monday 21 April 2008: The Committee of Inquiry's Findings on the Escape of Mas Selamat on Wednesday 27 February 2008. Online at: www4.mha.gov.sg/data/NewsFiles/c52_MinisterialStatement.pdf (accessed 1 July 2012).

Woodward, Mark. 1989. *Islam in Java: Normative Piety and Mysticism in the Sultanate of Yogyakarta.* Tucson: University of Arizona Press.

——. 2006. Religious Conflict and the Globalization of Knowledge: Indonesia 1978–2004, pp. 85–10 in *Religion and Conflict in South and Southeast Asia: Disrupting Violence,* edited by Linell E. Cady and Sheldon W. Simon. London: Routledge.

Wright, Robin. 2008. *Dreams and Shadows: The Future of the Middle East.* New York: Penguin Press.

Yahya, Maryam. 2006. *Polio Vaccines – Difficult to Swallow: The Story of a Controversy in Northern Nigeria.* IDS Working Paper 261. Institute of Development Studies, University of Sussex.

Yardi, Sarita and Danah Boyd. 2010. Dynamic Debates: An Analysis of Group Polarization Over Time on Twitter. *Bulletin of Science, Technology & Society* 30(5): 316–327.

Yezer, Caroline. 2008. Who Wants to Know? Rumors, Suspicions, and Opposition to Truth-Telling in Ayacucho. *Latin American and Caribbean Ethnic Studies* 3(3): 271–289.

al-Zarqawi, Abu Musab. 2004. *Text of Zarqawi Letter.* Online at: www.globalsecurity.org/wmd/library/news/iraq/2004/02/040212-al-zarqawi.htm (accessed 30 June 2012).

Zerubavel, Eviatar. 1991. *The Fine Line: Making Distinctions in Everyday Life.* Chicago, IL: University of Chicago Press.

——. 1999. *Social Mindscapes: An Invitation to Cognitive Sociology.* Cambridge, MA: Harvard University Press.

Zubaida, Sami. 1997. Is Iran an Islamic State?, pp. 103–119 in *Political Islam: Essays from Middle East Report,* edited by Joel Beinin and Joe Stork. Berkeley: University of California Press.

Index

Abbott, Andrew 14, 170, 175
Allport, Gordon W. 4–7, 9, 23–24, 26, 44n.5, 76n.4, 94, 143, 145–46, 152–53, 163

Bakhtin, Mikhail 78–79
Ball-Rokeach, Sandra 107, 174
boundaries 18, 168, 170
Bourdieu, Pierre 15, 78, 175
Bruns, Axel 125, 178
Bubandt, Nils 55, 96, 125, 139

categorization 3, 8, 11, 109, 167, 169, 175–76
Coady, CAJ 21, 48–50
Coady, David 25, 34–36, 44n.13, 50–51, 67
conspiracy theory 29–33, 36–38, 44n. 10, 54–58, 60n.8, 80
convergence culture 124, 177
counterinsurgency 67–68, 70–71, 73
counterpublics 78–79, 92n.1
crisis 1–2, 4, 6, 14, 17, 23, 91, 109

Das, Veena 79
DiFonzo, Nicholas 13, 76n.7, 76n.13, 94, 107, 108, 110, 153
Dundes, Alan 26

Fine, Gary Alan 11, 37, 42, 79, 91, 107, 108, 126, 146, 175, 179
Fisher, Walter 13

gossip 22, 27–29, 47–50
Gramsci, Antonio 14–15, 104n.2

Hopf, Ted 106, 110

Identity 108, 120–21, 135

Indonesia 14, 16, 94–105, 114, 116–17, 124–40, 168; Communist Party (PKI) 97–98; GERWANI 96–98; Java 15–16, 96, 98, 100, 102–4, 105n.1, 105n.11, 127, 132, 135; pro-government rumors 97–98; New Order 95–100, 102, 104; Suharto 14–15; 96; 98–104; Yogyakarta 96;
informal communication 5, 17, 29, 32, 78–80, 91–92
institutional logics 17, 170–72, 176
internet 176–78; see also new media; see also Twitter
Iran 78–92, 168; and death of Masoud Ali-Mohammad 89–91; and death of Neda Agha Soltan 88–89; elections 79, 80–83; post-election rumors 83–88
Iraq 61–76, 170–71; and rumors of bovine poisoning 61–62, 69, 171–72; and rumors about US military 62; and rumors of Weapons of Mass Destruction (WMD) 63

Japan 1, 169, 178
Jemaah Islamiyah 111–12, 126, 135
Jenkins, Henry 124, 177

Kant, Immanuel 22, 27, 39–41, 145
Kapferer, Jean-Noel 26, 69, 79, 160, 175, 179
Kelley, Stephanie 8, 63, 66, 75, 163–65
Knapp, Robert H. 8, 64, 19n.4, 77n.14, 160, 163

Malaysia 16, 111, 126, 132–36
Mas Selamat bin Kastari 108; escape 114–17; rumors about escape 118
master narratives 66, 68–69, 71–72, 74–76, 77n.18, 121; see also narratives

Index 207

meaning 11, 14, 19n.2, 68, 168, 173, 174, 175–76, 178
memetic isomorphism 131, 141n.12
Mohr, John W. 175, 176
Morin, Edgar 178
Mumbai 2008 Terrorist Attack 146–48
myth 14–16, 21, 94–95

Narrative 12–14, 16, 18, 25–26, 62–64, 67–69, 73–76, 79–80, 87, 92, 96–99, 106, 109–10, 118, 177–78; *see also* master narratives; *see also* shared narrative communities
narrative sedimentation 177
networked individualism 86
new media 16–17; 86–87
Noordin Top 16, 125–27, 138, 168; and autopsy rumors 127–30

Office of Strategic Services (OSS) 160–61

political communication 78, 63
political epistemics 168
producers 125, 131–32, 133, 136, 177, 178
propaganda 16, 64, 138–39, 159–61, 166n.10, 180n.2
public diplomacy 64, 124, 157–58, 159, 161, 164–65, 166 n.12
public opinion 43, 75, 78, 83, 158–59

Rosnow, R.L. 10, 24, 25, 146, 152–53, 163
rumor: affect and 91–92; ambiguity and 16, 23–25, 44n.5, 76n.7, 94, 107, 109, 118, 121–22, 144–46, 174; anxiety and 24, 145–46, 149–51, 153; credibility of 3, 11, 16, 61, 63, 65, 72–74, 91, 100, 110; definition of 3–5, 22–26, 46, 94, 144–45; plausibility of 5, 11–13, 16, 18, 33, 46, 51, 53, 58–59, 67, 74–75, 77n.14, 79, 110, 118, 121, 172, 175, 178; and power 3, 11, 14–16, 18, 168, 172, 179; and public policy 35–37, 39–44, 74, 169; and publicity 35–37, 43; reliability of 20–22, 33–35; as social problem 2–3, 169–70; study of 6–10,

148–51, 178; *see also* categorization, schema, symbolic power, testimony.

schema 13, 106, 109, 110, 121
Scott, James 16, 65, 95, 138
security culture 111, 122n.4
security symbols 113–14
sense-making 1, 14, 15, 17, 73, 107, 110, 118–20, 153–54
Shared Values Initiative 17, 161–62, 164–65
shared narrative communities 107–8, 117–18, 122
Shibutani, Tamotsu 3–5, 24–25, 32–34, 42, 107–8, 163, 169, 172–73
Singapore 111–12; and state communication campaigns 112–13; and terrorism 111–14
social cognitive structure 106–7, 110, 120; *see also* schema
social epistemology 20
strategic communication 17–18, 19n.1, 41–44, 63–65, 74–75, 137–38, 161–62, 166n.12, 169–71, 172–73; and message-influence model of 7, 17, 159, 165, 178
Sunstein, Cass 30–31, 35, 51, 54, 8
Swidler, Ann 174, 180n.1
symbolic power 14–16, 53

testimony 20–22, 46
thought community 109–10, 121
transmediation 76n.12, 124, 130–35
trust 14–15, 35–40, 36–37, 177
Twitter 60n.7, 93n.7, 144, 147–51, 154, 173–74, 177

urban legend 25–27, 180n.6
uses and gratification theory 159, 165

Weick, Karl 2, 107, 119–20
Wellman, Barry 86

YouTube 132–34

Zerubavel, Eviatar 11, 13, 109